D1481001

NEW MEXICO POPULISM

NEW MEXICO POPULISM

A Study of Radical Protest
in a Western Territory

ROBERT W. LARSON

WITH A FOREWORD BY HOWARD R. LAMAR

COLORADO ASSOCIATED UNIVERSITY PRESS
BOULDER, COLORADO

For my parents and sister

ACKNOWLEDGMENTS

Having spent almost five years working on the manuscript for this book, it is difficult to know where to begin in acknowledging all the help and support I received. As historians are always comfortable when proceeding chronologically, perhaps the best place to start is at the beginning. In this regard my grant from the Penrose Fund of the American Philosophical Society was an essential first. It helped me to meet the expenses that I incurred during the summer of 1969, when I began my research in New Mexico. Time is also important and a real debt of gratitude is owed to Dr. Darrell Holmes, former president of the University of Northern Colorado, and Dr. Frank P. Lakin, vice president. Through their auspices I received released time through the Bureau of Research at the university to start my research.

While working in New Mexico I was given help from a number of sources. In Santa Fe, the personnel at the State Records Center and Archives, the Museum of New Mexico, and the State Library were never reluctant to assist. Dr. Myra Ellen Jenkins, the state historian, was exceptionally helpful. Because of her remarkable grasp of historical materials for New Mexico, I was able to peruse the pertinent primary collections at the state archives most efficiently. Mrs. J. K. Shishkin, who was with the Museum of New Mexico before her retirement, and Mrs. Susan Henderson were also helpful and considerate. Librarians at the University of New Mexico in Albuquerque gave me invaluable aid, while those at New Mexico Highlands University made those beautiful drives from Santa Fe to Las Vegas most rewarding. My trip to Farmington to use rare microfilms of the Populist newspaper, the *San Juan Times,* was also profitable because of the kind support extended by the editorial staff of the *Daily Times* of Farmington.

Organizing and writing the manuscript was facilitated by the significant assistance I received when I returned to Greeley. I am grateful to Mr. Daniel A. Seager for making available an office in the old library building on campus. Others of the library staff at the University of Northern Colorado who extended help include Mrs. Virginia G. Costello, Mrs. Arlene Greer, and Mrs. Lucy Schweers. So many members of the university library staff headed by Mr. Thomas C. Harris gave me support, that I am hesitant to mention names for fear of omitting someone.

It is difficult to acknowledge some debts properly. In this category is the superb editorial assistance given me by two of my colleagues from the Department of English, the late Dr. Sam F. Freeman and Dr. Forrest W. Frease. Both gave unselfishly of their time and made excellent comments and suggestions for improving my study.

Readying a manuscript for publication is a necessary last step. Consequently, a grant from the Faculty Research and Publications Committee of the University of Northern Colorado to cover typing expenses was most important. I am also grateful to my typist, Mrs. Max Shirley, and to Mrs. Helen Stansbury, Mrs. Donna Jones, and Mrs. Sue Wright who lent their typing skills at crucial moments during the final stages of my work.

Dr. Howard R. Lamar, who was kind enough to write the foreword, deserves special mention not only for his willingness to do me this honor but because of his pioneering research on the political and economic developments of the territorial Southwest. Finally, a sincere thanks to my family and friends and to those treasured colleagues in my department and on the faculty who showed such an interest in the study.

Robert W. Larson
University of Northern Colorado
Greeley

CONTENTS

FOREWORD

Most historians of Populism never mention the Territory of New Mexico in their accounts, for Populism in the mountain West has been dismissed by so distinguished a historian as Richard Hofstadter as "mere silverism." But the comforting thought that genuine Populism wore only two hats, one Southern and one Midwestern, has been successfully challenged by Robert W. Larson's *New Mexico Populism: A Study of Radical Protest in a Western Territory.* He has probably coined a new phrase, in fact, for "New Mexico Populism" was distinctive, even unique, and it may well come to mean a form of social protest that was even more truly populistic than its midwestern or southern forms.

As Professor Larson reveals in the following pages, the movement in New Mexico was unlike either the agrarian railroad protests of Kansas or the crusade of the silver miners in Nevada and Colorado. New Mexican Populists were not obsessed with the silver panacea, or with Wall Street conspiracies and captains of industry. Nor did they exhibit in any recognizable form the familiar themes of racism, anti-Semitism, anti-Catholicism, or even anti-intellectualism. Few if any professional reformers or third party advocates could be found among their leaders. Their villains were not abstract forces or railroad rates, but clear and present local dangers that took the form of cattle and land monopolies, The Santa Fe Ring, and such ambitious individuals as Senators Stephen B. Elkins of West Virginia and Stephen W. Dorsey of Arkansas, who manipulated New Mexican land holdings for their own benefit.

It is true that these issues existed in New Mexico before the Farmers' Alliance and Populist movements arose, but what Larson points out is that local groups, often differing in economic makeup and political philosophy from county to county, sincerely or cynically adopted Populist ideas, rhetoric and methods to combat the forces of monopoly and corruption or to advance the cause of oppressed Spanish-American minorities. The result is a compelling tale of political intrigue, undercover agents — of whom the famous cowboy-author, Charles Siringo, was one —, violence and social protest of the most fundamental kind. Populism did not introduce these elements to New Mexican politics; they, too, were already there, but Larson's history gives the more familiar accounts of the land speculators and the Santa Fe Ring a new dimension and often a totally new meaning. Somehow the monolithic picture of the all-powerful Santa Fe Ring seems less accurate when we read that at one point five protest groups: the White Caps, the Knights of Labor, the urban Populists of Albuquerque and the farming Populists of San Juan County, and the Democratic Party, were simultaneously active in the Territory.

By tracing the long neglected and misunderstood histories of these local groups, Professor Larson is able to drive home his point that not only was New Mexico Populism more than silverism, it was almost everything but silverism. He has found that few if any of New Mexico's Populist leaders were primarily engaged in silver mining, and that while the territorial Populists made a great thing of silver in 1896, in the crucial year of 1894 silver received no special mention in the Populist local platforms.

Perhaps of equal importance, Larson has found that certain Spanish-American leaders, desperate to protect their people from the encroachments of Anglo-American land speculators, joined the Populist cause. Of the few Populist leaders elected to the Territorial Council, Pablo Herrera was the brother of the founder of the *Gorras Blancas,* or the White Caps, a Spanish-American group which was protesting Anglo invasion of the Las Vegas community land grant. Herrera's career, as well as that of Felix Martinez of Las Vegas, suggests that Spanish-American leaders could be as adept at using reform sentiment as Anglo-Americans.

His account of Alliance activity in Lincoln County, famous for its cattle war, not only discloses how Alliance leader Jasper Coe portrayed the Cattlemen's Association as an organization which sought monopoly control of the public domain, but throws new light on the relation between the Santa Fe Ring and the ranchers of that turbulent county. Yet far from being merely anti-monopolist, Coe and the Alliance espoused a low tariff, anti-immigration legislation, and participated in a cooperative.

By looking more closely at the famous fight between homesteaders and the Maxwell Land Grant speculators in Colfax County, Larson finds Populist ideas and methods being used by the former, and that in 1889 the Farmers' Alliance correctly opposed the proposed state constitution of that year as being a creature of the land-grant interests. Even school reform measures in the legislature — usually portrayed as an expression of Anglo-Protestant and Spanish-Catholic disagreement over public and parochial schools — takes on a new dimension as Larson follows the reform activities of the Populist leader, T. B. Mills.

Again, through a careful study of urban Populism in Albuquerque, Larson finds a more recognizable form of protest by merchants seeking better railroad rates and political reform. In the northwestern part of the territory, the fruit growers of remote San Juan County fought for reasonable railroad rates and irrigation development for a decade while voicing ideals which were identical with those of the national Alliance and Populist movements. Most surprising of all, Professor Larson tells us that only in the declining days of the Populist movement did the silver miners of New Mexico participate in the Populist movement.

The lucid manner in which this study explains the tangled and obscure story of New Mexico Populism is only one of the virtues of the book. It also helps explain the complicated political maneuvers by which trusted members of the Santa Fe Ring used Populism to advance their own careers or defeat a competitor within their own ranks! As a result the checkered activities of Governor L. Bradford Prince and Delegate Thomas Catron seem more explicable, while the efforts of Felix Martinez to employ a combination of Populist, White Cap and Knights of Labor dissent to promote himself and the Democratic party is a classic tale of political intrigue which even a member of the New York Tweed Ring would respect and admire.

Professor Larson has garnered the story of New Mexico Populism from local newspapers and the letters of little known participants. And while Populists never enlisted as much as ten percent of the voters in their ranks, this history of the movement at the village and county level is important for the fact that it reveals just how totally Populism affected the lives of certain individuals and groups, and how this small number had an eventual impact on territorial politics by joining the Democratic party.

Even so, Professor Larson has given us much more than a history of Populism at the grass roots level. By placing his findings in the context of the regional and national reform movements, he shows that even in New Mexico certain national patterns emerged, for there, as elsewhere, it was the Democratic party which embraced third party dissent to advance its own fortunes. But what is equally significant Larson describes how a pragmatic, multi-issue reform impulse could arise on the frontier, and especially a frontier which was more Spanish-American than Anglo-American. Moreover, territories are usually characterized as being concerned with the politics of development rather than the politics of reform, and New Mexico has often been cited as a prime example of the development-oriented single-party territory where reform could never succeed. Although reform did not win out there, Professor Larson has altered the old image and leaves us, instead, with a new appreciation of the way Populism affected the lives of individuals as they, whether for cynical or sincere reasons, struggled to change New Mexico's history. *New Mexico Populism* shows us how careful local studies can continue to enlarge the meaning of the most important third party movement in American history. Professor Larson has provided us with a fine model, in fact, for needed studies of Populism in other states and territories of the Mountain and Pacific West.

Howard R. Lamar
Yale University

1

NEW MEXICO: SEEDBED FOR POPULISM?

The cries of outrage heard throughout the West and the South during the stormy era of Populism were most audible in the Territory of New Mexico. True, they did not have the same impact as the shouts of frustration that reverberated so loudly in Colorado. Nor did Populist activity in the Southwestern territory ever approach the great successes in wheat-raising Kansas at the other end of the Sante Fe Trail. Nevertheless, chapters of the Southern Alliance actively operated in the territory on behalf of struggling farmers and stockmen. Assemblies of Knights of Labor were engaged in protest in San Miguel County. And, in 1894, the populist movement shifted its campaign from the county level and the struggle for a voice in the territorial legislature to a bold bid for the office of territorial delegate, New Mexico's only voice in the United States Congress. Fusionism, with all its dubious consequences, also had to be faced by the territory's small People's party in 1896. The two major parties, taking no chances, were apprehensive about the choice New Mexico Populists would make during that crucial year.

As with many other states and territories influenced by Populist ideas and programs, little has been written about Populism in New Mexico. A perusal of the index of *The New Mexico Historical Review* reveals no direct reference to Populism or the People's party. In 1966, Howard R. Lamar in his book *The Far Southwest, 1846-1912* dealt briefly with Populism in the context of territorial politics.[1] The present writer, in a book on the territory's statehood movement, devoted a portion of one chapter to the Populist protest.[2] But, on the whole, references to Populist activity in New Mexico have been few.

New Mexico Populism has needed a historian not only because it is important to recover this neglected phase of the state's past, but also because of the dearth of published histories of state and territorial Populist movements in the Rocky Mountain West.[3] To a lesser extent state studies are needed in other strongholds of Populism such as the Midwest and the South, although a number of fine monographs have been written about agrarian unrest and Populism in the Southern states, and Walter T.K. Nugent's study of nativism

1

in Kansas has revealed much about the movement in this important state.[4] Many ground-breaking articles have been written about local and state Populist movements, but the impact of these studies has been limited by the necessary brevity of this form of historical writing.

Notwithstanding the additional historical spadework that needs to be done to illuminate local, state, and regional Populism, some excellent synthesizing of the nature and direction of the overall movement has occurred to further refine and sometimes challenge the conclusions reached by John D. Hicks in his monumental *The Populist Revolt.* [5] Norman Pollack has endeavored to get at the grass-roots sentiment of Midwestern Populism, [6] while C. Vann Woodward has done much to reveal the essence of Southern Populism. [7] Unfortunately, no comparable effort has been made in the case of Western Populism, but perhaps no such effort should be made until more histories and biographies of a state or local nature are published for this region.

Richard Hofstadter in his revisionist treatment of Populism in *The Age of Reform,* although admitting that the mountain states of the West were one of the "three compact centers" of the national movement, dismisses Populism in this area as simply an emotional concern over the federal government's policy toward silver. "Silver is a special case," Hofstadter argues and separates Western Populism from the agrarian discontent that characterized the movement in the South and Midwest. "The free-silver Populism of the mountain-states variety," he concludes, "was not agrarian Populism at all, but simply silverism."[8] It will be the purpose of this study not only to chronicle the events of New Mexico Populism, but to respond to Hofstadter's interpretations and the interpretations of other historians of the Populist crusade. Populism in the Territory of New Mexico, in other words, will be related to the national movement. Evidence of the importance of silverism, agrarian discontent, antimonopoly sentiment, nativism, and other alleged trademarks of Populism was searched for with this intent, in order to place New Mexico in a correct perspective regionally as well as nationally. The results of the study, hopefully, will be to deepen to some extent an understanding of the general movement.

New Mexico's territorial status presents some problems in chronicling the discontent which eventually resulted in a full-blown Populist bid for power. Under the territorial system the power of the territory to influence national affairs was purposefully limited. The territorial delegate could not cast a vote in Congress. He could express the views of his constituents in congressional debate and serve on committees in the lower house, but these prerogatives were greatly diluted by his non-voting status. The territorial administration was appointed by the president of the United States with the advice and consent of the Senate; the governor, territorial secretary, and other high officials could usually be counted on to represent the views of the occupant in the White House in national matters. Territorial affairs were directly under the jurisdiction of the Department of the Interior in the late nineteenth century. An official with populistic views undoubtedly would have provoked an avalanche of protest mail from territorial citizens with orthodox political views, mail which the secretary of the interior could have used to force the removal of the objectionable official. In actual practice, however, the secretary of the interior was usually quite indifferent toward his territorial responsibility. Members of the territorial legislature were elected by the citizens of the territory, as was the delegate, but, according to New Mexico's Organic Act of 1850, all laws enacted by the legislative assembly had to be submitted to the Congress for approval. [9] Such approval was usually automatic, but not always. One could easily imagine the attitude that one of the conservative congresses of the late nineteenth century would have had toward a territorial law which radically restricted the activities of the railroads in the territory or curbed the power and acquisitiveness of big landowners in New Mexico.

Another problem faced by all territorial citizens, whether they were political rebels or not, was the great dependence of the territories on the federal government. Lewis L. Gould in his study of Wyoming politics from 1868 to 1896 has concluded that federal funds "emerged as an essential part of the economic health of the territory," and that the "persistent and orderly acquisition of federal appropriations" became the essential goal of Wyoming, as well as other territories of the arid West. [10] New Mexico with its rich historical heritage, its interesting synthesis of Anglo, Hispano, and Indian cultures, its long-known deposits of mineral wealth, and its centuries-old cultivation of the Rio Grande Valley and widespread stock raising does not fall perfectly into Wyoming's category. Wyoming, a state lacking in precious metals, is one of those Western commonwealths which aptly illustrates Frederick Jackson Turner's description of Western territories: "rectangular Territories . . . carved into checkerboard States, creations of the federal government, without a history, without physiographical unity, without particularistic ideas." [11] Nevertheless, New Mexico learned very early in its long sixty-two-year tutelage as a territory to look to the federal government for the expected largess and help.

The Republican party was the dominant party in the territory largely because of the willingness of the national party to promote programs regarded by many as vital to the territory's interest. They include tariff protection for wool and lead, the promotion of irrigation projects, an attempted solution to the land-grant question, and the maintenance of federal facilities, particularly military ones. These policies are in contrast to those initiated by President Grover Cleveland in 1885 which stressed limited government and tariff for

3

revenue and left territorial Democrats vulnerable to the charge that they were allied with a party indifferent to New Mexico's welfare. Recognizing New Mexico's dependence on the federal government, LeBaron Bradford Prince, territorial governor during the early Populist period, wrote a friend in Socorro on January 2, 1892, warning him not to participate in a plan to send to the Republican national convention a delegation opposing the renomination of President Benjamin Harrison. Prince, a Harrison appointee, claimed that the current administration had done more than any previous one in the disposition of public lands, including the establishment of a land-grant court in 1891 to judicate conflicting claims over the old Spanish and Mexican land grants. But the real thrust of his argument was that a territory had ''to depend so much on the National Administration that it would be foolish for it to act in an unfriendly manner even if there were some reasons.'' 12

Consequently, with New Mexico's territorial government so much under the thumb of the federal government and so heavily dependent upon Washington for helpful legislation and subsidies, it would seem an exercise in futility for a party such as the People's party to believe it could win power in the territory or do anything with that power if it should unexpectedly succeed at the polls. The well-known hostility of Populists toward Washington would make the People's party appear as a major threat to the growth and prosperity of the territory in the minds of many New Mexico citizens. The totality of Populism's indictment of the government's economic policies would alarm even those New Mexicans who recognized the defects of America's economic system. Yet, despite these liabilities, territorial Populists boldly challenged the two major parties, first on the county level, then on the territorial level. Did their audacity spring from deep conviction? Did they feel themselves to be the wave of the future? Whatever the causes, Populist motives will be examined in this study.

A study of Rocky Mountain territorial Populism brings up the question of whether it might not be more profitable to study Populism under statehood. There is a common impression that the great period of statemaking had passed before Populism emerged. But it is easy to forget that when the era of rising agrarian discontent began in the West, following the disastrous drought of 1887, there was only one state in the Rocky Mountain West, Colorado; the rest, Montana, Idaho, Utah, Wyoming, New Mexico, and Arizona, were territories. In 1890, the year in which third-party candidates won such surprising election victories, particularly in the Midwest, three of these mountain territories, Montana, Idaho and Wyoming, were proclaimed states by President Harrison. Yet New Mexico, Arizona, and Utah remained territories during the 1892 and 1894 elections, when the People's party made its most serious attempts to become a truly national organization. In 1896, the year of the Populist-Democratic fusion, Utah was proclaimed a state by Grover Cleveland, leaving only New Mexico and Arizona as territories in the Rocky Mountain region. Consequently, the Populist era began with an overwhelming preponderence of the Western commonwealths under the territorial system, but the balance shifted significantly toward state organizations as the period of protest and discontent reached its climax with Bryan's defeat in 1896. Territorial governments were almost as common as state governments in the Rocky Mountain West during the Populist era. Moreover, a study of Populism in New Mexico provides an unusual opportunity to discover how the political system of a territory responded to a concerted demand for change and reform.

A final factor to consider in writing the history of Populism in any Western state or territory is the undeveloped nature of these predominantly mineral-rich, spacious domains. Backward conditions were especially evident in New Mexico, whose emergence from the frontier environment was perhaps the most incomplete of all. Although the territory had made progress in developing its deposits of gold, silver, copper, and coal, confusion had resulted from its vast land grants, the titles to which were often muddled and up for "grabs." Extraordinary opportunities for individual aggrandizement thus provided a natural opposition to a semicollectivist movement such as Populism. Chances for acquiring a rich mining claim or title to a Spanish or Mexican land grant tempted even those with populistic or progressive views. If these seemingly matchless opportunities are added to the frontier individualism claimed for Westerners by Turner, then yet another obstacle to Populist success in New Mexico must be acknowledged. Yet, a People's party did exist in this unpromising seedbed for reform and, although the fledgling party did not flourish during two territorial elections, it did cause concern among many Democrats who were apprehensive that a Populist bid would detract significantly from their vote. As for the Republicans, they were tempted more than once to try to corrupt or absorb the would-be giant killer.

2

THE LINCOLN COUNTY
FARMERS' ALLIANCE

Protest and organized agitation were natural in Lincoln County, which in 1888 comprised the entire southeastern corner of the Territory of New Mexico. Small stockmen and farmers struggled for survival as ambitious cattlemen and cattle companies persisted in expanding their holdings in the county's rangeland. The county assessment rolls for 1888 show Captain Joseph C. Lea's cattle company owning 16,500 acres. [1] Most of this land, which extended along the entire Rio Hondo to its juncture with the Pecos, was purchased by the enterprising Lea during the period from 1879 to 1885. [2] Other big landowners included Charles B. Eddy, a transplanted New Yorker better known for his railroad and irrigation promotions; the British-incorporated Carizozo Cattle Ranch, Limited; Cox and Peacock; and the El Capitan Land and Cattle Company. [3] These large enterprises, not content with the sizable acreage they owned, were continually in search of water rights and exercised great political and economic power in the county.

Common to all stockmen whether large or small were the dry conditions that continued long after the summer drought of 1887. A Lincoln County newspaper, attempting to cheer up its readers, quoted the *Denver Republican* on October 11, 1888, to the effect that Colorado farmers were finding they could use less water in irrigation and still produce a satisfactory wheat crop. The precipitation being four and one-fourth inches less than average for the past seventeen years, "1888 will be known as a very dry year, unless the rain and snowfall between this time and the first of next January shall be exceptionally great." [4] Drought conditions were accompanied by unusually severe winters, such as the one in 1886-87, which swept the northern plains and caused cattle losses as high as 80 percent. In New Mexico, where winters were mild, depressed conditions in the cattle industry occurred later than in the north and were due primarily to low prices, overstocking, and excessive dryness. [5] On March 22, 1890, the *Stock Grower and Farmer* of Las Vegas expressed its concern over the continuing parched conditions in the West. "Rain is badly needed in the southwest. The

7

county [San Miguel] is very dry and the absence of spring moisture will result in heavy losses." [6] The adverse weather conditions compounded the problems already created by the cattle kings for the small operators of Lincoln County.

To cope with these challenges some of the small stockmen and farmers in the county organized chapters of the National Farmers' Alliance and Co-operative Union of America, or Southern Alliance. [7] Headed by Dr. C.W. Macune, this successful farm organization was spreading rapidly from its original home in Texas throughout the farmlands of the South. In New Mexico, chapters of the Southern Alliance were organized in neighboring Dona Ana County [8] as well as in Lincoln. Both the Lincoln and Dona Ana alliances were active, scheduling meetings throughout their respective counties, with local chapters rotating as hosts. The official voice of the Southern Alliance in southeastern New Mexico was the *Nogal Nugget,* published in the tiny community of Nogal, a trade center for mine and ranch supplies located twenty-five miles northwest of Lincoln, county seat of Lincoln County. [9] The paper was edited by J. E. Sligh, an energetic newspaperman who managed a ranch on the east slope of the San Andreas Mountains. He was active in Nogal Alliance No. 8, a chapter of the Lincoln County Alliance. [10] The paper regularly published the official directory for the Lincoln and Dona Ana county alliances and announced forthcoming meetings. On September 27, 1888, for instance, the *Nugget* notified Alliance members, who made up the bulk of its readership of less than a thousand, that the next regular Lincoln County meeting would be hosted by the Lincoln Alliance No. 13 in the town of Lincoln on the first Thursday of October. "Let us have big attendance. Do not fail to come in wagons, and bring bedding, etc., prepared to be independent. The Lincoln people will do the best they can for us, but to entertain the whole County Alliance is probably more than they will be able to do."

As was the case in places where the Alliance was active, a variety of social, political, and economic activities was sponsored by the Lincoln County organization. At the October meeting, so enthusiastically promoted by the *Nugget,* the re-establishment of a cooperative store at Nogal was to be the major topic of discussion. The first store had failed during the previous winter, because, as editor Sligh put it, the brothers failed to follow their leader. "The failure of the effort to induce the brethren to co-operate politically, was due to the same cause." The pages of the *Nugget* were replete with advice, given in a warm, fraternal manner by the editor or by one of the Alliance officers or by a reader. Some of the letters to the editor were critical, such as one by J.A. Akins, a special lecturer for the organization. He demanded that the charter for Seven Rivers Alliance No. 16 be withdrawn because it was the only chapter in the county that was not active. An "Alliance, like everything else, is worthless unless it is attended to properly." [11]

The Lincoln County Alliance was an active, lively organization operating in a hostile environment. The August 23, 1888, issue of the *Nugget* carried advertising by twenty-two ranchers in the county, including George W. Coe, one of the prominent partisans of the Lincoln County War and former friend of Billy the Kid. One merchant, whose advertisement appeared regularly, billed himself as the original "Cheap John," and claimed he had "everything" desired by Alliance people from a pair of duck pants or a calico dress to a farming plow.

It is difficult to assess the extent of farming in what was then an essentially stock-raising area. The territorial Bureau of Immigration, basically a New Mexico promotional organization, boasted in an 1894 publication that until "recently agriculture was very primitive, though yields were always phenomenally large." One must accept with caution this later description of agriculture in Lincoln County after its eastern flank had been partitioned into Chaves and Eddy counties. Nevertheless, the county must have had some valuable agricultural resources, as the bureau's publication described it as "dotted with thrifty farms." Irrigation was the key to an agricultural bonanza which would soon cover all the valleys with farms. Already vegetables were being raised amid the grapes and currants which "grow wild," and farmers could count on four or five cuttings of alfalfa a year. The bureau, in the best traditions of the old West, also covetously eyed the public domain, claiming that the best grazing and agricultural resources were on federal lands. [12]

The president of the Lincoln County Alliance was Jasper N. Coe. A cousin of George Coe, Jasper was an aggressive exponent of his organization's policies. [13] George Coe and Jasper's brother, Frank, were supporters of Alexander A. McSween who, along with the luckless John Henry Tunstall and cattle baron John Chisum, challenged the supremacy of a faction of powerful storekeepers and ranchers who developed Lincoln County after the Civil War and regarded all new arrivals as intruders. The entrenched faction, which had the support of Territorial Governor Samuel B. Axtell and other important New Mexico officials, managed to win a commanding advantage when McSween and three of his allies were killed while fleeing from Mc-Sween's burning home during an open war in the town of Lincoln in July of 1878. The victors were not satisfied with their success. While George and Frank Coe and other McSween supporters sought refuge in the nearby mountains, partisans of James J. Dolan and John H. Riley, successors to

9

Lawrence D. Murphy's mercantile firm in Lincoln and leaders of the triumphant faction, burned the Coe ranch to the ground.

Having lost everything, and confronted with a warrant for George's arrest, the two Coes had no recourse but to leave Lincoln County. They traveled to Sugarite, Colorado, to help a cousin, Lou W. Coe, move his cattle to the San Juan Valley. There they settled, along with Jasper (or Jap as they called him) on two ranches on the site of Aztec, present seat of government for San Juan County. [14] Although Jasper did not fight in the Lincoln County War, his sympathies obviously were with his kinfolk, and he once remarked to his son that Billy the Kid, who fought on the McSween side, was all right. [15] The Coes, particularly George and Frank, seem to have a penchant for getting into trouble. A little over a year following their arrival in San Juan country they became involved in another explosive range war as members of an allegedly anti-rustling organization known as the Farmington Stockmens' Protective Association. Although some lives were lost during the years 1880 and 1881, there was no bloody climax such as the one that occurred in the town of Lincoln in 1878. In 1882 Frank Coe, feeling the situation in Lincoln County had improved following Governor Lew Wallace's pacification of the area, returned to Lincoln to settle on unsurveyed land along the Ruidoso River. He was followed by his cousin George in 1884. Jasper, who had been in California with his family trying to make a new life, also returned to Lincoln County in 1884 to settle on land between his brother Frank and George. [16]

Why Jasper Coe assumed such an aggressive role in the Lincoln County Farmers' Alliance is not certain, but an examination of the county assessment rolls shows he was the poorest of the three. In 1888 Jasper had only four horses and three head of cattle, while his brother Frank had twenty-two horses and eighty head of cattle. The value of Jasper's property was assessed at $940, while Frank was worth $2,557 and George, $1,528. [17] Whether Jasper's rather marginal existence as a stockman motivated his identification with the Alliance, a group that had banded together for survival through cooperation, has not been determined, but his commitment to the organization was undeniable. Jasper Coe, or J.N., as he used his initials, was president of the local Lincoln Alliance No. 13 in the town of Lincoln, as well as leader of the county Alliance. He was an agent for the *Nogal Nugget,* the voice of the Alliance in southeastern New Mexico. [18] In 1890, when the organization decided to expand its activities throughout the territory, Jasper became president of the territorial Alliance. [19]

Coe's leadership of the county Alliance was forceful, for he was a strong-willed and pugnacious man. On August 16, 1888, he wrote a letter to the *Nugget* in which he vigorously defended one of the special land agents sent to Lincoln County to investigate land frauds. New Mexico's record of illegal land purchases was notorious. In 1884, the first year in which land-fraud statistics were made public by the General Land Office, the territory ranked first with 827 cases, followed by California with 574. Although Grover Cleveland has been given credit for launching the federal policy of restoring illegally acquired lands to the public domain, Westerner Henry M. Teller, secretary of the interior under Arthur and his commissioner for the General Land Office, had already taken steps to curb these fraudulent practices. By the end of the year 1885 seven special agents were investigating charges of fraud in the Territory of New Mexico. Under Cleveland's administration, in 1885 an even more determined team of men dealt with the problem of land frauds. Capable Lucius Q.C. Lamar, as secretary of the interior, and William A.J. Sparks, the new commissioner of the General Land Office, were committed to end the casual and questionable administration of public lands in the West. Their resolution was great despite the fact that the amount of land which could be purchased under the laws enacted by Congress was often inadequate for a semiarid region and that such a federal policy would further delay desperately needed land surveys. [20] Cleveland's appointment of George W. Julian as surveyor general of New Mexico was an especially bad omen for the big cattlemen of the territory. Julian, a septuagenarian, was a remarkably incorruptible man. Soon after he took office new cases of land fraud were reported and investigations were pushed with exceptional vigor. [21]

The big cattle operators in southern New Mexico were disturbed by the activities of a special land agent named R.P. Walker, who antagonized a large number of influential people in Lincoln County but found in Jasper Coe a bold and assertive defender. Walker became an ugly symbol for the national administration's allegedly repressive land policies. He was pictured by the Las Vegas *Stock Grower and Farmer* and the White Oaks *Interpreter* as a heartless man paid $10 a day to "hound and persecute" poor innocent settlers. [22] The *Weekly New Mexican Review* of Sante Fe claimed that Special Agent Walker was responsible for hundreds of cases threatening cancellation of land transactions. There was not "one scintilla of evidence to sustain the special agent's report, but hundreds of indictments have been brought in the courts against settlers with the same lack of evidence." [23] The *Socorro Chieftain* could not state the case against the administration's land policy strongly enough. The work of "the administration's land officials in this territory . . . has set settlement back five years." [24]

In response to such charges Jasper Coe posed the crucial question in the *Nugget:* Were the victims of Walker's investigations "poor men" trying to acquire 80 to 160 acres of land for homes, or were they "poor innocent" individuals who wanted to monopolize the waterfront along the streams of New Mexico? [25] The question was a vital one to small stockmen in the territory, for monopolizing water resources was a favorite technique of big cattle operators. Stephen W. Dorsey, the former carpetbag senator from Arkansas who established an enormous ranch in Colfax County, owned "all the springs" on 160 acres which controlled the "whole 10,000 acres back of it." [26]

Coe urged the *Nugget* to publish the national Republican platform. It was in such perfect accord with that segment of the press "subsidized" by the big cattle interests in New Mexico that Coe was ready to believe that the platform had been framed by Stephen B. Elkins himself. [27] Elkins was a former territorial delegate from New Mexico who had left the territory for the East. He later became Benjamin Harrison's secretary of war and an important United States senator from West Virginia. For years he had been a leading land speculator in league with cattle kings and other enterprising Anglos eager to exploit the resources of the territory. Territorial Governor Edmund G. Ross regarded him as one of the prime organizers of New Mexico's infamous land-grant combine, the Santa Fe Ring. "Smooth Steve" gained control of a large portion of the immense Mora Grant in the northern part of the territory, and, while he represented New Mexico in Congress, he sold stock for and worked in behalf of the Maxwell Land Grant. [28] Editor Sligh enthusiastically supported Coe's strong condemnation of the Republican platform. He insisted that the innocent settlers being harrassed by "spies and prosecutions," to quote from the platform, were in reality big cattle barons such as Charles B. Eddy and George Williams of Lincoln County. [29]

The leadership of the Lincoln branch of the Southern Alliance was staunchly Democratic, and, early in the fall of 1888, it began campaigning for the re-election of President Cleveland. Its concern was not only with the national Republican party and its devious platform, but with the clever shenanigans of the local party organizations in the territory. The effort of Republicans in Lincoln, San Miguel, and Colfax counties to organize so-called people's parties especially angered the *Nugget.* The Republican puppet party in Lincoln County was accused of "fence straddling" and representing neither party nor principle. And yet it was heralded as the "Peoples-Choice Party" by the *Leader* of White Oaks, a Republican newspaper regarded as hostile to the Alliance and to all "other labor organizations." [30] The attempt of this new party to win the support of the Alliance by calling itself the People's party and "yelling and whooping for Alliance men, and damning the

Cattle men, Rings, and Monopolies," would, in the opinion of the *Nugget,* ultimately fail, because it was insincere. [31]

Republicans, as organizers of these new "people's parties," had had years to show their honest concern for the little settlers of the territory. Yet, while in power, what did Republican officeholders do? They passed laws to protect the "Cattle Association monopoly" on the public domain. They robbed the people of their homes and gave the land to "fraudulent" grant claimants, fostering the most "stupendous system of Land Fraud ever known." They protected the railroads from taxation and from the "just demands" for lower rates. When special agents were sent by Washington to investigate charges of fraud and malpractice, they fought these honest investigators at every turn. Why then this tardy interest in small ranchers and farmers? Because these hypocritical politicians, as self-appointed "protectors" of the small and helpless, were eager to get people into "some kind of party where they can be voted as republican bosses dictate." [32]

Another concern of Alliance members in Lincoln County was the controversial quarantine law, enacted to keep cattle carrying the dreaded Texas fever out of New Mexico. Reflecting that strong fear of bigness which permeated Alliance groups and legitimate Populist organizations throughout the entire Populist era, the *Nugget* bitterly assailed the quarantine measure. It was not a legitimate law for the protection of cattle from Texas fever, but rather a measure to keep new stockmen out of the territory and to protect cattle association men in their *"monopoly of the public domain."* Every organized monopoly was calling for "protection" and the cattle association was a monopoly. Although the quarantine law was regarded as another piece of Republican legislation, another example of Republican concern for the "dear people," Governor Ross' proclamation to the county commissioners, ordering them to levy a quarantine tax on New Mexican beeves to pay for the cost of the inspection program, subjected even this liberal Democratic leader to attack. The purpose of the law was not to keep Texas beeves, as possible carriers of the disease, from entering the territory, but to keep thousands of small homesteaders from settling in New Mexico. "The quarantine law keeps out the cattle of small farmers, and as they can not leave the stock behind the farmers do not come. Thus the Cattle Baron is 'protected' from the man with the hoe and the plow." [33]

Fear of a cattle monopoly led the Alliance leadership in Lincoln County to identify with the struggle of other working people opposed to monopoly power, such as urban laborers, who as employees or consumers had to cope with manufacturing trusts. Almost four years before the St. Louis platform of the People's party called for the unity of the producing classes — ''The interests of rural and urban labor are the same, their enemies are identical.'' [34] — the *Nugget* began to show its genuine concern for the plight of urban labor. The protective tariff, long a favorite target of respectable Democratic politicians, provided an excellent departure point for a series of editorials highlighting the struggle between capital and the working class. Accepting Cleveland's belief that the tariff was the mother of trusts, the *Nugget* characterized the high, Republican-supported tariff as one in which ''farmers are 'protected' from selling their products at their own price, and are 'protected' from buying their goods in the cheapest market.'' The urban laborer was not much better off. The high tariff system shielded him so that he could not buy provisions and clothing in the cheapest possible market, but at the same time exposed him to the competition of the ''pauper and *peon* labor of the whole world.'' Because of the high, protective tariff, the farmer was compelled to pay $140 for $100 worth of wire fence, while his working brethren in urban American were required to pay $160 for $100 worth of cotton cloth. [35]

The lively *Nogal Nugget* was keenly aware of the political pitfalls it would encounter in advocating tariff reduction in the upcoming 1888 presidential election. Anticipating a favorite Republican campaign charge, it insisted that Cleveland was not a free trader in favor of permitting foreign countires to dump their cheap products on the American market, thus endangering the jobs of small wage earners. President Cleveland had never advocated the complete removal of all tariff barriers. Rather, it was the position of Cleveland and the Democrats to support those tariff adjustments which would ''compensate for any differences which [might] exist between the standard of wages which should be paid to America's laboring men and those of other countries.''

A much more effective way of protecting urban laborers from unfair competition, however, was to restrict drastically immigration from aboard. Revealing a nativistic attitude based upon economic considerations, rather than the racist or emotional ones claimed for agrarian protestors by Hofstadter, [36] the *Nugget* editorially condemned the policy which had allowed people to immigrate to America in unprecedented numbers during the eighties. The best way to provide true protection for the native workingman is through the ''restriction and prohibition of the immigration or importation of laborers from other countries.'' Those who now swarm to our shores have ''no purpose or intent of becoming our fellow citizens or acquiring any permanent interest in our country, but . . . crowd every field of employment with unintelligent labor, at wages which ought not to satisfy those who make a claim to American citizenship.'' [37] Although there might be some truth to this harsh criticism insofar as it involved the so-called birds of passage who crossed and recrossed the Atlantic at this time, it was quite unfair to lump all immigrants into one category. Scores of Europeans, as new Americans, were keenly concerned about almost everything they encountered in their adopted land, notwithstanding the confusion and bewilderment accompanying their first years in a new country.

Small farmers and stockmen in Lincoln County were concerned with other issues besides the so-called cattle monopoly and the tariff and immigration questions. Local problems, typical of those faced by any growing territory, also attracted the attention of the crusading little Alliance paper. The *Nugget,* in 1888, was especially troubled by the possibility that Lincoln County would be partitioned into three counties. Politicians should "go slow" before deciding to carve "three counties out of our present magnificent domain." [38] The creation of Chaves and Eddy counties out of Lincoln County the following year showed what little influence the Alliance organ had on the territorial assembly at Santa Fe.

One aspect of the Lincoln County Alliance that seems noteworthy was unwillingness of the organization to compel its members to adhere to the kind of discipline that would later become rather common among agrarian political organizations. The *Nugget* pointed with pride to the fifteen Alliance delegates who attended the last Democratic county convention and acted "just like any other delegates in that they worked individually for their personal preferences." Proud that all attempts to unite Alliance members into one voting bloc had failed, the Nogal weekly insisted that such freedom of choice and individuality must always be present if Alliance members were to continue to act according to principle. [39] Thus, that individualism so often associated with the American frontier was decidedly present in Lincoln County in 1888.

Although generally supporting a straight Democratic ticket, the *Nugget* shared that sturdy sense of independence with the membership of the county Alliance. Its editorial stands showed complete satisfaction with the Democratic candidates nominated for county office. President Cleveland, whose name would be reviled by Western farmers in a few years, was enthusiastically endorsed for re-election. But Antonio Joseph, the territory's Democratic delegate for the past four years, would not receive the journal's praise, because of his support of the proposed partition of Lincoln County. [40] Exhibiting a nativism which was undeniably racist and irrational, the *Nugget* attacked the incumbent delegate, insisting that "free-born American democratic citizens of Lincoln county . . . can affiliate with and vote for a pure bred Spaniard or Mexican, for they are a noble race of people, but when it

15

comes to voting for a Portuguese-*Nigger*-Mexican for our representative to Congress, who uses that position to assist in robbing our country of its fairest portions the democrats say 'No, not for Joseph.' '' [41]

Just how the Hispanos of Lincoln County responded to this vicious slur against Joseph could not be determined. Actually their numbers were small in this part of New Mexico. A perusal of the Alliance directories of that era for Lincoln and Dona Ana counties, and Colfax County to the north, yield not one Spanish name. Probably very few of the county's natives were pure-blooded; the term ''pure bred Mexican'' is delightfully incongruous in any case. Consequently, the *Nugget's* awkward, left-handed compliment to those with undiluted blood would have satisfied none but the most gullible. As for Delegate Joseph, an astute politician with ingratiating ways whose Portuguese father was a native of the Azores, [42] his response undoubtedly would have been to ignore such a crude attack. What the slur against Joseph's heritage demonstrated was that the *Nugget's* editor, J.E. Sligh, was intolerant of non-whites. If Sligh's views were as representative of Alliance thinking on this question as they were on the others, a virulent form of racism existed among many of the small stockmen and farmers in southeastern New Mexico. The Southern background of many of the Anglos in this part of the territory, symbolized by the association of the Lincoln organization with the Southern Alliance, would help to explain the contemptuous reference to Blacks used in describing the delegate's heritage; by italicizing only the word ''Nigger'' Brother Sligh was communicating most effectively with at least some of his Alliance brethren. The big question, almost impossible to answer, is how widespread was this intolerance of non-whites among the Anglo citizens of Lincoln County?

Misgivings about Joseph began to dissipate as election day approached. In early September, the Alliance paper was quoting favorable news stories about Joseph from other newspapers. [43] In early October, the *Nugget* was supporting the delegate against the candidacy of a man who probably had one of the best claims in the territory to being a ''pure bred'' Spaniard. Mariano S. Otero, Joseph's Republican opponent, came from one of the oldest most distinguished families in New Mexico. Partisan considerations had triumphed over considerations of blood.

Otero, a successful Bernalillo businessman and banker, [44] was pictured by the Democratic press as being an inept man who could no more help the citizens of New Mexico than a hen could ''hatch butterflies out of snow balls.'' Elected as territorial delegate in 1878, Otero was reported to have attended only twenty-one sessions of Congress. [45] Although he had introduced a few bills, several of which called for the settlement of private land claims, not "a single word" of his proposed legislation was ever enacted into law. Morever, even though he was a member of the House Committee of Weights and Measurements, records reveal that he did not attend a single committee meeting. [46]

As the office of territorial delegate was New Mexico's only voice in the nation's top deliberative body, the attitude of another county paper, the *Lincoln Independent,* towards this office is most revealing. "The truth is that in Congress the territorial delegates amount to little; they can not vote . . . and all they can do is talk and work before the committees. Hence it is very plain that we need experience and influence in our delegate and his care and industry as to our affairs." Joseph is such a man. The only positive thing that can be said about ex-delegate Otero, the *Independent* concluded, was that he was a skilled "operator at the festive game of poker." [47]

On election day, Alliance-supported Democrats triumphed in Lincoln County in one race after another. There was, of course, keen disappointment among county Democrats over Cleveland's loss to Harrison in the national election, but this disappointment was somewhat modified by Joseph's victory for a third term. [48] Members of the Lincoln Alliance, however, had taken to fighting among themselves even before the campaign ended, notwithstanding their precarious existence in a land of cattle kings. The issue that divided them was the collapse of the Co-operative Company, the Alliance-owned store in Nogal.

Philosophical differences over the principles of cooperative buying and selling had already split the leadership of the county organization. Editor Sligh was feuding with Jasper Coe and other leaders of the Lincoln Alliance, and the *Nugget* was no longer the "official organ" of the county organization. On October 4, Sligh, who was as ardent a proponent of the cooperative movement as C.W. Macune himself, was optimistic about a county Alliance meeting being held in Lincoln to discuss cooperative endeavors. Success would ensue if the brethren would only unite, he insisted. By early November, the *Nugget* was not only bemoaning the lack of cooperation, which resulted in the total failure of the Nogal store, but was lamenting the bitterness that had followed the store's collapse. "Brother is fighting brother. Brethren are trying to injure the property of other brethren! Charges are made that 'true Alliance principles have been forgotten.' " Stressing that spirit of collective action that the Northern and Southern Alliances and other farm groups had tried to instill into their members in the late eighties, the *Texas Farmer,* organ for the Texas Grange, was quoted for support by the distressed editor. Cooperation is as broad as humanity itself, and any departure "from this principle simply makes a business of a joint stock company."

Insisting that a farm cooperative was more than just a simple business enterprise, the *Nugget's* editor asserted that once the principle of cooperation is removed the "foundation timbers" of the cooperative must "fall to the ground." The Co-operative Company of Nogal, which was incorporated under the laws of New Mexico, had suffered such a fate. It had become "a tool in the hands of a few men" who wanted to advance their own special interests. Selfishness prevailed, and Alliance members, believing they would not receive a fair profit from their investment, failed to "subscribe and pay for stock."

As to what should be done about this business reversal, Sligh unhesitatingly offered his advice. Alliance members, who had subscribed and paid for stock, should meet and either decide to abandon the enterprise by selling their property or invest money to enable the cooperative to buy more goods. Or they should "adopt such measures as will induce others to unite with them and thus enlarge their capital." Their basic decision was whether to turn the Nogal cooperative into "a true co-operative store" or continue operating it as an ordinary joint stock company. The feuding editor, aiming his most telling barbs at Jasper Coe and his associates, insisted that a true cooperative store should be successful in any county where goods are bought and sold. "It cannot be otherwise. There is no chance of failure in such stores except that which might arise on account of a desire to reap the benefits which legitimately belong to others." Such greed and selfishness had "already hurt the Alliance" in Lincoln County. 49

The angry feuding of Alliance leaders was no new experience for Lincoln County. In the county's vast domain, which extended from the Manzano Mountains southward to the Texas border, individuality and sharp conflict had already given the people of Lincoln a permanent niche in American history. Ten years after the violent Lincoln County War men were still struggling with one another in the famous New Mexico county. In 1888, the major conflict pitted the instincts for survival of the small farmers and stockmen against the arrogant ambitions of the cattle barons. To many of the county's small operators the power of the cattlemen posed as great a threat as the industrial monopolies of the East posed to urban workingmen and small businessmen. Opposing the cattle monopoly in Lincoln County was very much a case of "bucking big business out on the plains," to borrow a term Robert G. Athearn used to describe the fight independent stock raisers had to wage against powerful stock grazers' associations. 50

Protest in this part of the Territory of New Mexico, then, was largely a reaction to ominous monopoly power. Problems such as sagging prices, adverse weather conditions, and a deflationary cycle, which were taking their

18

toll throughout much of rural America, had helped to create much of the discontent among small operators in the county. But the existence of a cattle monopoly, so-called, gave for many Lincoln citizens a tangible target for their outrage and distress. The organization to cope with all of these problems, notwithstanding its internal bickering, was the Lincoln County Farmers' Alliance. It was beginning to focus on issues the two major parties would avoid for years to come. A climate for agrarian discontent which would later result in a Populist political movement was thus being created. Whether Lincoln Alliance members would be attracted to the Populist label or prefer to stay with the Democratic party was yet to be decided. The emotions of many of them, however, had been sufficiently aroused to galvanize them into action long before free silver became the trumpet call for reform in New Mexico and throughout the rest of the Rocky Mountain West.

3

THE STRUGGLE IN COLFAX COUNTY

In the northeastern corner of the Territory of New Mexico sprawled Colfax County, its boundless rangeland dotted with strangely formed buttes and mountains standing like lone sentinels along what was once the most dangerous stretch of the Santa Fe Trail. Powerful cattle barons, such as ex-Senator Dorsey and his ally, J.W. Dwyer, grazed thousands of beeves in this ideal cattle country, and their economic power posed just as great a threat to the small stockmen and farmers of Colfax as that faced by the independent operators of Lincoln County. To survive, and to achieve the advantages of cooperation, many Colfax settlers felt it necessary to form Alliance chapters. Chapters were organized along the lines of the Lincoln County Alliance in Elizabethtown (later to become famous as a mining ghost town), Cimarron, Raton, Ute Park, and other communities scattered along the crest of the Sangre de Christos eastward across the plains.

The result of these efforts was a vigorous Colfax County Farmers' Alliance. Meeting on the third Wednesdays of January, April, July, and October, local chapters (in Cimarron, for example) rotated as host for the county-wide gatherings. [1]

The Colfax Alliance had its official journalistic voice in the *Wagon Mound Settler,* which the *Nogal Nugget* once accused of being timid in its defense of Alliance principles. The *Raton Weekly Independent* and the *Clayton Enterprise* were also sympathetic with the plight of the independent operators in the county. [2] The *Independent* ran a column entitled the "Alliance Department," devoted exclusively to news about the Colfax Alliance and its local chapters. Information about agrarian movements elsewhere was included in this column, such as the story carried on January 12, 1889, about the national conventions of the Southern Alliance and the Agricultural Wheel, held in Meridian, Mississippi, the previous month. The purpose of the concurrent meetings, important to the agrarian movement nationally, was merger, an objective finally achieved in September of 1889. "As neither the associated press nor the local press gave the event more than passing notice" the proceedings of the merger effort were printed in the *Independent 's* section reserved for Alliance activities.

Like those in the *Nugget,* such notices in the *Independent* breathed warmth and intimacy into the Alliance organization. The struggles of its members were revealed, but so were their joys and hopes — as, for example, a story about an oyster supper given by the Vermejo Park Alliance No. 28 in Colfax County. The supper was held at the home of an Alliance brother named Shy, since the local schoolhouse was too small. "Everyone came fortified with turkey, chicken and cake. Dancing commenced at eight o'clock and continued until ten, and the company repaired to supper . . . The bachelors related their experiences with tender passion, and wit and laughter was the order of the time." After an hour at the table, the party resumed its dancing "with added vigor until a late hour." [3]

But all was not joyful for the Alliance folk of Colfax County; indeed the oyster supper of the Vermejo Park Chapter was just a brief and welcomed respite. Many of them were engaged in a solemn struggle for economic survival. Big operators and powerful cattle companies, an unusually large number of which were operating in Colfax County, outranked even poor weather conditions and falling prices as major threats to Alliance members in the late eighties. Outfits such as the Scottish-controlled Prairie Cattle and Western Land and Cattle companies and the American-owned Illinois Live Stock and Palo Blanco Cattle companies [4] constituted the "cattle monopoly" in Colfax County. An even greater threat to the county's small independents was the Maxwell Land Grant and Railroad Company, a land monopoly that claimed 2,000,000 acres of land extending northward into Colorado.

The Maxwell Land Grant is the best known of the great land tracts granted in New Mexico during the Spanish and Mexican periods. It was one of 197 grants given to prominent individuals rather than to communities or Indian pueblos. Mexican Governor Manuel Armijo on January 11, 1841, awarded eleven square leagues to Carlos Beaubien, an influential French-Canadian from Taos, and eleven square leagues to Guadalupe Miranda, his collector of customs. The twenty-two-square-league Beaubien-Miranda grant was in harmony with the Mexican Colonization Law of 1824, which limited private grants to twenty-two leagues or approximately 97,000 acres. In return for this generous donation, Beaubien and Miranda were to settle the grant, located in what would later be Colfax County. Cotton, sugar beets, stock, and wool were to be raised by settlers brought into the area. It was hoped that such development would keep citizens of the expansion-minded United States out of the territory. Armijo, who granted similar tracts of land to other men, expected to share in the profits.

After Carlos Beaubien's death in 1864, his son-in-law, Lucien Bonaparte Maxwell, purchased the grant. Later he acquired Miranda's portion as well. Natives, and even Indians, felt secure living under the generous Maxwell, who was more like an easy-going manorial lord than a modern landowner eager to collect rents or oust intruders. Hispanos could graze their stock on his grant, and Maxwell's comfortable home in Cimarron was a gathering place for frequent guests. In 1870 Maxwell sold his 97,000-acre grant for a paper price of $1,350,000 to a group of land speculators. They included Jerome B. Chaffee, mine owner and power in Colorado politics, and Stephen Elkins and his closest associate in ''land-grabbing,''*Thomas Benton Catron. Maxwell was induced to use part of his profits to found the first regular bank in New Mexico, the First National Bank of Santa Fe. It handled the securities of what its new owners called the Maxwell Land Grant and Railroad Company.

The next development in this unusual real estate enterprise was the expansion of the boundaries of the Maxwell Land Grant to the extreme limits that the law would allow. The United States deputy surveyor of New Mexico, W.W. Griffin, was hired by the company to conduct a new survey of the grant's boundaries. As a result of his efforts, the company claimed a 2-million-acre plot instead of the 97,000 acres of the original grant, which had been confirmed by Secretary of the Interior Jacob D. Cox and the Congress in 1869. [5] In the meantime, an English cattleman named Wilson Waddington, whose ranch along the Canadian River was to become the basis of the famous Bell Ranch, [6] traveled to London and sold the grant as a 2-million-acre tract of land to a group of English buyers. To complicate the ownership of the Maxwell Grant, a group of Dutch financiers from Amsterdam agreed to a request by the new English owners to handle the mortgage of the land company.

A seesaw battle ensued between the company's owners, who wanted to push the Maxwell Land Grant well beyond its original boundaries, and those in government representing the viewpoint of the small settlers who opposed them. The settlers, of course, hoped to make Colfax County part of the public domain. The election of Chaffee in 1870 as Colorado's delegate to Congress and Elkins two years later as New Mexico's representative gave the company two forceful voices in Congress, but opposition to the land scheme in Washington did not diminish. The discovery of gold on the grant in 1867 had brought thousands of argonauts scrambling across the grant. Gold camps such as E'Town, or Elizabethtown, were soon crowded with miners indifferent to the claims of the Maxwell Company. Stockmen, primarily from Texas, moved

---

* The terms ''land-grabbing'' and ''land-grabber'' were commonly used in the Territory of New Mexico to describe land speculation.

into Colfax County at the same time, regarding the rolling grasslands there as part of the public domain. By 1873, the issue was clearly drawn. Did the range land of Colfax County belong to the company or to the numerous squatters, who saw no difference between this land and public lands elsewhere? A squatters' club was organized at Cimarron, and two groups were formed in Raton, one of which was willing to use force, if necessary, to resist the claims of the Maxwell owners. A ruling by the Department of the Interior on January 2, 1874, that the entire area was to be treated as public land greatly strengthened the will of the determined anti-grant squatters. [7]

The campaign to confirm the grant as a 2-million-acre holding received a major setback when the Maxwell Company went bankrupt in 1875. [8] But the bankruptcy proceedings seemed to have been a clever maneuver whereby the company owners could escape their creditors. Melvin W. Mills, a prominent Colfax County attorney and partisan Republican, bought the grant to cover a tax debt and, several months later, sold it to Elkins' law partner, Catron. But, in the end, the Dutch bankers involved in the company's operation managed to gain control.

With the size of the grant still in doubt, the company's promoters, unwilling to bring their questionable case before reform-minded Secretary of the Interior Carl Schurz, tried to win the support of Land Commissioner James A. Williamson. They wanted him to accept court decisions based upon land surveys as the ultimate determinate, rather than to use the Mexican Colonization Law of 1824 as a precedent. A quick survey, conducted by Stephen Elkins' brother and R.T. Marmon in 1878, resulted in a report which claimed almost 2 million acres of land for the grant. Because of favorable court decisions and friendly land-office rulings, the promoters were finally able to achieve practically everything they desired. On May 19, 1879, Williamson issued to the Maxwell Land Grant and Railroad Company patents of ownership for 1,714,764.094 acres of land. Court litigation continued, however, until 1887, when the expanded claims of the company were upheld in a decision by the Supreme Court, which tended to discourage further serious legal challenge. [9]

Lurking behind the scenes in the widely publicized controversy over the Maxwell Grant was the powerful Santa Fe Ring. Ill defined and secretive in its operations, this ring of lawyers, politicians, and businessmen managed to manipulate land grants throughout the territory, expanding their boundaries in much the same way as the boundaries of the Maxwell Grant were stretched. According to one of its staunchest opponents, Governor Ross, the Santa Fe Ring or Land Grant Ring was just one of many groups of schemers and speculators operating in the territory. ''Cattle Rings, Public Land Stealing

Rings, Mining Rings, Treasury Rings, and Rings of almost every description" were active in New Mexico. The center of this activity was in the territorial capital of Santa Fe, and the Santa Fe Ring was the "central head" for all operations. [10] Indeed the land monopoly created by the Santa Fe Ring was as much a cause of the radical agrarian protest, which was beginning to develop at this time, as was the cattle monopoly.

Elkins and Catron as leading promoters of the Maxwell Company had the dubious distinction of being the organizers of the Santa Fe Ring. The land-holdings of these two shrewd lawyers, which were acquired in a legal practice that often included defending native grantees and receiving land as a fee, were immense. Both men had part ownership in the Mora Grant, located south of the disputed Maxwell tract. Catron, whose law office became a nerve center for the Santa Fe Ring when Elkins moved to West Virginia, was the most proficient "land-grabber" of all. He eventually acquired the 593,000-acre Tierra Amarilla Grant, which straddled the Colorado border west of the Rio Grande.

Republican party members, enjoying as they did the patronage and support from Washington unbroken except for Cleveland's first term, were in a politically advantageous position to participate in the remunerative activities of the Ring. In addition to Elkins and Catron, Bradford Prince, Mariano S. Otero, and J. Francisco Chaves were Republicans, and were accused of Ring membership. But the organizers of the Santa Fe Ring were astute enough to realize that Republicans would not always control the government in Washington nor its appointees in New Mexico. Prominent Democrats were active too, such as two Catron law partners, Charles H. Gildersleeve and William T. Thornton. The latter was appointed governor of the Territory of New Mexico by President Cleveland in 1893. Most surprising of all was Delegate Joseph's activities in land speculation. Charged with being a henchman of Gildersleeve, Joseph was once accused of taking advantage of his own people in acquiring shares in the Chama and San Cristobal grants. [11] Even so, the personable little Hispano was popularly regarded as being antigrant and friendly to the cause of the small farmers and stockmen.

But the deft maneuvering of the Santa Fe Ring was to encounter frustration in Colfax County, where resistance to the Maxwell claims continued, although some settlers did decide to move elsewhere because of the bitter controversy over the grant. The Coe family, for instance, who were accustomed to frontier lands being opened to the public, having migrated from West Virginia to Missouri, preferred not to settle in Colfax County. Lou Coe passed through Colfax as early as the sixties and, sensing impending conflict, ended up in Lincoln County. [12] Other homesteaders, however, would stay and fight, greatly complicating the Ring's land-grabbing activities.

A different kind of resistance to the Santa Fe Ring occurred in the early seventies, when a group of grant owners living in Colfax County decided to fight total control of the Maxwell Company by Ring members. Led by one of the solicitors of the company, Frank Springer, these resident owners opposed the Santa Fe clique, represented in Colfax by the county probate judge, Dr. Robert Longwill. Serious violence erupted in September of 1875 when F.J. Tolby, a Methodist minister bitterly opposed to the Ring, was murdered. Longwill was one of those accused of the killing, along with Melvin W. Mills, who served as attorney for the Maxwell Company in Colfax County. The anxious judge, fearful for his life, eventually fled across the Sangre de Cristo Mountains to Sante Fe. When the territorial governor of New Mexico, Samuel B. Axtell, became an ally of the Sante Fe Ring, he was persuaded by Ring members that Judge Longwill could not possibly receive a fair hearing in Colfax County. Consequently, on January 14, 1876, the governor attached Colfax to Taos County for administrative and judicial purposes. The nervous judge could now be tried in a friendlier atmosphere. [13] Axtell's intervention in this conflict and in the Lincoln County War was to make him one of the most controversial figures in New Mexico history. One federal investigator sent to Colfax County even went so far in 1878 as to accuse the governor of planning the murder of Frank Springer. [14]

It was in such an atmosphere of violence and feverish legal maneuvering that Alliance members and other small settlers in Colfax County were to struggle desperately to save their modest landholdings. Although court decisions had gone against them, they did have the welcomed support of the strong-willed surveyor general, George Julian. Julian's sympathy for the small homesteaders infuriated the *Weekly New Mexican Review* of Santa Fe, a publication of the *New Mexican** which had consistently served the Santa Fe Ring and its interests in the Maxwell Company. "George W. Julian says Maxwell Land Grant [is] a fraud and ought to be thrown up for settlement, but after all congress and the courts have more to say than that." The *Weekly Review* insisted that the company had treated the squatters with "great fairness and in a great many cases with friendship." The stock and improvements of Colfax homesteaders had been purchased at fair prices. Yet, in response to the magnanimous policies of the Maxwell owners, there had been nothing but resistance and violence.

Much of the intransigence of the settlers in the county was due to the demagoguery of an exponent, like Rev. Tolby, of the faith of the Wesleys, the Reverend Oscar P. McMains. A staunch foe of the Maxwell Company, McMains was, according to the *Weekly Review,* the instigator of all troubles

---

* Also called the *Sante Fe Daily New Mexican.*

in the turbulent county. Opposition by the cleric was keeping both capital and immigration out of Colfax. The atmosphere of violence created by him had already claimed two innocent victims. A man was killed in the Colorado portion of the grant, and in the same area a home was burned by squatters. Was this a fair way to treat men whose only crime had been to recognize the legally established claims of the Maxwell Company? The *Weekly Review* also demanded to know what Colorado Governor Alva B. Adams would do about these crimes. [15]

The claims of fairness on the part of the grant owners infuriated the Alliance people and other so-called squatters in Colfax County. The Maxwell Company was not willing to compensate settlers at a fair price, they insisted. The *Independent* of Raton spoke for many of them when it stoutly maintained that the homesteaders in Colfax County were exhausted in their struggle for their rights. They were now ready to ''agree to any compromise which would pay them for their improvements and stock.'' But the company's stockholders would have to be willing to make a fair settlement. [16]

Some settlers, however, were unwilling to recognize the claims of the Maxwell Land Grant, despite the decisions rendered in behalf of the company by the highest court in the land. They insisted that the vast acreage of Colfax County was part of the public domain and should be opened to the public. A group from Fort Worth backed their position. The sympathetic Texans resolved that the order of January 2, 1974, by the Secretary of the Interior, which was supported in 1885 by Cleveland's Commissioner of the General Land Office, William A.J. Sparks, should be ''final and unreserved, be respected and enforced, and the entire tract, as required by said order, treated as public land.'' [17]

The warm support contained in this resolution, drawn up early in the year 1889, plus the obvious sympathies of Julian and Sparks, the Cleveland appointees, undoubtedly encouraged the settlers of Colfax County to continue their fight. Their persistence, however, was endemic of the pioneering spirit. The land was theirs; they had developed it and were at least entitled to first option. The fact that it was claimed by Dutch capitalists made the Maxwell enterprise even more intolerable, a total violation of the frontier ethic. Alien landownership, which was to inflame Populists in the nineties and would be denounced in their party platforms, was depriving Colfax homesteaders of rights regarded as inalienable. An Alliance member from Colfax County, who felt fortunate that his land was not on the grant, commiserated with those friends and brethren who were ''being oppressed by foreign capital. Every true American should do the same.'' [18]

A much more violent expression of anti-foreign feeling was contained in a widely reprinted letter sent to an Amsterdam newspaper. Dutch citizens were warned by the writer, who went by the initials L.H., not to come as "colonists to a country where life is in danger, where terror prevails, where the [Maxwell] company's agents are burned in effigy, and absent themselves when a campaign is on." The letter, a scarcely subtle threat against any Dutchmen bold enough to come to America and settle on the grant, painted a black picture of conditions in northeastern New Mexico. Would-be immigrants were told that half the cattle owned by the Maxwell Company would die because of unfavorable conditions of nature, and that the irrigation canals in the county lacked an adequate supply of water. The *Raton Weekly Independent,* in commenting on the letter, which appeared in both New Mexico and Colorado newspapers, seemed disturbed. It not only disapproved of the letter's tone of violence, but also of its discouraging assessment of livestock-raising conditions. A far better way to resolve the conflict in Colfax County, it stated, would be to have the grant company "buy" every claim for sale, and pay a fair price for all improvements. [19]

But the foreign-owned Maxwell Company was not the only "land monopoly" in the territory which disturbed New Mexicans. Aggressive American land claimants were as much a threat as alien capitalists. The *Las Vegas Daily Optic,* far more conservative than the pro-Alliance newspapers of Lincoln and Colfax counties, bemoaned the fact that "New Mexico should be so cursed with land companies and trusts whose purpose is not honest and whose every method is crooked." Referring to the immense size of the territory's land grants, it scored grant holders, such as the owners of the Maxwell Company, for the "perjury, and forgery" they used, in order to acquire "large strips of land that would in a European country be sufficient for several kingdoms if not empires." [20] Opposition to land-grabbers very obviously had not been silenced by the legal substantiation of the Maxwell claims.

The Maxwell Company urgently needed powerful political support, if it were to counteract the resistance to its claims. The enactment of the change-of-venue law by the territorial legislature early in the year 1889 provided the kind of assistance the land company sought. Supported by Republicans, the new law would allow an individual to request a change of venue. If the request were supported by the oaths of two disinterested persons, the individual would be granted his change and the trial would be removed to another county. The *Independent* spoke for Alliance members when it called the law a product of the clever machinations of the Maxwell Company. If the law was upheld, it would mean "a game of freeze out for every settler who has any rights whatever, either by title or improvements." Acquiring two "disinterested" persons on behalf of either the plaintiff or the defendent would not be at all difficult, the *Independent* insisted. False witnesses were easy to find, and the court could not inquire into the interests or motives behind the affidavits filed by the so-called neutral parties. County prosecutors were not even allowed to file counter affidavits. Thus, it became "absolutely mandatory" for the judge of a territorial district court to allow the change of venue.

By exercising its right to obtain a change of venue, the Maxwell Company was in an excellent position to move its cases against alleged squatters out of hostile Colfax County into a friendlier jurisdiction. The shift, of course, would increase the cost of litigation for the small settler, who could ill afford the expense.

> On the docket in this county are nearly a hundred cases of eject-
> ment which were brought against settlers by the Maxwell Land
> Grant company. Many of the defendents have a good defense both
> as to improvements and title. Many of these are poor, very poor.
> There are natives among them who have nothing in God's world
> but a few sheep, the little adobe house — the only one they ever
> knew or their fathers before them   and the little plat of land which
> gives them and their families their only sustenance. Can these
> people follow their ejectment suits into another county? Where can
> they procure the means even to travel or live upon [?]

In making common cause with poor Hispanos threatened by the new law, the Anglo-dominated Colfax Alliance and the Anglo settlers of Colfax County displayed a sympathy for their Spanish-speaking brethren not frequently uttered or sincerely felt. "It is cruel; it is unjust; it is wicked!" the *Independent* said of the change-of-venue law. "It is a law for the rich against the poor [,] the strong against the weak. It is but the tightening of the iron band of that mighty land monopoly which is surely grinding their bones into flour that it may make its bread." [21]

Alliance members were implored to take their case to Congress. Every member should "consider himself a committee of one to circulate a petition against the infamous change of venue law." Such petitions, if dispatched to Washington in impressive numbers, would "command respect." [22] A legislator claimed that the new change-of-venue measure was the "most outrageous law that the Republicans have yet fastened on the territory." He urged settlers in Colfax to send strong petitions of protest to Congress. [23]

A moment of exhilaration for many of the small settlers of Colfax occurred when Governor Ross vetoed the change-of-venue law on February 16, 1889. The governor made a particular point of condemning the ease with which a case could be transferred from one county to another. [24] But the victory, gratifying as it was to Alliance members in the county, was viewed with great caution, because of the difficulties Ross was having with his Republican-dominated legislature. The governor's problems with the territorial assembly were not new ones. In the previous legislative session, the Twenty-seventh, Ross had encountered much opposition to his programs. J. Francisco Chaves, a former Territorial Delegate who presided over the Council during the Twenty-seventh session, showed particular skill in thwarting Ross. [25] In the current Twenty-eighth assembly, opposition to Ross was even better organized. In 1888 the voters of the territory had given the Republicans a two-thirds majority in the legislature, and Colonel Albert J. Fountain, an attorney with a proud military record who became speaker of the House, joined with Chaves to oppose the governor. [26] Of 145 bills approved by members of the legislature, Ross signed only 47. The other 98 bills became law without the governor's signature or in spite of his veto.

Ross, a Democrat who identified more than any other nineteenth-century New Mexico governor with the workers and farmers, was forced to play a negative role throughout most of his gubernatorial career. He opposed the power of the Santa Fe Ring, becoming its most outspoken critic. He resisted the will of a majority of the legislators, exercising his veto power time and time again to block legislation he did not feel was in the best interests of the people. But the unfortunate result of Ross' actions was a record with few positive accomplishments. A measure to encourage homesteading by settling all titles to land grants was defeated. A bill failed which would have granted equal grazing rights and privileges to sheep owners. Measures calling for irrigation development and the establishment of a full-fledged public school system were blocked. [27] Consequently, no one was really shocked when the legislature overrode the governor's veto of the change-of-venue law on February 22, 1889. [28]

The quick restoration of the change-of-venue law by the Republican majority in the assembly assured the ultimate success of the Maxwell Land Grant and Railroad Company. The fight against land monopoly in the Territory of New Mexico continued, however. Several months before the change-of-venue law was enacted the independent farmers and stockmen of Colfax County faced a new challenge. During the 1888 election a new political organization that piously called itself the ''People's Party'' confronted them. To Alliance supporters this party looked suspiciously like a Republican device to encourage such ''land-grabbers'' as those associated with the Maxwell enterprise. Although the *Las Vegas Daily Optic* insisted that the new party was composed of both Democrats and Republicans, and formed to oppose the ''spiteful cliques and rings'' which had manipulated politics in Colfax County for years, 29 most Alliance members were dubious. When the conservative *Raton Range* endorsed the People's party of Colfax County, the *Nogal Nugget,* also fighting a new ''people's'' organization in Lincoln County, felt that its worst suspicions had been confirmed. This ''rank, rabid republican cow paper, cares nothing for people, except to vote them; yet the *Range* advocates a 'people's party'!'' 30 .

The *Nugget's* assessment of the Raton paper as a partisan journal notorious for manipulating popular causes had substantial basis in fact. The *Range* and another conservative newspaper voice in Colfax, the *Stockman* of Springer, were both owned by Stephen W. Dorsey and J.W. Dwyer, a pair whose unwavering resolve to expand their cattle spreads made them a decided threat to other stock grazers. M.W. Mills, in evaluating Republican strength in Colfax County in 1891, found much to criticize in the way these two Republican cattle barons were operating their biased news journals. They ''always take on the [Maxwell] Grant side and big money side and fool editorials every issue make them very unpopular and injure our cause.'' 31

Aware of the connections Republicans had with big cattlemen and grant owners, marginal operators in the county, whether members of the Colfax Alliance or not, were strongly attracted to the Democratic party. The *Independent* spoke for many of them when it enthusiastically backed Antonio Joseph and the ''Antigrant Democrats'' in the 1888 election. 32 A growing number of small stockmen and farmers believed that a vote for the Democratic ticket would be a vote ''in favor of destroying the grabbing system, by which mineral, agricultural and grazing lands have been taken from the people; [by] which grabbing system republican rule fastened up this territory.'' The investigations into fraudulent land acquisitions by such Cleveland appointees as George Julian and R.P. Walker encouraged 33 settlers to believe the land they squatted on was theirs. Most homesteaders in the county were therefore delighted when Joseph won his race against Otero. The Democratic showing in Colfax, stronger than throughout most of the territory, was received with enthusiasm.

Colfax voters had repudiated the ''self-styled reformers and howlers for law and order,'' chortled the satisfied *Independent.* Its reference was to the disappointed candidates of the ''People's'' ticket, only one of whom won a county office in the 1888 race. The sole ''glorious triumph'' was achieved by

31

the candidate for county coroner, who was elected by an overwhelming majority. The first corpse for the victorious candidate would be the People's party, which, according to the *Independent,* was in an ''advanced stage of decomposition.'' 34

The fight against the land-grabbers in New Mexico, so relentlessly waged in Colfax County during the 1888 election, shifted to a special convention assembled in Santa Fe. There on September 3, 1889, a group of citizens met to draft a constitution which would hasten the territory's admission to the Union. The convention, which had been proposed by the same legislative body that overrode Governor Ross' veto of the change-of-venue law, 35 was called to correct the belief held by some congressmen that New Mexico was not interested in statehood. Opponents of admission had made telling references to the fact that no recent effort had been made in the territory to draft a constitution and submit it to Congress for approval. This alleged indifference was one of the excuses offered by the territory's detractors to drop New Mexico from the Springer omnibus bill, by which statehood had been approved for Montana, Washington, and the Dakotas earlier in the year.

The hopeful delegates to the constitutional convention were in serious trouble from the very beginning. Territorial Democrats, feeling that they had not received adequate representation at the convention, refused to participate; only one Democrat was represented among seventy-three elected representatives. When the convention considered a provision for the establishment of a secular school system, the leaders of the Roman Catholic Church in the territory attacked the proposed constitution. Finally, the damaging accusation was accepted without much hesitation in Colfax County that the constitution approved by the delegates in late September was a ''land-grabber's'' document. According to this charge, the constitution's general tax on large landowners was insufficient for the revenue needs of the proposed state. The elite souls of the privileged land monopoly would thus be allowed to shift the tax burden to the cattlemen and farmers of the territory. 36

As the election approached to ratify the new constitution on October 7, 1890, opponents intensified their attacks. Jacob D. Crist, an active Democratic leader and editor of the *Santa Fe Sun,* used his paper to condemn the ''so-called bosses, the rich land grabbers, railroad lawyers, and professional politicians, who have arrogated to themselves the authority to make and present a constitution to the people that intrences [sic] their special interests . . . at the expense of the masses.'' Fourteen Republican convention leaders were listed in the *Sun* along with individual landholdings totaling an astonishing 9,457,166 acres. J. Francisco Chaves, who presided over the convention, was regarded as typical of the land-hungry leaders responsible for the controversial Santa Fe constitution. As attorney for the 89,405-acre San

Clemente Grant and the slightly smaller Canada de los Apaches Grant, estimated at 88,000 acres, it was obvious where he stood on the land-grant question. Of interest to Colfax County residents was the participation of Frank Springer, who not only represented the Maxwell Grant but also the claimants to the Las Vegas Community Grant in nearby San Miguel County. The active role of cattleman Charles B. Eddy, reputed to control 20,000 acres of Lincoln range land, did not escape the attention of Alliancemen in that part of the territory. Eight grants, in addition to the Tierra Amarilla and Mora holdings, were associated with one of the convention's most prominent leaders, Thomas B. Catron, who owned some of the grants and represented claimants to the others. Mariano S. Otero, who was again nominated to oppose Joseph in the 1890 race for delegate, was accused of having an interest in the Ojo del Espiritu Santo and Bernalillo grants and six others. Republican leadership had effectively exploited the opportunities provided by the Spanish and Mexican land grants during the territorial period, and would continue this exploitation, the *Sun* insisted, when statehood was achieved. "Let some Diogenes with his lantern look for a clause in that constitution which will hurt a land grant." [37]

The special-interest image of the constitution, when added to the growing religious opposition and intense political partisanship that marked the days preceding the crucial vote, dimmed prospects for approval by the referendum. A majority of voters on October 7 showed their lack of enthusiasm for the controversial document by decisively rejecting it 16,180 to 7,493. [38] The defeat of the Republican-drafted instrument improved Democratic prospects for the regular election scheduled the following month. Joseph's undeserved reputation as an anti-grant political leader eager to clarify the entire land question was enhanced in the Democratic press during his race against Otero to represent New Mexico in Congress. Shortly before the election the partisan *Sun* boasted of Joseph's past efforts to settle land titles in the territory. It praised his efforts to clarify the grant question by working in Congress for the creation of a court to judicate all conflicting claims. A story in the *Deming Headlight* was cited to show the extent of Joseph's interest in this all-important territorial issue. In 1887, at the request of the New Mexico Bureau of Immigration, Joseph and other prominent citizens traveled to Washington, D.C., to lobby for the land court bill. The delegate worked "faithfully and zealously" to get such a bill through the House. Otero, Joseph's perennial opponent, also agreed to lobby for the land court bill but got no farther than St. Louis, where he lost interest in the project and returned to New Mexico. [39]

More important for troubled stock grazers and farmers in the territory were the races for the legislative assembly. The year 1890 was a fateful one in the

West, as third-party movements were beginning to flourish in the wheat-raising country to the east and north of New Mexico. The fervent Populist crusade would result from these electoral challenges in Kansas, Nebraska, and the Dakotas. These states were part of an immense L-shaped area demarcating agrarian discontent in the United States, the cotton belt of the South forming the bottom line. Agricultural unrest throughout the extensive region was in response to sharp price declines, appreciating debts, and the reckless power of the railroads. In New Mexico, added irritants were the alarming monopoly efforts of the cattle barons and grant holders. The great question in the territory was whether Democratic successes in the legislative races would break the Republican strangle-hold on New Mexico politics. Would a Democratically controlled territorial assembly have the courage and conviction to challenge the land monopoly or cattle monopoly — the two terms being practically interchangeable in Colfax County? The struggle for leadership in the Twenty-ninth legislative assembly in 1890 could have far-reaching implications for agrarian elements in counties such as Lincoln and Colfax. But much more dramatic was a protest occurring in San Miguel County. Its development would have the most significant influence of all on the direction of agrarian radicalism in New Mexico.

4

THE SAN MIGUEL PEOPLE'S PARTY

In December of 1889, Sheriff Lorenzo Lopez of San Miguel County and Chief Justice Elisha Van Buren Long of the Territorial Supreme Court telegraphed an urgent plea to Governor Prince, who had replaced Ross in the spring, asking for immediate delivery of fifty rifles and enough ammunition to meet an impending attack on the Las Vegas jail. [1] Such a desperate situation had not occurred since the summer of 1888, when Governor Ross considered sending fifty militiamen to Springer, as the district court convened, to prevent violence over the Maxwell Land Grant controversy. [2]

Ross' concern had been with Colfax settlers openly expressing their outrage; Prince's concern was to be with a secret native organization terrorizing its adversaries. Governor Ross had been forced to cope with the anger of independent operators who feared the loss of their land to an immense foreign-owned monopoly; Governor Prince would have to deal with small Hispano settlers defending a different kind of land grant — the communal holding known as the Las Vegas Community Grant. San Miguel County was to provide the most extraordinary example of radical protest and unrest in the territory. Native settlers, threatened by loss of their land, organized into a secret, oath-bound organization called the White Caps. Their goal was to prevent any further encroachments by Anglo ranchers on their large communal holding, which dated back to the Mexican period when the Luis Maria Baca family received the Las Vegas Grant in the 1830's.

Miguel A. Otero, who in 1897 was appointed the first Hispano governor of the territory, has provided one of the most vivid descriptions of the White Caps, or *Las Gorras Blancas,* as the natives called them. One night more than a hundred *Gorras* passed by his house on horseback, riding two abreast with white caps drawn over their faces to avoid recognition. They rode solemnly through the new town located by the railroad, East Las Vegas, and through the old town, West Las Vegas. Their armed appearance communicated an unmistakable message to the frightened townfolk, who hastily removed themselves from the path of the mysterious entourage. [3]

At other times, such subtle forms of intimidation were replaced by violence. White Caps would engage in terror and destruction, cutting down wire fences and scattering the stock of those people they regarded as intruders. Even homes and barns on the grant were burned. As a result of numerous night raids conducted during the summer of 1889, twenty-three persons were arrested by Sheriff Lopez and placed in the Las Vegas jail. Threats of a break-in by friends and neighbors of the *Gorras* prompted the telegram to Prince in December by Lopez and Justice Long imploring the governor to send rifles and ammunition. Four months later, with the campaign of terror seemingly unabated, San Miguel Probate Judge Manuel C. de Baca urged Prince in a letter to organize a militia to deal sternly with the White Caps. [4]

Prior to these pleas for gubernatorial intervention, there had been almost a decade of smoldering resentment against newcomers to the county. Governor Prince, in a detailed report to Secretary of the Interior John W. Noble, traced the origins of White Cap activity back to about the year 1880. At that time certain persons interested in ranching began to purchase the interest in the Las Vegas Grant of some of the heirs of the original settlers. The people of Las Vegas regarded the huge 496,446-acre tract as a ''Community Grant'' open to anyone who wanted to use its water and pasture land. When many of these new settlers, with their Anglo concepts of land tenure, began to claim absolute ownership of certain portions of the grant and to fence their claims, hostility erupted. Although most of the land purchases were modest ones in the early eighties, a few were as large as 10,000 acres.

In 1887 an important test case regarding the legality of these recent land acquisitions was brought before the district court. It involved an Anglo buyer and a defiant native claimant to the grant by the name of Padilla. Chief Justice Long, presiding over the trial, took an entire year to study the matter before he announced his decision in favor of Padilla. A jubilant three-hour demonstration greeted the judge's popular ruling in the case of *Millhiser* vs. *Padilla,* and the decision greatly bolstered the morale of the Hispanos in San Miguel County. It also reinforced their conviction that the grant belonged to the community at large and that all intruders better beware.

Purchases on the grant or adjacent to it continued, however, and a sharp increase in native militancy was marked by the organization of the White Caps, probably in the year 1888. Fence cutting and serious destruction to property, starting in the summer of 1889, led in November to the indictment of twenty-six people and to the arrest of a comparable number the following month. The threatened jailbreak to free those twenty-three who were incarcerated, which prompted Sheriff Lopez's anxious plea for help, never materialized. The accused were later released on bail. In the spring of 1890 all the cases were dismissed by Chief Justice O'Brien, a Harrison appointee who replaced Long. O'Brien's decision was unavoidable. The county district attorney, Miguel Salazar, could not obtain witnesses to any of the depredations committed by the White Caps. Governor Prince reported to Noble that these dismissals were particularly unfortunate because they encouraged many citizens of Las Vegas and environs to believe that all future offenses against so-called trespassers on the grant would go unpunished. [5]

The governor's pessimistic evaluation of the new Hispano attitude was supported by prolonged violence following Justice O'Brien's action. White Caps increased their terror activities against Anglo ranchers, whom they regarded as land-grabbers. They extended their night raids beyond the Las Vegas Grant into adjoining ones. Roaming bands of White Caps were even active in the neighboring counties of Mora and Santa Fe. Old Benjamin F. Butler, the contentious ex-Union general, stated in a letter to Prince on July 9, 1890, that a total of twenty-five acts of destruction had been brought to his attention. As owner of 400,000 acres of land in New Mexico, the self-professed radical who once ran for the presidency on the Greenback ticket could not tolerate this kind of protest. He demanded that Prince conduct a full investigation. Wilson Waddington, whose spread on the Canadian River had been fenced for twenty years, received a threatening letter from a group of White Caps. As translated by his son-in-law William J. Mills (who later became New Mexico's last territorial governor) the letter has an almost apologetic flavor:

> This notice is with the object of requesting you to coil up your wire as soon as possible from the North to the South sides. They are fences which are damaging the unhappy people and we request you further coil up your wire as soon as you can to the agricultural land, and if you do not do it you will suffer the consequences from us. Your Servants. The White Caps.

The determination of the night-riding *Gorras* was so strong that even the old Mexican patriot, General Nicholas Pino, who had lived on his Galisteo ranch for forty years, was ordered to remove the fences from his property. [6]

Prince, reacting to strong pressure from Washington, wrote to all twenty-five persons whom Butler had cited as victims of the White Caps. He also wrote to Justice O'Brien, District Attorney Salazar, Sheriff Lopez, the chairman of the Board of County Commissioners, and prominent citizens of Las Vegas asking for information and advice as to how to cope with the *Gorras.* Governor Prince was no political novice; he had been in some heated battles before. The aristocratic New Yorker, a descendent of Governor William Bradford of Plymouth Colony, had run afoul of Senator Roscoe Conkling by accepting the appointment of naval officer of the patronage-generating New York customhouse. Conkling blocked the appointment in the Senate as part of his feud with President Hayes over Civil Service reform. Persona non grata with New York Republican leaders, Prince accepted the post offered by the Hayes administration of chief justice of the Territory of New Mexico in 1879. [7]

Although a zealous justice, who promptly disposed of 1,184 civil and 1,483 criminal cases during his three-year tenure, [8] Prince acquired his share of enemies. His exceptional interest in the rich mineral wealth of his adopted home created suspicions. He invested in so many gold and silver mines [9] that he had to maintain an office in Flushing, New York, to handle his increasing mine properties. To many this was proof that the stately, bewhiskered New Yorker was just another acquisitive carpetbagger. [10] He was also accused of having aligned himself with the land-grabbing Santa Fe Ring. According to Miguel A. Otero, Prince was associated with the Ring while serving as chief justice and holding court in Otero's bailiwick of San Miguel County. [11]

The governor had, however, achieved undeniable prominence during his decade in New Mexico. He was a leader in the statehood movement. [12] He played an active role in the Trans-Mississippi Congress and other organizations to promote the West. And his distinction as an outstanding layman in the Episcopal Church had brought him widespread attention throughout the years. Catron, jealous of Prince's growing importance, had blocked the ambitious Easterner's bid for the office of territorial delegate in 1884. But Prince's appointment as chief executive of the territory had provided him with an opportunity for political distinction that he was unwilling to allow the *Gorras* to destroy.

Governor Prince had been aware of the growing menace of "White Capism" for some time. The numerous complaints of ranchers to him or to his superiors in Washington had already convinced him that some drastic action on his part was essential. But he was unable to cope directly with the problem during the spring of 1890, because of his involvement with the statehood movement. The territorial Bureau of Immigration had requested the governor to appoint a delegation of influential citizens to go to Washington and lobby for admission. Prince, with his delegation of twenty-nine prominent New Mexicans, was in the national capital from April to the end of May. On his return he was confined to his home for three weeks with nervous exhaustion. It was not until July that he regained the strength to devote full time to the urgent crisis caused by the White Caps. [13]

Once recovered, Governor Prince promptly followed up his dispatch of letters to victims of the *Gorras* and to important San Miguel officials and citizens with a dramatic proclamation in English and Spanish. Issued on August 1, it stated unequivocally that further disorders would not be tolerated. Prince also met with the Most Reverend J.B. Salpointe, archbishop of Santa Fe, and the clergy of San Miguel County to see if the influential Catholic Church might not intercede with those elements of the native population involved in the secret organization. He organized a committee of seven Las Vegas leaders, including the mayor and three county commissioners, to arrange a public meeting on August 16 to discuss the problems caused by the night raids. The meeting produced a shock: four-fifths of those in attendance proved to be in sympathy with the "fence cutters." [14] In his August 12 report to Secretary of the Interior Noble, Prince even urged his superior to use his influence with the War Department to use troops garrisoned at Santa Fe and Fort Union to patrol the tense area between Las Vegas and Lamy. Noble brought the governor's irregular request to the attention of President Harrison and Secretary of War Redfield Proctor. But in a letter dated August 19 Proctor replied that he and the president agreed that Prince should work with his local district attorney and marshal until such civil authority was challenged in a way that would shatter the public peace.

Employing another tack, Prince, after receiving information about four blatant cases of fence cutting outside the Las Vegas Grant on pre-empted or homesteaded property, made another request of Noble. He asked for $500 to assist him in arresting the guilty parties, as fence cutting on these properties was clearly a federal offense. He also solicited help from United States District Attorney Eugene A. Fiske, a docile ally called "Prince's poodle" by some of his detractors. Fiske, too, was eager to prosecute the *Gorras*. In the end, however, he had to admit that, despite an able and honest grand jury, he could not find sufficient evidence to justify prosecution. Disappointing to Prince was the fact also that Noble apparently never sent the money requested. [15] The case was most illustrative of the problem. It was almost impossible for Fiske or any other prosecutor to get a member of the White Caps to testify against his organization for fear of reprisal. And it was equally difficult to get an outsider who could identify any of the *Gorras*, as they operated at night, their faces concealed and their assaults varied to avoid detection.

After meeting with Archbishop Salpointe and the priests of San Miguel, Prince went to Las Vegas to meet with the leaders of the Knights of Labor in the county. This colorful organization, considered radical by many people at the time, was to contribute to the development of Populism as a national movement in a most significant way. Although the organization was fading in power and influence in the early nineties, several leading Knights played an important role in the first national convention of the People's party. These Knights were largely responsible for the tough transportation plank in the 1892 platform, which called for the nationalization of railroads. [16] In San Miguel County the Knights of Labor had been an active and growing organization, the bulk of its membership probably drawn from railroad employees in the area. Its increase in strength and numbers had paralleled the growth of the White Caps to a remarkable degree. The *Gorras,* interestingly enough, had taken almost as great an interest in labor matters as the Knights. Teams hauling railroad ties, for instance, were often halted by masked White Caps and, if the drivers were not charging contractors enough for their hauls, the ties were unloaded and chopped up or burned. [17] This intrusion into the labor field became so serious that, on July 23, the officials of the Atchison, Topeka and Santa Fe Railroad announced that rail ties would no longer be purchased in the Las Vegas area, a decision which was to cost the local economy $100,000 a year. [18]

Salazar, the county district attorney, asserted in a letter to Prince on July 23 that he had three reliable witnesses who knew how the *Gorras* was founded and by whom. According to these witnesses (undoubtedly terrified, as they could not be found to testify) the founder was a native New Mexican named Juan Jose Herrera. He had returned to San Miguel some two years ago after a stay in Colorado or Utah. Herrera , in the organization of his secret society, had seven lieutenants who effectively controlled the growing number of recruits and placed them under oath not to divulge any information on pain of death. Herrera's two brothers helped him keep discipline: Nicanor, considered the meanest brother by a Pinkerton investigator, and Pablo, who had served a sentence for murder. [19] The Herrera brothers were successful because of their resistance to the alarming intrusions on the Las Vegas Community Grant. Salazar estimated in his report that there were as many as 700 members in the organization. Moreover the numerical strength of the group was on the increase, its disruptive activities being expanded into adjacent Mora County at the time.

Perhaps most significant was the fact that the resourceful Juan Jose, sensing the need for a respectable front, had decided to use the Knights of

Labor for that purpose. Evidence that the White Caps had successfully in-filtrated the assemblies or lodges * of the Knights of Labor in San Miguel was quite substantial.

When Governor Prince met with the leading Knights of San Miguel County, Juan Jose and Pablo were there. Prince was outraged by what ap-peared to him to be collaboration between the terrorist group and the labor organization. An August 1 letter to Terence V. Powderly, the national leader of the Knights, expressed concern. He insisted, firmly but politely, that Powderly exercise all his power to prevent the Knights from being used as a cover by the *Gorras* for their lawless activities. Prince stated that there simply were not enough Knights to justify the fifty local assemblies in the county affiliated with the national organization. Nor were there enough union members to have made possible the impressive thousand-man procession which marched during the last Fourth of July celebration.

Prince's assessments were at least partially correct. Three Master Work-men from Local Assembly 4636 wrote Powderly a week later, pleading with him to forbid further expansion of the organization in San Miguel County. The three admitted that, until 1887, the local Knights had made common cause with the native population in the county. They resisted land-grabbers on the Community Grant through an organization known as the "Las Vegas Land Grant Association." But when Juan Jose Herrera began to organize more assemblies, a move accompanied by an upsurge of violence, the three Knights and a number of their associates began to have misgivings. Especially disturbing to them was the admission into the labor organization of so many "Mexican people . . . of the poorer class." If this trend continued, they warned Powderly, no one could foretell the consequences. [20]

The slur against the new native members of the organization, although it might have been directed only against those who were White Caps, was probably another example of Anglo prejudice against native New Mexicans. Regardless of how effectively Anglos and Hispanos could work together in the territory, there was usually enough strain to complicate their relations. The tension went back to the conquest and before, although the situation was obviously quite different during the Mexican period. [21] The temptation is to use the anti-Hispano remark as yet another example of nativism among groups that would later organize and lead the People's party.

---

* The local assemblies of the Knights were referred to as lodges in some of the New Mexico papers.

A more genuinely contemptuous remark can be attributed to Republican conservative Melvin W. Mills, the Colfax attorney associated with the Maxwell Grant. In an August 2, 1891, letter to Prince critical of statehood, Mills characterized the natives of the territory as "ignorant people" unfit to govern. "What shall become of the White Cap element when they get to running the State I do not propose to conjecture," he wrote. Whether Prince's views were those of his old political ally is questionable. If they were, he would never admit it publicly and would be hesitant to reveal it privately.

The San Miguel Knights were probably less prejudiced than most Anglo groups in New Mexico. They were, however, decidedly disenchanted with the type of Hispano politics being practiced in the county. Conservative Republican politics, long dominant in San Miguel County, caused much of their distress; family factionalism was an even more disturbing element. A feud involving Eugenio Romero and his brother-in-law, Sheriff Lorenzo Lopez, was seriously fragmenting the county's political life.

Eugenio Romero was a tough Republican boss who knew all the angles. A perpetual candidate, he was always running for the best-paying job and justifying his conspicuous presence in public affairs with the remark: "The people, they wanta me." When it came to paying the assessments expected of all good officeholders in the county, Romero could be relied upon to settle without a complaint. He simply would wait until all of his subordinates had paid him and then pay his assessment in one lump sum, his own lien on the total campaign fund invariably being a substantial one. Such tactics could work only if there were no other strong personality around. Lorenzo Lopez, however, was not the sort of person to be completely eclipsed by the old *jefe,* and soon he began to challenge Romero's power. [22] By 1890, the feud had blossomed into a full-scale political confrontation, and Democrats were charging that the Lopez and Romero factions were so desperate that they were using White Caps to destroy each other. [23]

Even before the Lopez-Romero feud reached its peak, many citizens in the county, including Republicans, Democrats, and Knights, had become thoroughly disgusted. In the 1888 election F.A. Blake, editor of the Las Vegas *News,* and a group of Knights founded a "People's party." [24] The name, of course, was not a new one in San Miguel or elsewhere in the territory. In 1876, as a matter of fact, a People's party held a September convention in Las Vegas to nominate candidates for the November election. During the same month "the People's Convention of Dona Ana County" was meeting in Mesilla to nominate candidates and endorse Trinidad Romero for the delegate's race. [25] People's parties, as has been recorded elsewhere, also had been organized in Lincoln and Colfax counties.

42

The *Nogal Nugget* felt the same suspicions toward the San Miguel People's party organized in 1888 as it felt toward the People's parties of Lincoln and Colfax counties. The new party was a front for the Republican party. It was supported overwhelmingly by the Republican county press, including Blake's Las Vegas journal. [26] In its critical assessment of the situation, the *Nugget* was only partly correct. Blake was a Republican, but he was more of an opportunist than a party workhorse who would try to organize and manipulate a front group to advance his party's interests. The Las Vegas editor, having a high opinion of himself, felt he had been bypassed by the Republican leadership in San Miguel County. His organization of a new party was probably as much an effort to spite the Republican chiefs in the county as it was to advance himself. As for the Knights involved in the formation of the new party, their motives seem to be sincere. Notwithstanding the anti-Hispano remark of the three leaders corresponding with Powderly, the members of the labor organization had stood squarely with natives of the county against encroachments on the Las Vegas Community Grant. The ideals of the Knights of Labor as a national organization would also tend to insure the sincerity of their motives. Of particular significance is the fact that the party that Blake and these Knights had organized became the first genuine People's party in the Territory of New Mexico. From this modest beginning, a Populist movement was to grow into a territory-wide party affiliated with the national organization. Its early leaders, moreover, would be drawn from the troubled county.

The Knights involved in the organization of the new party represented three assemblies that had existed before the union's rapid expansion following the White Cap outbreak. Knights from East Las Vegas, West Las Vegas, and Tecolote spearheaded the third-party effort. Their ideals, according to Blake, who was himself a Knight, were the same as those of the union itself, "principles first and men second." Public officials were to be responsible to the "whole people," but were never to forget their obligations to the party that elected them. Economic and "equitable administration of public affairs" was to be guaranteed in such a way that justice and "equal protection" would be afforded to all. The laboring men who organized the San Miguel People's party declared themselves unequivocally opposed to bossism. They insisted that their officers should follow the guidelines adopted by the party and leave crucial questions to a majority vote of the rank and file.

The first bid for power by the new party was no more impressive than the dismal showing of the Lincoln and Colfax People's parties. Only 140 votes were polled by the infant political organization in 1888. But soon after their disappointing performance the "white-cap troubles" occurred, giving the Knights an opportunity to push their union organization into other parts of the county. The result was that, prior to the 1890 election, "a large minority, if not a majority" of San Miguel voters were organized into active assemblies of the Knights of Labor.

As the labor organization grew in numbers and influence, aided by the White Caps who so effectively underscored the deep anxieties of the San Miguel natives, the attitude toward the young People's party began to change. Although the new organization was jeeringly called the "burro party" by its detractors, with the approach of the 1890 election the divided Republicans and Democrats of the county were not so confident as they sounded. One skillful Democratic vote getter, Felix Martinez, carefully reassessed his political career in light of the threat posed by the new party. [27]

Only thirty-three years old at the time, Martinez already had been successful in the mercantile and real estate businesses. A dapper Hispano with a trim moustache and well-combed hair, Martinez was a born promoter. His life would be crowded with promotional schemes, but it was in politics that he would show his most exceptional talents. Concealing a natural aggressiveness and utilizing an excellent command of both Spanish and English, the polished Martinez was able to gain rapid prominence in the Democratic party. In 1884, he ran for county treasurer. He was so popular that, although the Republicans were accustomed to carrying the county by 1,500 to 2,000 votes, Martinez lost his race by only 200. In 1886 he became county assessor, and in 1888 he was elected to serve in the territorial House of Representatives. [28] In 1890, although he was able to dominate the San Miguel delegation to the territorial Democratic convention, [29] he was beginning to perceive the difficulties of being a Democrat in a predominantly Republican county. Prior to the county convention of the People's party in 1890, Martinez came close to renouncing his Democratic connections, even though, in Blake's opinion, he was never in sympathy with the principles of the Knights of Labor and if he professed any interest in their program it was a "sham." [30]

When Felix Martinez attended the 1890 political convention of the San Miguel People's party, it was evident from the very beginning that he would be one of the major influences in the new party's councils. Although a newcomer, the "little martinet" was able to deny to Charles F. Rudulph, a popular county politician, the coveted sheriff's nomination. Martinez finally consented to allow Rudulph to run for the office of county superintendent, a position the frustrated office seeker won in November. An even more solid indication of the new member's almost instantaneous leadership in the party was his selection to chair the People's convention and his appointment to the small and exclusive executive committee. [31]

44

Other sources of support for the San Miguel Populists were the disaffected county Republicans. Sheriff Lopez, engaged in his bitter struggle with his brother-in-law, decided to join the promising reform party. [32] More important for the future growth of Populism in the territory was the support of Republican Theodore B. Mills. T.B. Mills, as he usually was called, was a remarkably cultured man for the rustic frontier environment he had chosen for his home. Handsome and dignified, he came from an illustrious family; his grandfather had fallen in the War of 1812 at the head of his regiment. Born in Ohio, Mills was graduated from Oberlin College and became an avid book and newspaper collector; he owned one of the most "select and comprehensive" private libraries in the territory. [33]

A Civil War veteran, "Colonel T.B." had come to Las Vegas by way of Arkansas and Kansas. He had been a member of the Kansas state legislature and president of the King Bridge Company, a firm engaged in bridge building throughout the West. In 1878, he came to New Mexico and immersed himself in various business enterprises. He purchased the Hot Springs in Las Vegas and made it a valuable property. An energetic local booster, he gave a promissory note to the builders of the Santa Fe Railroad, to whom he eventually sold the Hot Springs. [34] Although he later reneged on his note because the railroad company failed to build a depot near the plaza of the old town, [35] he and the other Las Vegans who gave such notes were probably responsible for hastening the arrival of the railroad in 1879. Later Mills went into a real estate partnership with his son, Byron T., a lawyer active in Republican politics who once served as chief deputy to Miguel A. Otero when Otero was county clerk. [36] The extroverted Mills, who was an active Mason, [37] ultimately proved his eminence in Las Vegas business circles by becoming president of the Las Vegas Real Estate Exchange. [38]

His economic acquisitiveness was typical of the Western empire builder. Mills seems to have had a hand in everything from real estate [39] and livestock investments to mining claims. Land-grabbing, that favorite New Mexican brand of speculation, did not escape his attention. Although his interests in land grants in Old Mexico and near Tierra Amarilla, in the northern part of the territory, [40] may not have brought him much in the way of material wealth, his investments in mining netted him some promising properties. During the year 1890 the forty-nine-year-old speculator, sporting the heavy moustache which was one of his trademarks, was associated with the Socorro Mountain Mining Company. [41] Several years later, Mills was in the field, working a regular shift on some of his claims in the Cochiti mining district. [42] Combining his penchant for action with a fine mind, Mills edited during the eighties a biweekly newspaper, the *Mining World.* [43] He also wrote a

Handbook of Mineral Laws, and Guide to New Mexico, mentioned by Hubert Hugh Bancroft in his *History of Arizona and New Mexico, 1530-1888.* [44] Despite a poor literary style, evident in his private letters, he was chosen to prepare a description of San Miguel County in a book promoting the 1884-85 World's Exposition at New Orleans. [45] In 1893, the personable Mills was made president of the Western Columbian Club, a prestigious organization to promote the World's Columbian Exposition in Chicago. [46]

Mills served in the territorial House for one term after being elected at the polls by a convincing majority in 1884. [47] But he, too, apparently became discontented with the clannishness and factionalism of Republican politics in San Miguel County. Consequently, this unusual convert to populistic politics joined the promising new party organized by Editor Blake and the local leaders of the Noble and Holy Order of the Knights of Labor. As was the case with the wily Martinez, Mills' prominence enabled him to achieve quick recognition. The 1890 convention of the People's party, while it confidently organized itself so that delegations from each precinct in San Miguel became precinct committees, elected Mills to chair its key coordinating committee. [48] More important, the former Midwesterner was nominated by the People's party for a seat in the Territorial Council.

Probably the most newsworthy act of the county convention was the nomination to the territorial House of burly Pablo Herrera, brother of the founder of the White Caps. The move, which would greatly complicate Governor Prince's campaign to destroy the controversial secret society, seemed to crown the creation of a most unusual coalition. Dissatisfied Democrats and discontented Republicans were allied in a party organized by members of a utopian union movement. Now White Caps were moving into important leadership roles in the fledgling political organization. Prince was dismayed at what appeared to him to be a politicalization of the White Cap movement. He shared a view held by a growing number of New Mexico leaders that a few active and educated men — Mills and Martinez best fit this category — were playing upon the emotions of simple, uninformed people. The result was White Cap lawlessness. The selection of Pablo Herrera must have reinforced the governor's view that the protest movement in San Miguel County was a conspiracy.

Chief Justice O'Brien was more specific than Prince in feeling that the *Gorras* in the new People's party were being deliberately used by ruthless politicians. His description of these devious leaders brings to mind the patrician Mills. A few wicked, designing men were behind the White Cap movement, O'Brien insisted. ''Some of them are aspirants for political favors, and some of them *educated Americans,* base enough to mislead the thoughtless natives in hopes of political preferment.'' The justice felt that these clever plotters were most responsible for the depredations which finally brought the concerned Prince hastening to the county for his on-the-spot investigation. "The poor dupes who actually destroy the fences are blameless when compared with the wicked leaders who inspire and plan the midnight depredations that disgrace the territory." [49]

The flurry of new political activity in San Miguel County now increased the difficulties of the official effort to suppress the White Caps. A surprisingly vibrant third-party movement in the county was a serious challenge to the dominant Republican party, its supremacy already threatened by the destructive Romero-Lopez feud. The editor of the *Las Vegas Daily Optic* tried to minimize the new threat by calling the People's party "a mongrel association of dissimilar elements." [50] But his heavy humor was due more to alarm than to feelings of superiority or contempt. The new third party was, quite obviously, becoming the vehicle for protest in San Miguel County. The Democratic party, which had assumed that role in Lincoln and Colfax counties, was neither strong enough nor bold enough to lead the kind of political opposition the times demanded against the so-called land-grabbers on the Las Vegas Community Grant. Democrat Joseph, the incumbent delegate, expected to retain most of the votes of those attracted to the new party in his race against Otero, because of his warm relations with the Knights of Labor in the county. [51] But the first genuine People's party in the territory, more radical than the Alliance-supported Democratic organizations elsewhere, was to provide a significant new dimension to the upcoming 1890 election.

5

1890—YEAR OF CHALLENGE

An attitude of discontent was common throughout much of the West in 1890. Farmers in the wheat-belt states were becoming discouraged with their plight; some had grown disenchanted with the system itself. The price of such staples as corn and wheat continued to drop. To debtor farmers these price declines meant less money to make mortgage payments. In 1866 the price per bushel of wheat was $2.062, but by 1892 it had dropped to $0.831. [1] The price decline in agricultural products was part of a deflationary trend that had affected the entire nation, but its effects were especially serious for farmers. Added to the persistent drought in the Great Plains, which began in the summer of 1887, the steady appreciation of currency that resulted from the disastrous price declines compelled many Midwestern farmers to face a dismal future. Compounding their problems was the arrogance of the railroad owners, who customarily charged all the traffic would bear. The power of these transportation barons was enormous, causing legislators in Kansas and Nebraska, for example, to bow to their lobbying and their inducements in the form of free railroad passes or other scarcely subtle bribes. Land, free or cheap, was a sacred goal of most of the small farmers west of the Mississippi, but the major railroad corporations had received Western land grants from the federal government that exceeded the German Empire in size. [2] To many farmers these vast holdings constituted part of a national land monopoly.

By contrast, the people of the urban East appeared to be prospering, their growing political power causing alarm among many agrarian groups. The opulence of the capitalist class was made most evident by the gaudy Victorian palaces of Newport or New York City, which symbolized financial success for the most talented or the boldest. But even the working class and the lower middle class seemed to be enjoying a better life. Urban laborers, for instance, were benefiting from the price decline on agricultural items by lower food prices. Many of them were employed in industries with a rising wage scale. Laborers employed in one New York brewing firm saw their daily wages gradually rise from $1.30 in 1866 to $2.00 in 1891. With an ever-increasing number of new gadgets and labor-saving devices, life in the East appeared glowing, in contrast to the simplicity found on lonely wheat farms of the West. But rural America compared unfavorably in other ways, too. In population, people living in the country had declined to only sixty percent of the national total by 1890. The drop was a significant one from the ninety five percent recorded in 1790. The weakening of the farmer's political base largely caused by this percentage decline only added to his feelings of helplessness. [3]

The Northern and Southern Alliances and other farm groups that emerged in the troubled eighties had done much to raise the hopes of Western farmers. But the efforts of these farm organizations to adjust the political and economic system of the nation, so that the small agrarians could compete on a basis of at least some equality, had not succeeded nearly so well as the enthusiastic campaigns to end loneliness and isolation through sponsored social activities. Direct political action seemed increasingly necessary, if there was to be any hope. Since the two major parties appeared to many of the farmers to be indifferent, new third parties or Alliance-endorsed factions within the major parties began to take on a new allure. In 1890 these infant political organizations were springing up throughout the West and the South. The seeds of Populism had been sown.

With New Mexico's frontier isolation coming to an end, the territory would be affected by the ebb and flow of these currents of discontent. Although the territory had always been influenced by national issues to some degree, the arrival of the railroads in 1879 significantly increased New Mexico's involvement in the affairs of the country. Recognizing the changes that had already been wrought by the coming of the transcontinentals, Governor Prince, in a letter to Washington on April 23, 1892, asserted that rail transportation, which now made travel to the national capital a trip of less than a week, had revolutionized territorial politics. Whereas political rule prior to the railroads was accomplished by ''coercion, threats and bulldozing,'' politicians now had to take cognizance of entirely new conditions. ''Modern and American systems'' were needed to make the more nationally integrated body politic of New Mexico work. ''The native people will not stand what they did 15 years ago,'' the governor warned. [4]

In this provocative letter Prince was attacking the methods of his political rival, Tom Catron. He was not referring to the sharp increase of native intolerance toward such controversial practices as land-grabbing. The hostilities of small landowners, both Hispano and Anglo, toward the alleged land and cattle monopolies operating in the territory would not be shared by the aristocratic Prince. And yet the alarm felt by Alliance members in Lincoln and Colfax counties and by the Knights and even the White Caps of San Miguel was creating a climate of opinion favorable to the growth of a larger protest movement. New Mexico's population growth would feed this increasing dissatisfaction by bringing into the territory new immigrants, many of whom embraced convictions similar to those of the more disenchanted residents. During the eighties, according to the 1890 census, the population of New Mexico grew by 40,717 people, bringing the total to 160,282. Much of the increase could be attributed to the natural growth of the indigenous population. But by 1900 twenty percent of the 196,310 New Mexicans were from outside the territory, 2,053 of them from Kansas, the center of agrarian protest in the Midwest. [5]

New Mexico agriculture was also growing in importance. With interest in reclamation intensifying during the 1880's, cultivated acreage increased to 787,822 in 1890. A total of 156,691 acres had fallen under the plow during the preceding decade. In the nineties, largely as a result of irrigation, the total acreage under cultivation would rise to 5,130,878. According to the May 8, 1891 issue of the *Rio Grande Republican,* the amount of cultivated land in Colfax County increased five times over the previous year. [6] Agricultural cultivation advanced despite an average territorial lending rate of 10.05 percent interest in 1890. [7] Although New Mexico's agrarian economy was more oriented toward a local market than that of neighboring Arizona, its economic welfare was becoming more intertwined with that of the nation.

Even more important to the territory's national involvement was the booming mining economy which, more than any other industry, pulled New Mexico into the arena of national controversy during the nineties. The previous decade had been one of mining prosperity, with Governor Prince remarking some years later that the territory was spotted with mining camps, each of which regarded itself as a second Leadville, Colorado. [8] The production of silver was gaining the greatest prominence, for strikes were being made almost everywhere in the mountains of New Mexico. New and promising mines were opened up, especially in such counties as Sierra and Grant in the silver-rich southwestern corner. Silver had displaced gold as the leading precious metal mined in the territory. Prior to 1880, the production of gold had outstripped the sought-after white metal by almost three to one.

From 1885 to 1889 a dramatic reversal in the economic importance of the two metals occurred. Silver production climbed to $19,113,000 and gold production dropped to $3,808,000. But unfortunately for the silver industry, the price of silver was on a dangerous decline. In 1885, when silver mining was rapidly expanding, the price of silver was $1.33 an ounce. By 1890, however, it had dropped to $1.05 an ounce. Silver production declined during the five-year period by more than forty percent. [9]

Stock grazing was the major enterprise in the territory, and the late eighties saw sheep raising, New Mexico's oldest industry, maintaining itself at a remarkably even level. But in the cattle industry there were serious price declines caused by overproduction. The price per head of cattle in 1886 was twelve dollars, which was considerably below the national average. By 1889, it had dropped to only seven or eight dollars. Even though the number of beeves increased by 135,000 in 1887 and 1888, the total assessed value of stock declined by $1,200,000 during those years. The drop in cattle prices hurt the small rancher, often a marginal producer, much more than the large operator. And these low prices, when added to the fear of monopoly, accounted largely for the agitation in the cattle-raising counties of New Mexico.

Profits in the sheep-raising industry, on the other hand, rose slowly over a seventeen-year period. The gross income per rancher increased from 32 cents a sheep in 1883 to 54 cents in 1899. Nationally this industry seemed least affected by the economic adversities that plagued the West. The value of sheep, as a matter of fact, reached a peak price during the depression year of 1893. Herd improvement probably accounted, at least in part, for the relative stability of the industry in New Mexico. While the average sheep produced only two pounds of wool at sixteen cents a pound in 1883, by 1899 the wool yield per head had increased to 4.15 pounds at thirteen cents a pound.

An indication that the economy of the territory was still partly localized, despite the arrival of the railroads, can be seen in the stable price level of alfalfa. While the national average value of alfalfa hay dropped $1.09 per ton from 1885 to 1894, the price of the important stock feed in New Mexico remained stable. There were even instances of increases reported. In 1885, the price per ton in the territory was fifteen dollars; in 1894, it ranged from ten to twenty dollars per ton. [10]

This growing integration of the territory into the national picture, both politically and economically, was reflected in the deliberations of the two major political parties during the year 1890. Meeting in their territorial conventions in early autumn, Republicans and Democrats felt compelled to pay greater attention to national issues than they had in the past. Local issues, of course, were dealt with; Republicans, for instance, in their September gathering, defended the controversial constitution they had drafted in 1889 against charges it was a land-grabbers' document. That same convention had reconvened on August 18, 1890, to amend the constitution so that public school taxes would not be collected at the lowest level. The amendment was to assure the Roman Catholic Church of its customary local sources of school revenue, [11] but it did not appease Catholic clergymen. The defeat of the constitution by a better than two-to-one margin in early October revealed to many Republicans that they were in serious trouble with the electorate.

But because of the territory's increased national identification, territorial Republicans would have to be on the defensive on national issues, also. With territorial leaders being appointed by the Harrison administration, it was almost mandatory that Benjamin Harrison's record be supported. In response to this obligation the Republicans, who again nominated Mariano S. Otero as territorial delegate, passed a strong resolution commending the Sherman Silver Purchase Act as good "protective silver legislation." [12] The Sherman Act, passed by Congress in July, committed the government to buy, at the commercial price, 54 million ounces of silver a year. The sum was the estimated annual output of all the Western silver mines. The new measure differed from the earlier Bland-Allison Act,which had pledged the treasury to buy from two to four million dollars' worth of silver monthly. [13] Territorial Republicans, unable to anticipate the disastrous drop in the commercial price of silver during the next several years, felt confident that their stock with the silver miners had been bolstered by the legislation. One development that the convention delegates were able to anticipate correctly was the creation several months later of a Court of Private Land Claims. Confident that such a court would resolve the bitter controversies over land grants, the Republican convention thanked President Harrison, who would sign the appropriate legislation on March 3, 1891, for his part in making such a court possible. [14]

The Democrats, who met in Silver City, decided to use the maligned constitution of 1889 as a weapon to regain control of the territorial legislature and to keep Antonio Joseph in Congress. They attacked the proposed state constitution by resolution, listing such objections as the unfair apportionment and the one-percent limit on state taxes, which they claimed would shift the tax burden to the less able. [15] Joseph was nominated to run on an anti-grant platform, [16] despite his past connections with the Santa Fe Ring.

Turning to national issues, the Democratic delegates, dissastified with the Sherman Silver Purchase Act, supported a resolution endorsing the free coinage of silver. [17] Seizing on what would become the dominant issue in the West even before the Populists could organize on a territory-wide basis, the Democrats furthered their image as the party of the little man. Many of the delegates who gathered at Silver City were in territorial industries that suffered from serious price declines. Unlike Republicans, who traditionally had been associated with the healthier sheep-raising industry, a large number of the Democratic delegates were in the cattle business. Depressed prices in this industry had significantly affected the range country from Colfax County southward into the "Little Texas" area of the territory's southeastern corner.

Although national issues were given the greater share of attention at the two party conventions, local political issues in the end proved most durable. Not surprisingly, political oratory in the fall campaign was warmer in those counties where dissatisfaction was greatest. In San Miguel County, for instance, where the first bona fide People's party in the territory was making a second electoral bid for power, concerned Republicans were exploiting the White Cap issue for all its worth. Pablo Herrera's candidacy for a seat in the Territorial House made the new People's party especially vulnerable to the charge of "White Capism." But the Democratic party could not escape that damaging accusation either. Primarily because the Knights of Labor were giving their enthusiastic support to Joseph, the Republicans were using a guilt-by-association strategy against their major rivals. In every White Cap area where Joseph campaigned the issue was brought up and used against him and his party. The *Gorras* had infiltrated the Knights and the Knights were supporting Joseph — convincing proof that Joseph and his party were not at odds with these native night riders. In San Miguel County, where the Knights of Labor were able to muster 2,000 marchers during the campaign season in another big Las Vegas parade, [18] the use of the White Cap issue produced telling results. Even in Santa Fe and Mora counties, where there were fewer Knights and White Caps, the unfair association of the Democrats with the violence of the *Gorras* became a favorite Republican campaign technique.

Republican legislators, eager to maintain their political control in the changing territory, insisted that New Mexico was "on the verge of a revolution and riot and bloodshed." They pilloried the San Miguel White Caps for their destructiveness and for the shame that they had brought to New Mexico, always implying that the Democrats were in league with them. The Republican *New Mexican* of Santa Fe did not hesitate to express its biases. The Democrats were responsible for the White Caps, it bluntly told its readers as the excitement of the campaign mounted. [19] An issue to match the politically dangerous association with the Santa Fe Ring, so effectively used by Democrats, had been found by Republicans in White Capism.

The Democratic press, squarely on the defensive on this issue, disowned any White Cap support for the party. The "devil may care" attitude of the *Gorras* was severely rebuked by the *Santa Fe Sun,* acting as the partisan news voice of the Democrats in the territorial capital. The "lasting disgrace" to New Mexico resulting from this group's behavior was lamented. As for the serious charge leveled against the Democrats by the *New Mexican* that they were responsible for White Cap violence, the *Sun* was indignant. It reprimanded the Republican journal for dividing honest men on a purely "non-political issue."

Joseph was defended as a man who had done more for the territory than all the other delegates from New Mexico put together. The charge that he was "hand in glove with the White Caps" was dismissed as a "piece of baseless ingratitude." Joseph's strong supporters, the Knights of Labor, that "most honorable body of organized laboring men in the world," were also defended. To brand the Knights as White Caps, "as is done by some papers, and then charging the White Caps with every crime in the calendar, is an insult to every laboring man who has honestly sought to better his conditions by organizing with his fellow laborers for this purpose." Membership in the Knights was lauded as a "badge of honor." As for the fact that a few Knights were White Caps, it was an "outrageous insult" to indict an entire organization for the acts of a few. The peppery newspaper urged all Knights to respond on November 4, election day, in a "masterly" and decisive way by voting "against the rich bosses who deliberately insult the poor working men because they organize themselves for their own mutual benefit." [20]

Because of the potency of the White Cap issue in San Miguel and Santa Fe counties, Democrats tried to turn it around and use it against their Republican taunters. In San Miguel the "rapid growth" of the *Gorras* was attributed to the fact that the two feuding Republican factions, the Romero and Lopez factions, were deliberately using the White Caps to destroy one another. The failure of Miguel Salazar, the Republican district attorney of the county, to win convictions against those alleged White Caps arrested in 1889 was also cited.

Turning to neighboring Santa Fe County, the *Sun,* three days before the election, reported the presence of White Caps in the southern part of the county. The alarming development had already caused one or two serious demonstrations during the preceding ten days. More sensational was the journal's accusation that the rapid growth of the movement in Santa Fe County was the handiwork of the powerful Republican *jefe,* Tom Catron. According to the story, Susano Ortiz, chief witness against certain prominent citizens arrested because of the White Cap mania, had been overheard to say in a conversation on the streets of Santa Fe that the White Caps were not going to vote Democratic, but support the "Republican ticket" instead. Ortiz also boasted that he had met with White Cap leaders southeast of Santa Fe in Tecolote the night before, and had gone back to the capital city to get additional money from Catron so he could return to the masked conspirators and pay them more. Pure hypocrisy screamed the *Sun;* the White Caps were being "bought up for the Republican ticket," while the *Santa Fe Daily New Mexican* was making a "terrible noise" against the Democrats. [21]

Remaining on the offensive the *Sun,* on November 1, added another charge to its list of accusations. Republican managers had hired "reckless fellows, so-called White Caps, to come into the city [Santa Fe] and join the Democratic parade to-night in White Cap dress for the purpose of inciting a riot and assisting them in their scheme to fasten White Capism on the Democratic party of this county.'' Consequently, on the eve of the election, the bitter White Cap issue was submerging the more fundamental and substantive local and national issues in northern New Mexico. Also, all parties, the Republican, Democratic, and People's party of San Miguel, felt compelled to cope with numerous and ingenious charges of aiding and abetting the *Gorras.*

Land-grabbing and other related issues were not forgotten, however; after all, the White Caps had organized in response to the serious threat to the Las Vegas Community Grant, and the state constitution drawn up in Las Vegas in 1889 had been defeated largely because it appeared to favor ambitious landowners and speculators. The Maxwell Land Grant and the controversial change-of-venue law were still the key issues in Colfax County.

In Lincoln County, the cattle monopoly remained the paramount issue as far as many of the small stockgrazers were concerned. The *Nogal Nugget* was sold to the Lincoln County Farmers' Alliance in 1890, allowing the crusading farm group, which by this time owned several other newspapers, to control the editorial policies of the journal. The *Nugget* changed its name to the *Liberty Banner* and a new editor was hired. He was J. E. Wharton, who lowered subscription rates from two dollars to one dollar a year, making it the cheapest paper in the territory. [22] Thus, the fundamental issues motivating agrarian protest in such states as Kansas and Nebraska were being kept alive in New Mexico by the newspaper outlets of the Farmers' Alliance.

Territorial politics were changing significantly in 1890. For years they had been dominated by the Republican party or had been under the control of the Santa Fe Ring under what Professor Kenneth N. Owens has called a ''noparty'' system. [23] But now new or breakaway parties were moving into the picture. The People's party of Lincoln County, although still unable to dispel its reputation as a creature of the Republican party, again fielded candidates in 1890. The growing strength of the genuine Populist movement in San Miguel was convincing proof of what a popular reaction to land-grabbing could do to the traditional political pattern. But the increasing political independence found in isolated San Juan County, where one of the most successful People's parties would soon take root, provided a different kind of threat to party unity.

San Juan, located in the Navajo country of northeastern New Mexico, was attached to Rio Arriba County in a large legislative district entitled to one vote in the Territorial Council. The county had approximately 500 electors as compared to Rio Arriba's 2,300. [24] But the population of San Juan was growing steadily because of substantial strides in production of cereal crops and fruit on irrigated lands. Wheat raising was important; in a few years the county would boast a crop yield of 20 to 40 bushels an acre. Although the first fruit trees had been planted only five years earlier, by 1891 twenty-three thousand would be in production and by 1892 approximately fifty thousand. Much of the cereal and fruit produced in San Juan was set aside to feed the miners in the busy silver camps of western Colorado. And irrigation was important to the county's continued growth. Once called "one of the garden spots of the world" by the New Mexico Bureau of Immigration, the county would see twenty thousand acres of land in the San Juan Valley put "under the ditch" by the mid-nineties. But the actual potential for irrigation in the county's three major river valleys, the San Juan, Animas, and La Plata, was conservatively estimated at one million acres. [25]

Farmers in the prosperous county, feeling isolated from the distant capital at Santa Fe, were growing resentful of San Juan's political subordination to neighboring Rio Arriba County. In the autumn of 1890 both the Republican and Democratic parties of Rio Arriba nominated candidates for the Council without even consulting the party leaders of San Juan. The *San Juan County Index,* published in the county seat at Aztec, demanded that both local parties decide on San Juan's candidate for the lone Council seat. It urged Democrats, who were to meet in Largo in mid-October, to nominate a candidate acceptable to the Republicans meeting in Flora Vista three days later. The citizens of San Juan County thus hoped to demonstrate that they were "not to be led by the nose . . ." [26] Such independence portended future defiance in the young county and symbolized the growing fragmentation of party politics in New Mexico during the fateful year of 1890.

Voters assembled at the polls throughout the territory on November 4. If the number of party rebels participating was not as large as in Colorado or the depressed wheat-raising states to the east, the determination of the disenchanted voters seemed just as great. In 1890 a new American political party was being created. Still not unified, its name varying from state to state, the Populist movement would not result in a nationally organized party until 1892; its ultimate cohesiveness as a separate third party had to be preceded by emergence of the independent protest parties so strong in the Midwest.

The Democratic party, however, would rival any success that the new party movement in New Mexico might have. Similar to their counterparts in the South, Democrats would attract and channel much of the agrarian discontent so vital to Populism. As the returns of the 1890 vote began coming in it became obvious that most of the dissatisfied voters in the territory were going to reject monopoly control and land-grabbing by voting Democratic in the county and legislative races. Fear of White Capism was overcome in the north central counties as Democrats chalked up impressive wins. Two Republican representatives from Santa Fe County were replaced by Democrats. [27] In San Miguel, the most populous county in the territory, the People's party did triumph, but this did not disturb such Democrats as J.H. Crist, editor of the *Santa Fe Sun.* He congratulated Felix Martinez, the ex-Democrat, for his part in the victory. Crist claimed that the people of San Miguel County by asserting themselves against the dictatorial Republican bosses had at last ended Republican "Ring rule" in New Mexico. [28] In Colfax County the acrimony over the Maxwell Land Grant controversy had not been forgotten as the entire Democratic ticket, except for the candidate for sheriff, was elected. [29]

Democrats did well throughout the rest of the territory too. In San Juan County they elected their candidate to the territorial House of Representatives. [30] In Lincoln County the entire Democratic ticket was elected. George Curry, who became territorial governor of New Mexico in 1907, was Democratic county chairman at the time. He attributed the victory of his party to the Lincoln Populists who split the Republican vote. Thus, the charge leveled by the old *Nogal Nugget* that the Populist party in Lincoln County was only an offshoot of the Republican organization was borne out. Democratic victories in the southeastern corner of the territory were due largely to the propinquity of Democratic Texas. But the Democratic tide seemed especially strong in 1890. For instance, in Chaves County, recently severed from Lincoln, the Democratic candidate for the key office of sheriff defeated Pat Garrett, who had gained immortality for having shot Billy the Kid on July 14, 1881. [31]

When all the votes were tallied the Democrats emerged with a two-vote majority in the lower House of the territorial legislature. William Burns, who won his race in Sierra County in the mining-rich southwestern section of the territory, was subsequently selected by the Democrats as speaker of the House. The Republican margin in the Council was narrowed; there were now seven Republicans and three Democrats, plus T.B. Mills, one of two Populists serving in the upper House. [32] "The Republican 'land-grabbing' bosses will positively not organize the 29th legislative assembly," mocked the Democratic press. The era of "fraud and intimidation has passed." [33] In the most important territorial race, the contest for delegate, Joseph once again triumphed over Otero (his margin in this race was 2,054 votes). [34]

New Mexico Democrats by their successes duplicated the feats of their parent organization in 1890. Nationally, the party increased its strength in the United States Senate and wiped out a seven-vote majority in the House, electing 235 Democrats to 88 Republicans. Populistic candidates gained seats in the Congress too. Just as Mills and Pablo Herrera were elected to the territorial assembly from San Miguel, independent third-party candidates were elected to the national legislature. In Kansas, shrewd Jerry Simpson, attired in rags to capitalize on the charge he was ''Sockless,'' won a seat in the House of Representatives, while William A. ''Whiskers'' Peffer defeated the established Republican veteran, John J. Ingalls, for one of the Jayhawker state's two Senate seats. Eight other independents were elevated to the national House, and in the Senate John L.M. Irby of South Carolina and James H. Kyle, a preacher from South Dakota, joined Peffer to form a small bloc independent of the major parties.

In the South most Southern Alliance members remained loyal to the Democratic party in 1890. Fearing a split among white supremacists in their organization because Southern Bourbons were characterizing their group's cooperation with the Colored Alliance as a first step toward the creation of a ''niggers' party,'' a majority of the Alliance members stood pat. Nevertheless, the Southern Alliance succeeded in electing to the House approximately 35 Democrats pledged to Alliance policies.

Fusion was also important in the 1890 election: many of the 52 congressmen representing the South and the Midwest were elected because of the cooperation of one of the two major parties with the new independent forces. On the state level, where the important triumphs were mostly in the Midwest, third-party candidates won three governorships and seized control of both houses of the legislatures of seven states. The lower house in a half-dozen more states fell to the command of independents representing the mounting agrarian protest in the country. [35]

To succeed at the polls was one thing,but to bring about important legislative changes was quite another. When the Twenty-ninth Legislative Assembly convened in Santa Fe on December 29, 1890, Mills tried to implement a few of the demands which had caused so many people to move toward political independence in 1890. On the sixth day of the session the Populist leader introduced Council Bill No. 23, ''An Act to regulate transportation of freights by railroad corporations and to prevent their pooling of their earnings.'' As the essence of monopoly in New Mexico was either land-grabbing or the greed of the cattle barons, Mills' presentation of a memorial from the Commercial Club of Las Vegas calling for protection of the Las Vegas Community Grant was another attempt at reform. [36] His prominent role in promoting educational change was also important in light of the significance attached to public education at this time by many farmers and workers. [37]

In most of his legislative efforts Mills failed, a fate common for one advocating change before there is adequate public support. His bill proposing railroad regulation was sent to the Committee on Railroads, where it quietly died. Legislative support for small landowners on community grants also failed to materialize. A bill calling for the confirmation of such grants was submitted to the Committee on Municipal and Private Corporations, on which the hostile Catron served. Two other reform measures were rejected by the Council, both of which were introduced by a twenty-five-year-old Republican legislator from Silver City, Joseph A. Ancheta. Undoubtedly reflecting the concerns of mine workers in his part of New Mexico, one of Ancheta's bills called for the prompt payment of wages to laborers every month, the other for protection of mine employees. [38] Control of the Council by conservative Republican leaders, however, was to stymie such reform legislation.

In the area of educational improvement, however, Mills and his allies were more successful. The question of public education in New Mexico was a complicated one. Because of the reluctance of the Roman Catholic Church to surrender its virtual monopoly on education among the natives of the territory, many ordinarily progressive Spanish-speaking leaders were suspicious of public-supported education. Governor Ross had worked diligently for the creation of a truly effective tax-supported educational system, only to be balked by such leaders as Tom Catron, who opposed the governor's efforts because the Republican Old Guard wished to maintain its useful alliance with devout Hispano leaders in northern New Mexico. [39] But support for educational reform in the Twenty-ninth Assembly was much stronger. Ancheta, although a graduate of Notre Dame University and a native, worked side by side with Mills in support of a public school system. The assistance given by the young Republican was deeply appreciated by Mills who, as a member of the key Committee on Education, [40] was equally dedicated.

But Mills and Ancheta were not alone; Governor Prince wanted a full-fledged public-supported educational system organized during his tenure. Chagrined by the fact that not one public school in Santa Fe had been opened "a single day" during the past year, Prince called for a ten-month school year, the expenses to be borne by a general tax and local district taxes. His recommendations, presented in a 34-page message, were partly accepted by a legislature so divided that even the selection of a public printer produced a major debate. The Democratic House and the Republican Council created a territorial board of education, a teacher-training institute, and territorial and county superintendencies. Local taxation for educational purposes was also provided. But the assembly refused to prohibit employment of non-certified teachers and failed to provide travel expenses for members of the territorial education board and teacher institute. [41] Prince was satisfied, though. When he wrote President Harrison to tell of his success, he asserted that the new school law would bring the standards of the "Mexican communities" up to American ones in a short time. [42]

While the educational reforms enacted by the legislature received some attention, an attempted assassination involving three men prominent in the fight for public education stole most of the headlines. The incident occurred on the night of February 5, 1891, when rifle and gunshot bullets shattered the window of an office in the Griffin Building on Palace Avenue where five legislators were gathered for a committee meeting. Of the five only Ancheta was hit; Mills, Catron, Pedro Perea, and E. Stover escaped injury. The would-be assassins fled on horseback, eluding a posse which pursued them for seven miles along the Old Pecos Road. Ancheta, although receiving wounds to the neck, face, and shoulder, recovered. The *Albuquerque Citizen** insisted that the bullets were intended for Mills, Ancheta, and Stover in retaliation for the conspicuous role all three men played in the passage of the school bill.

The public was outraged at the attack, and Governor Prince responded immediately. He offered a $5,000 reward for information leading to the arrest of the men involved in the attempted assassination. A joint resolution unanimously passed by both houses the following day authorized the governor to make any such reward worth $20,000. [43] Prince went even further, secretly communicating with the Pinkerton Detective Agency in Chicago. The agency's Denver office dispatched the famous Spanish-speaking investigator, Charles A. Siringo, to New Mexico. Believing that the shooting of Ancheta was directly tied to White Cap violence, officials sent Siringo to San Miguel, where he managed to ingratiate himself with the Herrera brothers, particularly Nicanor. He also won membership in the Knights of Labor without going through the probationary period. Generously entertaining White Caps with money supplied by Prince, Siringo masqueraded under the name of Charles T. Leon. He eventually came to the conclusion that the Knights and the *Gorras* were separate organizations, a fact among others making it difficult to identify the actual culprits in the attempted assasination. The threat of the White Caps was not minimized, however. Siringo's superior, James McParland, the agency's Denver superintendent who gained national attention for his role in breaking the power of the Molly Maguires, compared the night-riding *Gorras* with the Mollies of Pennsylvania. "The secret society of White Caps is traveling in the same direction in New Mexico." [44]

---

* Sometimes called the *Albuquerque Daily Citizen* or the *Albuquerque Evening Citizen.*

61

During the early stages of Siringo's investigation he began to suspect that the attempted assassination was the work of Francisco Chavez, Democratic sheriff of Santa Fe County, and the White Caps of Tecolate. As the five-month investigation progressed, the Pinkerton agent narrowed his suspects down to Sheriff Chavez and a close ally. He concluded that Catron was their intended victim. The corpulent Republican, who should have been an easy target, had been standing near the window through which the shots were fired. He was evidently marked for assassination because of his role in a feud which would shortly become one of the best known in New Mexico history. Catron was a supporter of Francisco Gonzales y Borrego, a turncoat Democrat and bitter rival of the Santa Fe sheriff. [45] The conclusion was that the bullets were not fired to protest educational reform, but to eliminate the prominent Republican for his unwise involvement in a Democratic feud.

Mills' presence at the shooting gave at least one Populist successful in the electoral challenge of 1890 the publicity that a new cause usually needs. The erroneous report that the San Miguel legislator was one of the intended targets because of his prominent support of educational change might even have dramatized the growing demand for reform in New Mexico. But the limited electoral triumphs of the new party in 1890 were to produce another event which, if it did not match in importance Mills' involvement in the Ancheta affair, did provide one of the more humorous incidents of the young reform movement. During the waning days of the Twenty-ninth session — a session disappointing to those who had campaigned for reform in 1890 — Pablo Herrera broke a long silence. Although the recently elected Hispano spoke good English, he had been content to sit quietly with a cynical expression on his face. Now, however, the disgusted Populist rose and made a speech. He told his House colleagues of the dreary years he had spent in the penitentiary, and then commented on the sixty days he had just served in the legislature. In his opinion, the time he spent in the penitentiary was more enjoyable and worthwhile than his service in the territorial assembly. Miguel A. Otero later commented on Herrera's speech in these words: ''Without wishing to reflect on the character of any member [Herrera insisted that] there was more honor, truth, and honesty within the penitentiary walls than he ever saw in the House, and in the future he would much prefer a sentence in the penitentiary than to be elected as a member of the House of Representatives in New Mexico.''

Many Populists throughout the country were to express their disenchantment with the system during the nineties, but few would do it more effectively than Pablo Herrera. A year and a half later, for example, Populists pushed through their national convention in Omaha a resolution by which no governmental official — state, local or national — could serve in a Populist convention. But even this repudiation does not quite reach the heights of cynicism achieved by Herrera that day in the Twenty-ninth session. His colleagues were in an uproar, laughing and cheering, and the speaker was compelled to order a fifteen-minute recess while members gathered around Herrera to shake his hand. [46] A levity had been reached during that session which would be difficult to attain in the troubled months ahead.

6

THE 1892 ELECTION

Eighteen ninety-two was an eventful year in the farmlands of America. After years of falling prices, compounded by rising mortgage foreclosures resulting from the collapse of the Western agricultural boom in 1887, wheat farmers in the Midwest were prepared to take even greater independent political action. The perpetual threat of the merchant's crop lien in the South and the alarming decline in the price of silver in the West brought support from these regions too. The refusal of the Southern Alliance to join a new political party at a farm-labor convention in Ocala, Florida, the month following the third-party victories of 1890 dampened the enthusiasm of some. But disenchantment with the two major parties was too strong to derail a new party movement altogether. A mass meeting of interested people from thirty-three states and territories was held in Cincinnati on May 19, 1891. The strong desire of many of the delegates for a new political party to speak for the people was unmistakable. The convention passed a resolution creating a People's party and established a national executive committee. A meeting was scheduled for February of the following year to find out if other reform organizations could be united under the new party banner.

In 1892, on Washington's birthday, the proposed convention met in St. Louis. Enthusiastic delegates listened with delight to Ignatius Donnelly's eloquent delivery of the preamble he had written for the platform of the new party. Delegates representing organizations such as the Southern Alliance, the Northern Alliance, the Knights of Labor, the National Colored Alliance and the Farmers' Mutual Benefit Association greeted the Minnesotan's delivery with zeal. When he concluded hats and papers were tossed into the air and cheering delegates waved wraps and umbrellas in approval. The convention, carrying out its patriotic design, called for a national convention to meet in Omaha on the Fourth of July. Moreover, to assure grass-roots support, a committee of five was selected to draw up the convention call. It invited all those who approved of the preamble and platform adopted at St. Louis to hold open meetings in the towns and villages throughout the country, on the last Saturday in March, to elect delegates to the Omaha convention. As it later worked out, each state was entitled to eight delegates at large with four additional ones from each congressional district, setting the maximum number for the July 4 convention at 1776. [1]

But in 1892 the People's party in the Territory of New Mexico was not prepared to extend its political activities outside the boundaries of San Miguel County in any significant way. The Democratic party had absorbed much of the protest fever in the territory, and Joseph's apparent renomination only strengthened his party's image as a defender of the people. The territorial delegate was solid on those issues which were gaining the widest acceptance among farmers, small stockmen, working men, and miners. His advocacy of silver coinage underscored the stand for free silver that the territorial Democratic party had taken two years earlier. His friendship with the Knights made him particularly popular in those northern counties where the organization had acquired strength. And, despite his quiet land investments, he still had the reputation of being a staunch opponent of the land-grabbers.

The most immediate threat to the Populist organization in San Miguel, however, was not the popularity of the easy-going territorial delegate, but the manipulations of that strong-willed newcomer to the People's movement, Felix Martinez. Using his position as a member of the party's executive committee, Martinez soon made himself controversial. He was accused by newspaperman Blake of working to annex the Populist party to the Democratic party. Operating on a ''sub rosa'' basis, Martinez had spent the last two years plotting to ''drag'' the new party into the Democratic organization. His plan was to induce the Populist members of the last legislative session to take part in the Democratic caucuses and ''not act as a party independent of both the old ones in the house of representatives.'' [2] In his efforts, Martinez was completely successful. While Mills, as one of two Populists serving on the Council, often used his independent judgment, San Miguel Populists in the House were active participants in the Democratic party caucuses. By forfeiting their independent decision making, the People's party thus lost an excellent opportunity to hold the balance of power in the Twenty-ninth territorial legislature. As there were only eleven Republican representatives to nine Democrats, the four Populist votes in the House could have been decisive on many issues. [3] In its refusal to act independently the Populist bloc sacrificed the opportunity to control the course of legislative action ''in the interest of the people as a whole.''

Martinez's successes in Santa Fe during the legislative session were duplicated in San Miguel County, where he gradually assumed a commanding position in the county organization. The founders of the party grew increasingly resentful. Blake probably spoke for a good many of the Knights of

Labor involved in the organization of the party in 1888 when he accused Martinez of putting the "people's party into the contemptible position of [being] a side show to the democratic circus." [4]

Another problem faced by the San Miguel Populists was their close association with the White Cap movement. Undoubtedly the work of the *Gorras* had sparked the party's growth in 1890, but it had also immersed it in an ever-deepening controversy. The long-range disadvantages of this association became more evident as time passed. Fortunately for the political harmony of the county the influence of the White Caps had declined sharply since Governor Prince's personal intervention in the summer of 1890. Their loss of power and influence was due to several factors, the role of the governor being one of them but the decrease of Anglo encroachments on the Las Vegas Community Grant unquestionably being another. The removal of those detested fences was crucial. It not only reduced the necessity of violent action on the part of the *Gorras,* but made the alternative of political participation much more attractive. Pablo Herrera's lone term in the legislature as a Populist representative was symbolic.

But before the White Cap menace would totally disappear from the scene, opposition to the *Gorras* would grow and further splinter political activity in San Miguel. A counter organization, called the United Protective Organization, made its appearance in the county seat of Las Vegas. The *Santa Fe Daily New Mexican* claimed as many as 3,000 members for the new group by February 18, 1891. The Catholic Church in the territory went on the attack, too. On March 5, 1891, the *Revista Catolica,* a Jesuit newspaper in Las Vegas, urged Catholic members of the secret White Cap society to refrain from further violence. Notwithstanding this plea, the *Gorras* continued their controversial existence. Archbishop Salpointe felt compelled to intervene directly a year later to prevent a threatened merger between the White Caps and that equally secret organization, the religious brotherhood of the penitentes. [5]

The White Cap issue had already aggravated the Lopez-Romero feud in San Miguel County. Sheriff Lopez's decision to join the People's party had further convinced the followers of Republican boss Eugenio Romero that Lopez and his associates were in league with the *Gorras.* The Romero faction had even charged that Lopez and his new-found political friends were allied with the notorious Society of Bandits of New Mexico. Such a charge was unfair, since the Society of Bandits of New Mexico — or the Forty Thieves as it was often called — was nothing more than a group of desperados. One historian has characterized the society as an Al Capone organization. [6] It represented neither third party nor pressure group, but rather was an instrument of the infamous Las Vegas Tavern owner Vicente Silva, who later killed his wife and brother-in-law and was himself slain by his associates. Murder was almost commonplace with the society. Miguel Otero, a biased Republican observer of San Miguel politics, later told that one of Silva's men put a notice in a Romero-controlled Spanish-language newspaper, *El Sol de Mayo,* repudiating his involvement with the group. The man was later tried and executed by Silva for his disloyalty. Because of such terror tactics Romero formed the Mutual Protection Society to oppose the Society of Bandits. The wily Republican officeseeker, alleging that Lopez's People's party and Silva's gang were part of the same parcel, also organized a new party, the *Partido del Union* or Union party.[7] Consequently, even though the White Caps were slipping into oblivion during the early nineties — Pablo Herrera, the group's most energetic leader, was killed by Lopez's brother a couple of years later [8] — they continued to confuse and fragment politics in San Miguel.

Political disorganization and new party alliances were becoming increasingly common in the Rocky Mountain West at this time, especially after 1892, when the silver issue was dominant. However, the groundwork for the celebrated silver crusade was being laid in New Mexico and other Western states and territories even prior to the 1892 election. Of the two major parties in the territory, the Democrats had responded most decisively to the silver question, declaring for free coinage in 1890. Their early action placed New Mexico Republicans on the defensive. Further equivocation by the Republican party might be interpreted as indifference, or worse yet, as opposition to free coinage.

Thomas B. Catron, an astute political weathervane, comprehended the importance of silver sooner than most of his party associates. This extraordinary man had dominated New Mexico politics for close to two decades. As the recognized leader of his party he had framed its policies, written its platforms, "controlled its conventions, represented the party at national conventions, and was a member of the republican national committee." [9] Catron was, in short, "Mr. Republican" in New Mexico and he intended to remain so. But what good would his leadership be if his party were to be pulled down by a weak stand on silver?

For Catron, New Mexico's most successful land-grabber, politics was a powerful instrument to protect his holdings. His accumulation of Mexican land grants is a story in itself. Arriving in the territory in 1866 as a young lawyer from Missouri, Catron was quickly made district attorney of the third judicial district. Two terms in the Territorial Council as a representative of Santa Fe County and a conspicuous role in the New Mexico Bar Association further enhanced his power and prestige. But a successful legal practice that included defending the rights of Hispano grantees to their landholdings gave him wealth to match his political prominence. So successful was this aggressive Anglo in these land-grant cases that the land he acquired through legal fees or separate purchase gave him the reputation in 1883 of being one of the largest landowners in the nation. [10] As some of his landholdings were acquired under questionable circumstances, political involvement seemed the only way to cope with his numerous detractors. It was for this purpose that Catron worked diligently to manipulate the quasi-political Santa Fe Ring, acting as its undisputed head after Elkins' departure for the East. "Mr. Republican" had far too much at stake to let the silver issue get the best of him.

Catron was one of many important Western politicians who began to gravitate toward James G. Blaine as a possible presidential candidate in 1892. Concern for the declining price of silver had become evident in the mining counties of southern New Mexico, where a silver convention held in El Paso was looked upon with exceptional interest. [11] President Harrison was regarded as being unfriendly to silver coinage. Silver Republicans in Congress, including the influential Senator Henry Moore Teller of Colorado, believed that Harrison had used his executive power to defeat free coinage measures in 1890 and 1892. [12] Moveover, there was a widespread belief that the president would not hesitate to use his veto authority if a free coinage measure should pass both houses. Blaine, on the other hand, was regarded as being more sympathetic to the Western silverites.

The move toward the popular Blaine, who was then serving as secretary of state under Harrison, revealed the extent of desperation among Westerners within the party. The "Plumed Knight," suffering from a chronic case of Bright's disease, was probably too ill to campaign for public office. His commitment to silver coinage was questionable, at best. On June 8, 1892, the *Rocky Mountain News* of Denver printed a letter written by Blaine in September of 1891 to Colonel A.L. Congers of Ohio, in which Blaine allegedly denounced the concept of free coinage.[13] Nevertheless, there was a strong feeling held by Teller and his Senate colleague from Colorado, Edward O. Wolcott, that if as president Blaine could not support free coinage, at least he would not use his power to oppose it. As a result, many Westerners, including Catron, looked with keen interest at the draft-Blaine movement being organized by Matthew S. Quay of Pennsylvania and Thomas C. Platt of New York, powerful senators who had quarreled with the president over patronage matters.

Governor Prince, a party loyalist, was concerned over the early maneuvering of Catron and his allies. They wanted to gain control of the territorial convention scheduled to meet in the spring to select delegates to the June meeting of the Republican national convention in Minneapolis. Picturing his rival as a longtime foe of the national administration, Prince claimed that Catron had favored Russell A. Alger for the presidential nomination in 1888. Now he was attempting to block the president's renomination in 1892 by supporting Blaine, who admittedly had "much popular support." Catron's determined anti-Harrison campaign, moreover, was no recent development; as early as April, 1891, he announced himself as delegate to the territorial convention to choose delegates to the Minneapolis meeting. [14] As the territorial gathering was not scheduled until a year later, on April 14, 1892, the extent of Catron's careful preparations was remarkable. Prior to the territorial meeting, he had recommended that a maximum number of delegates be sent to Minneapolis to represent the territory, in order to give more of his supporters an opportunity to attend the national convention. According to one of Prince's confidants, Catron had even promised the inhabitants of Clayton and Folsom a new county in return for their support, if he were successful. [15] Prince tried to counter these efforts with letters to Republicans attempting to show the folly of opposing the president's renomination. He stressed the territory's utter dependence on Washington and the consequent danger of offending the national administration. [16] In a circular letter sent by the governor on January 14, 1892, to party leaders throughout the territory, Prince warned that Harrison would be the only candidate nominated at the Minneapolis convention, as Blaine's anticipated withdrawal from the race would remove all opposition.

Blaine's subsequent announcement that he would not be a candidate had a mixed effect on his disappointed Western boosters. In Colorado, the leading silver-producing state, Teller and Wolcott refused to accept Blaine's word as final. By June the slogan "Blaine and Free Coinage" [17] had become the rallying cry for silver Republicans of the Centennial State. With silver production having eclipsed the output of gold in New Mexico, Catron's response to Blaine's decision was important. Territorial Republicans and Democrats awaited his next move with anticipation. So did San Miguel Populists, who were struggling to maintain their independent existence and hoping the national Populist movement would restore the party fortunes.

Whatever Catron's future course would be, he had resolved to control the April territorial convention scheduled to meet in Silver City, in the heart of the silver-producing country. Old and loyal associates such as W.L. Rynerson, New Mexico's national committeeman, and Tranquilino Luna, one of the territory's largest sheepmen, were committed to support him. Other "anti-administration" leaders backing Catron were John Riley and John Bail. His main opposition was Harrison's chief appointee in New Mexico, Prince, and such political allies of the governor as Eugene A. Fiske and E.G. Stover of Albuquerque. Miguel A. Otero, an opponent of Prince in Republican politics, alleged that the move by Catron and his allies to control the Silver City convention was not to stop the president's renomination, but to show Harrison who the real Republican leaders of the territory were. They wanted the president to realize how distasteful the reappointment of Governor Prince and U.S. District Attorney Fiske would be to territorial Republicans. [18]

Silver coinage was becoming a major issue in New Mexico in 1892. It would soon challenge in importance those issues which had generated such strong emotions in the Farmers' Alliance and the Knights of Labor and other protest organizations. Even so, Catron, riding the silver bandwagon with his support of Blaine, was not entirely certain he could defeat Prince and the Harrison loyalists. Unaware that four uncommitted delegates from San Miguel County were leaning toward him and that Nicholas Galles of Sierra County and W.J. Whitmore of Socorro County had decided to support him at the Silver City convention, Catron decided to guarantee victory. He would put pressure on the delegation from Taos County, where, because of his good relations with Hispano leaders, he enjoyed much popularity. Jose Julio Vigil of Taos was approached. Vigil possessed six proxies in addition to his own vote. According to a notarized affidavit sworn by Vigil, Catron offered to pay him expenses to Silver City plus fifty dollars if he would agree to support the Catron slate of presidential delegates. When the elderly delegate refused, he was arrested at Lamy while waiting for the Silver City train on the charge that he carried a falsified name. He was detained there until the following day. Upon his release the incensed delegate rushed to Silver City, arriving there during the final hours of the convention. [19]

But the strong-arm methods allegedly used by Catron to acquire the Taos votes did not turn out to be the most surprising event at the Silver City meeting. Outmaneuvering Prince, Catron unexpectedly introduced a resolution endorsing Harrison's renomination. According to Prince, the Catron resolution led to a takeover of the Silver City convention by ''new converts'' to the Harrison cause, [20] with sixty-two delegates, or two-thirds of the convention, controlled by Catron and his supporters. With supreme arrogance the Catron people allowed the governor's backers, the so-called party loyalists, to filibuster for an entire day. Then they nominated their own slate of presidential delegates, including Catron and Tranquilino Luna, John Bail, Miguel A. Otero, W.J. Whitmore, and Nicholas Galles. [21]

Prince was dejected over his defeat at Silver City. In a letter to Secretary of the Interior Noble, written a week or so after Catron's victory, he insisted that the ''real friends'' of the president should have been the ones sent to Minneapolis as delegates. He feigned surprise that Harrison's secretary of war, Stephen B. Elkins, longtime associate of Catron, had sent a note of congratulations to the victorious Catron. He criticized his rival's methods, which he asserted would never have been tolerated in the East, using the false arrest of Vigil as a prime example. [22]

Meanwhile, territorial Democrats met a month later in Santa Fe to nominate two delegates to the Democratic national convention scheduled to meet in Chicago. The Democratic meeting was controlled by Judge William T. Thornton, who, significantly in a territory controlled by rings, was a partner in Catron's Santa Fe law firm. The pressure of the silver issue on Catron was considerably diminished when the Democrats, although sending an uninstructed delegation to Chicago, adopted a resolution endorsing the candidacy of ex-president Cleveland, a known "gold bug." [23]

New Mexico's delegates attended national conventions dominated by gold forces, suspicious of bimetallism but still afraid to condemn free coinage. In Minneapolis, Blaine's last-minute resignation from the cabinet had greatly encouraged Quay and Platt and the more persistent silver Republicans from the West. Colorado's junior senator, Edward O. Wolcott, was given the honor of nominating the old party favorite. In his eloquent oration, he called for avenging Blaine's defeat by Cleveland in 1884 by giving him another chance to run against the Democratic leader, who was expected to be renominated. But Blaine never had a chance. President Harrison, as expected, had solid control of the Republican delegations from the South and enough strength outside this region to win the nomination. The leading silver-producing states — Colorado, Nevada, and Idaho — unanimously supported Blaine, but the vote in the other mining states was split among Harrison, Blaine, and William McKinley, with Montana surprisingly giving all of its votes but one to the president. In the territories, where the power of the national administration was always felt, Harrison's margin over Blaine was 14 to 2. The Catron-led delegation to Minneapolis accounted for almost half of the president's territorial majority. A plank in the Republican platform favoring at least limited silver coinage — "the Republican party demands the use of both gold and silver as standard money" — minimized the potential political damage to the ambitious Catron for his unwillingness to support the cause of "Blaine and Free Coinage."

On June 21, following the Republican convention, the Democratic national convention assembled. Western silverites again found themselves out-numbered. Cleveland was nominated in a convention kept in session by party leaders until the balloting was completed in the early hours of the morning. Concessions to silver Democrats were not significant. Adlai E. Stevenson of Illinois, who was sympathetic to the silver cause, was nominated vice president, an obscure position unless the president should die. The

Democrats, like the Republicans, endorsed a cautious silver plank. But this commitment was a guarded one, the party insisting that the parity of values of both gold and silver be maintained. Both planks alluded to the necessity of some international conference or agreement to insure parity. Partisanship on the silver issue was not eliminated, however. The Democratic plank condemned the Sherman Silver Purchase Act for its ineffectiveness.

The way was prepared for the Populists to take a strong, unequivocal stand on free coinage. But the angry delegates who gathered in Omaha in July had other issues to deal with, such as the power of the railroads and the declining economic position of the farmer. Even so, Republicans and Democrats were concerned about the kind of silver stand the leaders of the new party would take. Because of their apprehension, silver senators in both parties worked to pass the Stewart Free Coinage bill on July 1, three days before the Populist convention opened. This vote allowed twenty-nine senators to go on record for silver coinage. The victory of the silverites did not unduly alarm the leadership of the two parties in Congress, however, as a rules committee report submitted in behalf of the Stewart bill was rejected by the House on July 13. [24]

Because of the deft equivocation by both major parties on the silver issue, this politically explosive question did not achieve the prominence it was to enjoy four years later. Free coinage was one of a number of controversial planks adopted by the Populists at Omaha in a platform which also included such demands as governmental ownership of railroads and the elimination of alien landownership. Bold resolutions gave the platform an even more radical character with their advocacy of such proposals as a graduated federal income tax and the direct election of United States senators. The Populist silver plank was, nonetheless, the strongest offered by any national political party that year. ''We demand free and unlimited coinage of silver and gold at the present legal ratio of 16 to 1.'' But the misfortunes that plagued the Populists in 1892 did much to weaken the force of this honest silver declaration. The sudden death of Leonidas L. Polk of North Carolina removed from presidential consideration the man most capable of bringing the South into the Populist column. The unwillingness of Walter Q. Gresham, the attractive Republican reformer from Indiana, to accept the nomination deprived the Populists of a candidate with a national image. [25] In the end, the party had to turn to a professional third-party man, General James B. Weaver of Iowa, former Union officer and Greenback presidential candidate in 1880. Although James G. Field, an ex-Confederate from Virginia, was nominated for the vice presidency to give the ticket a sectional balance, the two Populist leaders could not match in extraordinariness the party platform with its unequivocal call for free coinage.

The national issues generated by the political conventions in 1892 would have to be dealt with in New Mexico. Candidates for the office of territorial delegate were particularly susceptible to the new political currents of 1892. Candidates for county and legislative races, of course, could remain absorbed with local issues. Catron's triumph at Silver City appeared to prepare the way for his selection as his party's delegate. Opposition to the powerful Republican boss did not seem great, although one prominent Republican from the northeast believed Prince would be a stronger candidate in his part of the country, and Catron more potent in the counties to the south. [26] But with opposition effectively cowed Catron had little difficulty making his claim on party leadership. He was nominated in Las Vegas on August 25 as the Republican choice for the territory's lone voice in Congress.

The selection of "Tom" Catron had a telling impact on all election races in New Mexico. Because of his power, wealth, and aggressiveness, the conservative Santa Fe Republican would become a major factor in the campaign regardless of his intent. Democrats could be expected to wage the most partisan kind of campaign, while Populists, still few in number, could rob the Democratic party of its more reform-minded voters if the Democrats failed to take a tough stand against such a conservative foe. Even within his own party there was resentment. Prince stated that Catron was the "most arbitrary and dictatorial of men." No one could get along with him without "absolute submission" to his stubborn will. "Through all kinds of administrations no one having grave official responsibility has been able to keep on good terms with him. Those who are not his 'peons' he considers his enemies." [27] M.W. Mills of Colfax County warned Catron to "give up his foolish methods of antagonizing people who would co-operate with him." [28] The Colfax Republican wrote Prince on August 22, three days before the Las Vegas convention, that the "army of Mr. Catron haters scare me."

The Democrats met in Albuquerque in August to select their candidate for territorial delegate. Joseph was the front-runner to succeed himself at the meeting, but there was substantial opposition this time. Harvey B. Fergusson, an able attorney who had moved from White Oaks in Lincoln County to Albuquerque, was supported by a group of Democrats from the southern part of the territory. They included the controversial Albert Bacon Fall of Las Cruces, who in those days was a Democrat. [29] Joseph had already served four terms, and some Democrats were unhappy with the little Hispano from Ojo Caliente. His failure to get statehood for the territory had hurt his reputation, and in the eyes of many his longevity in office had resulted in overexposure. Nevertheless, the silver Democrat, enjoying an undeserved anti-grant image and maintaining his connections with progressive groups such as the Knights of Labor, remained to many voters a more attractive alternative than the more liberal Fergusson. Moreover, Joseph's native heritage continued to be a major asset in an area where Spanish-speaking citizens remained a solid majority. [30] With such advantages for the incumbent, Fergusson was unable to garner enough votes to unseat Joseph, who was nominated for an unprecedented fifth term.

In San Miguel County, where the Populists maintained their important foothold, the leadership of the People's party began to proclaim the great benefits that fusion with the Democrats could bring. But many rank and file Populists were now aware of the national People's movement as embodied by the Weaver-Field ticket. Recognizing a possible conflict between local aspirations and national goals among Populists, Martinez, T.B. Mills, and Blake fell back on a favorite and safe political issue: What will happen to the territory if Catron is victorious? Against this political background, negotiations were opened between Blake and the other founders of the San Miguel People's party and leading county Democrats. But Felix Martinez, using his power as a member of the prestigious People's party executive committee, decided to avoid the endless bickering that more democratic participation usually brings. He convinced T.B. Mills, chairman of the county committee, to issue a call for the county convention without bringing the members of the county central committee together to discuss such important matters as the apportionment of delegates. Having arranged a convention without a set apportionment or binding instructions, Martinez began informal discussions with some old-time Democrats from East Las Vegas. He promised them spots on the ticket if they would agree to give two or three Knights places, to satisfy the founders of the new party. [31]

When the county Populist convention met in October, suspicion and tension resulting from the talk about fusion filled the air. The Republican *Las Vegas Daily Optic,* hoping to exploit distrust among Populists and Democrats, asserted that the People's party was reneging on its promises to allow the Democrats five places on the county and legislative slates. Democrats would not again be ''deceived'' by such insincere promises. [32] The *Albuquerque Democrat** apparently believed the *Optic;* it launched a scathing attack on Martinez three days later, on October 14. Insisting that the People's party had actually ''gone to pieces,'' the *Democrat* maintained that ex-Democrat Martinez was unprepared for ''great political emergencies.'' His ''large and noisy tongue'' had wrecked everything. [33] On the following day, however, when it was discovered that the Democrats had done exceedingly well in their fusion arrangement with the Populists, the journal

---

*Sometimes called the *Morning Democrat.*

75

reversed itself. Martinez was now heralded as a "consumate leader and wise politician for which he has so long been given credit and which have made him the strongest man of any party in San Miguel County." The Albuquerque paper was exuberant about the eleven of sixteen places it claimed were given to the Democrats. It happily announced that the fusion ticket was also "solid for Mr. Joseph." [34]

If Democrats were elated, a number of prominent San Miguel Populists were not. Blake, who wanted to be nominated for one of San Miguel's two seats on the Council, was so embittered that he bolted the convention, taking his closest allies with him. [35] The burro skin had been stripped off the People's party, and "slapped" on in its place was the skin of the "Tammany Democratic tiger." He accused Martinez, who chaired the convention, of pushing through a program and ticket of which most delegates were "utterly ignorant." [36]

The actions of the convention represented a resounding triumph for Martinez. Martinez, along with J. D. Veeder, was nominated by the fusion body for a seat on the Territorial Council. [37] Thus, the able T.B. Mills was displaced after only one term in the upper house. Mills' immediate reaction to this move cannot be ascertained, but in the coming months he broke politically with Martinez. Lorenzo Lopez was again nominated for the office of sheriff, which further inflamed the Lopez-Romero feud. Eugenio Romero, who was the Republican choice, insisted it was now his inning, Lopez having already served two terms. [38]

By far the most controversial action of the fusion meeting of the Populists and Democrats was the nomination of one of the Herrera brothers for an important county office. Juan Jose Herrera, founder of the *Gorras,* was nominated as probate judge for the county. While many Democrats were surprised, San Miguel Republicans reacted more violently. The Herrera family must be "exterminated from the politics of San Miguel County," the *Optic* declared. The existence of such an element in the county simply could no longer be tolerated. But the newspaper did caution: This "must be done at the polls, though." [39]

Except for Dona Ana County, where a People's ticket was put together, [40] San Miguel was the only county where significant third-party activity took place in 1892. But, surprisingly, there was no move in San Miguel to follow the example of the national organization in its independent bid for power, nor was there any evidence uncovered to indicate a close relationship between the local and national movements. Mills did have the financial resources and the interest to attend the Omaha convention. It is clear though that Felix Martinez, the master manipulator, had no intention of associating his adopted party with the national People's party. From almost the beginning Martinez strove to unite county Democrats with the new party, to put an end to the dominance Republicans had long enjoyed in San Miguel. In the process, he drove out that element of the People's party most responsible for its organization. The future of the party as an independent political organization was now in serious doubt.

With Catron running as the Republican choice for delegate, however, it was not a good time for dissident Populists or Democrats to sulk. Although the power of this office did not vitally affect the everyday life of the territory, the office provided the best means by which citizens could express their views on national issues. Besides, there were the legislative and county races, which did influence the welfare of most citizens in a meaningful way. The outcome of the race for delegate could affect these local contests just as the results of a presidential race often influence state and congressional elections.

The Democratic press was ingenious in exploiting Catron's vulnerabilities. The candidate's immense landholdings became a favorite target allowing the Republican's opponents to level all sorts of charges. Taking up an issue stressed by the Populists in their Omaha platform, the *Albuquerque Democrat* asserted that Catron was openly "advocating the right of aliens to hold great bodies of real estate, in order that he may find sale for some enormous tracts of land which he claims to own." Supporting alien land ownership was serious enough, but the Republican candidate was also accused of opposing the partition of "large grants into convenient homes for farmers and others."

Catron was also pictured as a tax evader. He had a long record of resisting settlement near his land grants in the fear of increased land value resulting in higher taxation. More serious was the charge that he had defeated a public-school bill in 1889 believing it would increase the taxes on his grants. His opposition to the school bill of 1891, which Governor Prince and Mills so vigorously supported, was attributed to the same motive. [41] Feigning a concern for Catron's welfare should he be defeated, the *Democrat* assured its readers that Catron would "continue to practice law in Santa Fe for years to come and go right along absorbing all the land grants in sight." [42]

Catron's stand in favor of statehood, important now that the silver controversy had been neutralized, was also put in the worst possible light. The Santa Fe Republican was not interested in the benefits statehood might bring to his fellow citizens, but favored admission so he could be "a prompt candidate for the United States senate." [43] The *Albuquerque Democrat* could have added that Catron expected the value of his landholdings to rise after admission. [44] Joseph was still regarded as the more likely of the two to win New Mexico statehood, in the opinion of partisan Democratic journalists. [45]

77

Controversy over Tom Catron's political methods permeated all phases of the 1892 contest. The Grant County Democrats stated that Catron had been the author of twenty-five years of questionable legislation and had a record of shameful "manipulation" of legislative contests. Supporting Grover Cleveland, their presidential standard-bearer, the Grant Democrats contrasted Catron's career with the familiar motto associated with Cleveland: "a public office is a public trust." [46] On November 3, the *Albuquerque Democrat,* exploiting Republican disaffection with Catron's candidacy, asserted that Prince was so disgusted he made a trip to southern Colorado during the heat of the campaign to work in behalf of the Republican ticket there. That the governor was disenchanted cannot be denied. He wrote his friend M.W. Mills on August 3 that Catron's election would cost the candidate "a great deal more money than it would anyone else to get the same number of votes." When a man is nominated with the understanding that the election is to be "carried by money he must buy everyone [,] even his own people." Despite his dislike of Catron, Prince did campaign for him in Deming, Silver City, Albuquerque and other communities. Moreover he was hurt when Catron's campaign manager, A.L. Morrison, chairman of the Republican central committee, refused to accept his offer to speak for Catron in the eastern counties because of the derogatory remarks Prince had supposedly made about the Republican standard-bearer. [47]

But Catron was not the sole target of campaigners in 1892. Joseph took a few lumps too. On September 17, he was criticized by the *New Mexican* for having allegedly remarked that the prospects for statehood would be improved if he were re-elected and the citizens of the territory chose a Republican legislature. Such a balance would show that New Mexico was open to both parties. Another emotional issue was the tariff. For years Republicans had boasted that their tariff stand had given protection to the mining and wool industries of New Mexico. Judge Thornton met this issue head on, attacking the tariff on lead as being a liability rather than an asset to New Mexico miners. The exclusion of the Mexican ore, he insisted, had produced a scarcity of fluxes, thus increasing the cost of smelting. [48]

Because of the equivocation of both national parties on silver, this issue was put into limbo for the balance of the 1892 campaign. Catron was relieved, in view of his desertion of the Blaine cause; the occasional surfacing of the silver question was his constant dread. Such a situation occurred while he was campaigning in Kingston in the southern part of the territory. After a speech in which he declared he was "unalterably in favor of free coinage of silver," the candidate smugly sat down. A Republican song book was taken out and his campaign manager, Morrison, began leading the burly miners in a campaign song to the tune of "Tramp, tramp, tramp the boys are marching." The martial tune and the inspiring words swept the miners along in a rising enthusiasm. ''For an honest vote for all and an honest count to all every man will vote for Harrison and Reid.'' Then: ''No-free-coinage-heresy ''— half of the group stopped and looked around in bewilderment — ''by our votes can ever be . . .'' By this time Morrison was practically standing alone, [49] while Catron no doubt was searching for a place to hide.

New Mexicans were interested in the national campaign, too. Democratic papers were enthusiastically for Cleveland, the *Albuquerque Democrat* heralding the popular nominee as ''The Nation's Choice.'' His election, the paper declared, would mean ''an honest pure administration of public affairs — free from robbery of the masses and classes.'' [50] Republican journals, of course, were for Harrison, but without the same kind of excitement. The frigid little president simply could not inspire such emotions.

James B. Weaver's Populist campaign received scant attention in the territorial press, unless the news was unfavorable to him. An egg-throwing incident involving a young Georgia Black is a case in point. The dignified ex-Union general had been a controversial figure during his campaign in the South. It was common knowledge that during the war he had carried out orders to seize supplies from civilians in Pulaski, Tennessee, for the benefit of Confederate refugees; consequently he was on the defensive. When the young Black was arrested for throwing eggs at General Weaver, newspapers in New Mexico and throughout the country found one more opportunity to ridicule the Populist movement and its candidate. ''If the Weaver boom is, throughout, as much of an ado about nothing as is the claim of his having been insulted in Georgia, then the whole thing is the biggest farce ever before the country.'' [51]

As election day approached, both major parties were apprehensive, particularly about the Catron-Joseph contest. M.W. Mills, an astute political observer, had predicted that the Republicans' choice for delegate might lose by as much as 800 to 1,000 votes in the eastern part of the territory. [52] On the eve of the November vote, he found cause for optimism. Catron may ''scratch through'' yet, he wrote on October 29. When the ballots were counted, however, Joseph's total was 15,799 to Catron's 15,220. [53]

Joseph's close victory was primarily the result of a decline of Republican strength in certain crucial counties. In populous Bernalillo County, for instance, the Republican vote fell from 2,042 (Otero's count in 1890) to 1,947. Joseph, on the other hand, bettered his 1890 margin by more than 500 ballots, winning 1,914 votes. [54] The Democratic resurgence in Bernalillo was largely the result of feverish work by a coalition of Democrats and independent Republicans, who resented the ''boss rule'' exercised by Mariano

S. Otero and his "ring" of henchmen who had long governed the county. [55] In Valencia County, where Republican leader Colonel J. Francisco Chaves was able to deliver votes with the same facility that enabled him to drive his immense flocks of sheep to market, the Republican vote dropped from 1,510 in 1890 to 1,350. The perpetually outmanned Democrats could garner only 123 ballots for Joseph. [56]

Another important factor in the election's outcome was Antonio Joseph's durable strength in the eastern counties, where serious protest against land-grabbing and monopoly had begun in the late eighties. Negating Catron's successes in such traditional Republican strongholds as Santa Fe and Rio Arriba counties, Joseph outpolled his rival in every eastern county. In Lincoln County, one of the cradles of Alliance activity, Joseph gathered 684 votes to 400 for his rival. In Chaves County, partitioned from Lincoln, Catron could win only 63 votes out of 325 cast. To the north, in Colfax County, arena for the struggle over the Maxwell Grant, Joseph won handily, 918 votes to 632. His victories in Mora, Guadalupe, and Eddy counties completed his electoral sweep of eastern New Mexico.

In sparsely populated northeastern New Mexico, Democrats also demonstrated their vote-gathering supremacy. In San Juan County, Joseph proved he had strength among agricultural elements, winning the county by a vote of 251 to 185. But despite the incumbent's consistency in winning county majorities, Catron, by adding Grant, Socorro and Sierra counties in the silver-producing region of New Mexico to his victory column, came within 579 votes of the four-term delegate. [57]

The most important vote, however, was in San Miguel, where the greatest number of ballots of any county was cast. The election campaign there had been marked by exceptional bitterness. A joint debate was held in the county courthouse on the eve of the election involving Populists and Democrats on one side and the Republicans on the other. It ended practically before it began when Republican Eugenio Romero, the first speaker, denounced his opponents, led by Martinez, in a heated tirade. [58] As news of the final count became known, however, it was obvious that about all the Republicans could do was to rant against the potent alliance of Democrats and Populists. The *Las Vegas Daily Optic,* conceding that the entire People's ticket had probably won, tried to take some consolation in its belief that the victorious margin of the Populists would be reduced from the 1890 sweep. [59] Martinez showed his political acumen when he predicted before the balloting that Joseph would win by 800 to 1,000 votes. [60] Joseph's final 864-vote margin was another confirmation of Martinez's capabilities as a party leader. Although the 2,629 votes cast for Joseph were 757 fewer than his 1890 tally [61] and the showing of the People's party was not so good as it had been two years earlier, the Populist foothold in the territory's most important electoral county was still a firm one.

The results of the 1892 election in San Miguel demonstrated to both Democrats and Populists the importance of fusion. Joseph's winning margin in San Miguel County was greater than his 579-vote margin in the territory. Had the Democrats not cooperated with the San Miguel Populists, Joseph undoubtedly would have lost his race for delegate. The Democrats knew this and so did the Republicans. If the new party could retain its strength, it would hold the balance of power in future elections, just as it had held the balance of power in the lower house during the previous legislature. What the leaders of the People's organization would do with their potential power remained to be seen.

The Democratic triumph in the delegate's race was matched by Democratic successes in the fight to control the Thirtieth Legislative Assembly. In the House, Democrats increased their representation from nine to fifteen, holding a seven-vote margin in the new body. Two seats were gained in the new Territorial Council, the Republican margin having been cut to one. [62] The party of Jefferson and Jackson would exercise much greater influence during this session than the previous one. And much of its new strength was due to fusion with the Populists. The election of the entire fusion ticket in San Miguel, including two members to the Council and three to the House, spelled the difference between a narrow margin and a decisive one in the House of Representatives.

The key role of San Miguel County in the outcome of the 1892 election was appreciated by the Republicans. Charging fraud, San Miguel attorney George W. Pritchard challenged the legality of the elections of Lorenzo Lopez as sheriff and Juan Jose Herrera as probate judge. The elections of other county officials were also questioned. Pritchard asserted that 98 Republicans were not allowed to vote in Arroyo de los Yutos because there were not enough tickets. Also, according to him, Republican tickets were removed from the ballot boxes in Los Alamos and replaced with Democratic ones, and at least a thousand members of the People's party had failed to pay the required poll tax, using either fraudulent receipts to vote or none at all. [63] Echoing the Republican's charge, Max Frost, in an editorial in the *New Mexican* on November 16, insisted that when there were ''enough votes in San Miguel County for the White Cap ticket'' the leaders of the People's party stopped counting.

Electoral reform was one of the major issues dealt with by the new legislature which convened in December. Ballots were no longer to be numbered or marked by election judges or clerks, nor would a voter be prohibited from changing a ballot by substituting a name of his own choice. [64] The Thirtieth Legislative Assembly, more progressive than most of its predecessors, went even further. It eliminated the undemocratic poll tax. [65] Moreover, to expand educational opportunities, thus assuring a better-educated electorate for the future, the legislature established normal schools at Las Vegas and Silver City. [66]

The plight of the small landowner was given attention too. The legislature jointly memorialized Congress to extend by one year the time for filing land claims before the Court of Private Land Claims. Such action was necessary because many of those who had not filed were illiterate or unfamiliar with the English language. Describing these people as ''exceedingly poor'' and often elderly, the legislators urged the federal government to be compassionate. [67]

The new legislature, however, was not to be progressive in the same way that some of the Populist-dominated bodies in the Midwest were. The Thirtieth session ignored a number of important areas in its legislative program. Nothing was done to disturb the status quo sufficiently to produce cries of outrage from land monopolists or cattle kings. A regulatory act creating the office of coal-oil inspector was passed, which undoubtedly represented some deviation from the standard laissez-faire approach. There was no important railroad legislation enacted, though, such as the regulatory measure proposed by Populist leader T.B. Mills during the Twenty-ninth session. [68] As a matter of fact, better rail transportation was considered so essential in New Mexico that there was a law on the books which gave railroads tax exemption for six years following completion of their tracks. The Thirtieth assembly amended this incentive by providing that the six-year exemption apply only to those railroads which had begun construction. [69]

Despite Joseph's victory and the election of a predominantly Democratic legislature in 1892, New Mexicans who wanted more drastic overall reform for the future were disappointed. Democrat Cleveland did edge Harrison for the presidency but the reform ticket of Weaver and Field won only 22 electoral votes. All of these came from two sections of the country, the wheat-raising Plains states and the mountain West. In the popular column, the Populists could claim only nine percent of the total vote. Congressional victories and gubernatorial and legislative successes in certain Midwestern and mountain states did provide hope for the future. But a grand triumph of the little people of the nation, which was naively anticipated by some Populist supporters in 1892, did not occur.

82

The aftermath of the 1892 election revealed how fragil the Populist and Democratic alliance in San Miguel was. Old-line leaders of the People's party watched with resentment as Felix Martinez promptly identified with the Democrats after the election. Hoping to win appointment as United States marshal, the man most responsible for the successful fusion ticket in San Miguel had gone to Washington with a delegation of prominent Democrats to see Grover Cleveland about federal appointments in the territory. [70] Although Martinez was unsuccessful in his quest for office, many Populists wondered what the future of their party as a separate, independent entity would be under opportunistic leaders such as Martinez.

7

THE POPULIST TERRITORIAL BID

The months that followed Cleveland's election victory were difficult ones for most Americans. The depression, which began in 1893, proved to be the most serious one that the United States had experienced up to that time. Farm prices dropped to even lower levels; businesses failed; banks and loan companies, particularly in the West and South, collapsed; mighty railroad corporations went bankrupt; and unemployment soared to unprecedented heights. President Cleveland blamed many of these economic woes on the Sherman Silver Purchase Act, which he claimed had compelled the United States to deplete its valuable gold reserves by buying silver. Using all of his executive powers, he pressured Congress into repealing the act. His success in this effort was felt in the Territory of New Mexico and the other states or territories of the mining West. Mining companies, which had been limping along because of declining silver prices, were forced to close down altogether. The impact of these shutdowns on the economy of the surrounding area aggravated the other economic problems caused by the depression. Even in New Mexico's more localized economy there were serious difficulties.

Politically, Populists from the territory and elsewhere had recovered from their disappointment with the 1892 election. Their strategy for the upcoming 1894 election was to blame both major parties for the Depression of 1893. Although bitter with Democrat Cleveland's role in the repeal of the Sherman Silver Purchase Act, the populistic *San Juan Times* of Farmington was unwilling to leave the Republicans blameless. "One of the funny things about the panic," it editorialized, "is that it was produced largely by Republican laws and will be used, because its climax came under democratic rule [,] to boost the Republican party back into power. Thus wrongs enacted by a party is [sic] to be the means of re-electing it to power." The ones who have suffered, according to the *Times,* are the common folk who do not "understand the working of political machines." 1

The fusion movement in San Miguel County, which had prevented independent political action on the part of the Populists in 1892, began to come apart soon after its successes in that campaign. The major cause of disintegration was the man most responsible for the movement, Felix Martinez.

Martinez had first alienated the original leaders of the People's party when he handpicked the party ticket during the 1892 nominating convention. In the campaign that followed he allegedly "bled the candidates for the people's party for every dollar they could raise." He then disbursed a sum of $12,000, on which he "never rendered an account," to friendly voters, so that they could pay their poll tax. After the election Martinez insisted on naming all deputies for the county offices and determining the salaries they could draw. He received a handsome commission for his efforts, "no question[s]" asked. The results of these arbitrary actions were disunion among the members of the People's coalition and anger among the new county officials, who decided to "rebel against having rings in their noses." 2

The resourceful Martinez was determined to build a new power base in the county, however. Borrowing the name of Eugenio Romero's Union party, he organized those elements of the old party still friendly to him into a coalition described by the *Las Vegas Daily Optic* as "simply the democratic party with a strong wing or faction of the republican party attracted to it." In August of 1894, Martinez and other political leaders held an important meeting at the county courthouse. There a serious attempt was made to expand the new political union by wooing the Independent party, a group of Republicans who bolted their party four years earlier, and some wayward Populists. Despite their lack of success, the *Optic* was bitter. It stated that "no principle great or small" was involved in the creation of either the Union or Independent parties, both were merely "skillful manipulations to capture county offices." The Republican journal also believed that the members of the Independent party ulitimately would cast their "undivided vote" for the Democratic ticket as would the Union party, which was "the old democratic party."

The remarks of the *Optic* about the San Miguel People's party were equally unkind. "Its principles, objects and aims have been allowed to fall to the ground, without even the . . . cloak of a name to cover them. Bitter personal feeling dispersed this weak representative of the national populist party, in this county, like a fog before the noonday sun." The best solution for the political chaos caused by the serious fragmentation of parties in San Miguel County was, according to the *Optic,* for all ex-members to realign with their old national parties after the 1894 election. They should reorganize in conventions and start over. Union party men would return to the Democratic fold. Members of the Independent organization would decide between the two major parties. As for the unhappy Populists, they "could crystalize into one heterogeneous mass the disaffected voters of all classes and parties and adopt principles and platforms divergent enough to suit them all."3

Populists in New Mexico were in the process of reorganizing even before the *Optic* gave its unsolicited advice. But the center of the third party's reconstruction was to be in Bernalillo County rather than in the cradle of the territorial movement, San Miguel. Stretching north to Rio Arriba and San Juan counties, Bernalillo, which along with San Miguel was one of New Mexico's two most populous counties, extended all the way to the Arizona border. The county was much larger then than it is today.

In late August of 1894, the *Evening Citizen* of Albuquerque reported a significant step in the shift of Populist activity to Bernalillo. [4] T.B. Mills had left San Miguel County in 1893. [5] He had moved to a place near Cochiti, then part of Bernalillo County, to work a mining claim. The former Populist leader had, according to the Republican journal, appointed himself leader of the People's party in Bernalillo. He was also engaged in an effort to call a party convention. "The Colonel," as Mills was often called in the press, [6] was a political boomer, and it was predicted that he would make things lively if given half a chance. [7] The news report confirmed another fact: prospector Mills' unceasing search for the Big Bonanza had not dampened his enthusiasm for politics. He was committeed to use his powers of persuasiveness to bring about a rebirth of Populism in the territory.

Serious opposition to Mills' efforts was found in Bernalillo, the home of several contenders for party leadership. M.P. Stamm, a prominent wholesale produce merchant from Albuquerque, [8] was one of them. He had impressive connections with some of the national leaders of the Populist movement. Operating his business in the Wheelock and Stamm Building in the commercial section of the city, Stamm was a serious-minded man whose views harmonized closely with the more ideologically committed elements of his party. He was Mills' strongest potential rival. Thomas F. Keleher, who was in the wool and hides business in Albuquerque, was another contender. [9] Keleher, however, seemed more inclined to support the aspirations of Stamm. Other leaders in Bernalillo included Ben Myer, Colonel Brady, and a man named W.A. Skinner, none of whom had achieved prominence in county or territorial affairs. The *Albuquerque Democrat,* more concerned about the impact of Populism on Democratic fortunes than it would care to admit, described the Bernalillo People's organization as "large, respectable, enthusiastic and honest." Skinner was large, Stamm was respectable, Keleher was enthsiastic, and Meyer was honest. But this "Big Four" was just about all the new party amounted to. [10]

The sarcastic assessment of the *Democrat,* however, was inaccurate and unfair. Mills may not have had eminent competitors, but the resurgence of New Mexico Populism in 1894 involved many determined people. In Gallup, for instance, local Populists held an ''enthusiastic meeting'' during the first week of September. James Maloney, a local leader, presided; a man named Charles Brown was chosen as chairman and a permanent Populist organization was established. One feature of the organizational meeting in Gallup was the scheduling of six lectures by a Dr. Longstreet, an ''eloquent and convincing'' advocate of Henry George's Single Tax. [11]

Rivals for control of a rejuvenated People's party were also found outside of Bernalillo. In San Juan County, where resentment against both major parties remained because of the county's subordination to Rio Arriba, Populist sentiment was exceptionally strong. Fred E. Holt, editor of the *San Juan Times* in Farmington, was an avowed Populist who expressed the most basic sentiments of the discontented farmers in his county. On August 17, he published an urgent appeal for money from M.C. Rankin of Terre Haute, Indiana, treasurer for the national Populist committee. It was signed by H.E. Taubeneck, the national chairman, and other committee members. Endorsed by Holt, the appeal outlined an unusual plan for fund raising whereby a thousand of the more prosperous Populists of the country would contribute five dollars apiece. Ten thousand supporters would each donate a dollar; 20,000, fifty cents; 30,000, thirty-five cents; and a million, ten cents. Because the People's party was composed of the ''great common people of the country, who are poor and honest,'' this system was essential. The party ''has no millionaries, bank or railroad corporations upon which to call for campaign funds.'' Exuding that optimism so characteristic of Populist rhetoric, the framers of the appeal insisted that, if the People's party took advantage of the ''blunders and infamy of the present administration,'' it would have no trouble gaining the ''balance of power in the next congress.''

On August 18, the county committee of the San Juan People's party met at Aztec for the purpose of setting dates for the party's primaries and county conventions. Meeting in the office of a Dr. A.H. McFarland, representatives of nine precincts, including Farmington, Aztec, Flora Vista, and Bloomfield, were present. One noteworthy feature of the gathering was the presence of two Hispanos as members of the county committee, Juan N. Jaquez of Largo and Juan B. Valdez of Blanco. [12] Although their representation cannot be cited as convincing proof that nativism did not exist among San Juan Populists, the percentage of Spanish-speaking people in the county was lower than in the two neighboring eastern counties, Rio Arriba and Taos. Therefore, pressure to have native representation in the agricultural county was not great. Editor Holt showed a careless confidence about the new movement. ''The way the Republican and Democratic officeholders are trying to seek refuge beneath the wing of [our] Populist party show[s] our cause is a strong one.'' [13]

Populism was spreading into the southern part of the territory, too. In Sierra County, where repeal of the Sherman Silver Purchase Act delivered a death blow to many mining camps, there was a strong move to organize a county party which would involve leading citizens. When the party ticket was finally put together, it included Thomas Murphy, the first sheriff of Sierra County, and Robert West, who owned the biggest house in Kingston. Both men were Populist candidates for the office of county commissioner. [14] In Grant County, in the southwestern corner of New Mexico, inflamed miners and other citizens were determined to organize a party that would represent them. "The populists of Grant county are on the warpath, and the democrats of that area are disrupted," crowed the Republican *Evening Citizen.* [15]

Mills would have to attract support in these new Populist areas, if he were to have a major voice in the resurgent movement. Fortunately for the ambitious Populist leader, he had the distinction of being a two-term legislator, while practically all of his competitors enjoyed no such eminence. Recognizing this attribute, the *San Juan Times,* in late September, called Mills the "great law maker of the territory." It boasted of his work on the Council in developing support for public education, asserting that a liquor-licensing law he framed was largely responsible for the "beautiful school edifices in every town and city" in New Mexico. His work in acquiring such prerogatives for women as the right to hold property and the right to sue was mentioned. The law he spearheaded for the incorporation of cities and towns was cited as another tribute to his effectiveness. [16] Such projects were very much in harmony with Populist doctrines of equality and popular rule. [17] Perhaps it was due to an uncomfortable awareness of Mills' potential leadership that the *Evening Citizen* decided to characterize him as a run-of-the-mill officeseeker. "Col. T.B. Mills is crying in the Cochiti wilderness for the populist nomination for territorial delegate." [18]

The former San Miguel legislator had to act quickly, however, if he intended to use his adopted county to launch a new political career. Stamm and Keleher were already busy organizing a county party which they would eventually head. In late summer, a petition was circulated among the voters of the county calling for a mass meeting in Albuquerque on the twelfth of September.

> We, the undersigned voters of Bernalillo county, having lost our faith in the ability and integrity of both the republican and democratic parties to legislate for, and in the interests of the great wealth producing classes of America . . . do . . . sever our allegiance to both [old parties]. [19]

On September 12, Populists from all over the county gathered in Albuquerque for an organizational meeting in Grant's opera house. The meeting began with the ubiquitous Single Taxer, Dr. Longstreet, delivering a lecture. With Stamm acting as chairman and Alexander Stevens as secretary, the delegates then got to the serious business of the convention. The ''result was the birth of the populist party in this portion of New Mexico.'' Acting on a motion by Keleher, the following members for the county central committee were selected: Stamm, W.W. McClellan, and F.M. Eddings of Albuquerque; William Bowers and Ellis Winters of Gallup; J.C. Holt of Bland; and J.G. Johnson of Allerton. One newspaper noted that several familiar Democractic names comprised a majority of those elected. [20]

Surprisingly, Mills had been left off the Bernalillo central committee. There was still hope for him, however, in the territorial meeting scheduled at the same time for selecting an executive committee for New Mexico and a nomination for territorial delegate. Albuquerque had been chosen as the site; the city was hosting a territorial fair and the railroads were offering a special rate of one and one-half cents per mile. Fred Holt, editor of the *San Juan Times,* arranged to attend both the Populist territorial convention and the fair, proudly exhibiting good San Juan apples at the latter. Although he failed to earn a prize — one must assume his political mission was more important anyway — he could boast of having been the ''sweepstakes'' winner at the fair two years earlier. [21] The Populist political convention was designed to match its festive rival. Lafe Pence, Populist congressman from Colorado, had been scheduled to address a mass meeting on the twelfth. He was a ''good talker'' and a ''royal welcome'' was planned for him. [22]

T.B. Mills issued the call for the first territorial convention of the Populist party. This action probably indicated that, although Mills could not gain control of the Bernalillo organization, he still expected to receive support from other counties in the territory. The call recommended a number of proposals that the delegates were urged to consider; some were from the 1892 Populist platform, others from earlier declarations. A few seemed to represent more local or recent concerns. On the top of the list was the increasingly popular demand for free coinage. It was followed by the more controversial call to nationalize the railroads and telegraph lines. Reiteration of such familiar Omaha resolves as the direct election of United States senators, a graduated federal income tax, and restriction of undesirable immigration was also made. Reflecting the tensions caused by the recent Pullman strike, Mills suggested that the convention condemn military interference with civil authorities in time of peace. Territorial Populists were also urged to proclaim themselves in favor of the right of laborers to organize for their ''mutual benefit and protection''; widespread denial of this right had first been cited in the preamble of the Saint Louis platform. Compulsory arbitration was another topic suggested. In the area of participation in government, the abolition of the electoral college was proposed. Such a recommendation appeared in both the 1891 Omaha resolutions and the 1891 Cincinnati platform.

But the territory-wide Populist gathering was also urged to support issues of more local interest, including admission by popular demand of New Mexico and other Western territories into the Union. The Populist recommendation that surplus or unused lands be reclaimed by the federal government and held for ''actual settlers only'' was modified. Mills proposed that arid lands, of which there was an abundance in New Mexico, should be turned over to the states or territories for irrigation.

Other topics suggested by Mills were the development of reciprocal trade arrangements between the United States and the bimetallic nations of the Western Hemisphere and an inheritance tax in which estates would be divided equally among heirs rather than being put in the hands of trustees. The protection of American industries under certain necessary conditions was also advocated. Mills probably felt that a declaration calling for limited tariff protection was essential for a fledgling party in a territory where the protection of wool and lead was regarded as vital. The Populist leader concluded his call with a statement of principles carefully defining America's priorities. ''A prosperous nation protects its agriculture first, manufacturing next, and commerce third. This can only be brought about in a republic by the votes of the people.'' [23]

With a determination to reorder the nation's priorities, delegates from almost every county assembled in Albuquerque. In actual numbers this new bid for power was not impressive, but the aspirations of those who attended were. Meeting in the Wheelock and Stamm building on September 13, following the mass meeting of the preceding day, delegates were called to order by J.M. Evans of Sierra County. A committee on resolutions was appointed to formulate a party program, and a territorial executive committee was organized to administer party activities. Members selected to serve on the executive committee were Stamm, the chairman, Bernalillo; Dr. M.M. Milligan, San Miguel; Thomas Murphy, Sierra; Fred E. Holt, San Juan; Sig Lindauer, Grant; Robert Machel, Santa Fe; and E.A. Dow, Valencia. [24] Besides the strong Anglo composition, there was both on and off the committee the usual urban make-up common to Populist leadership elsewhere. [25] Stamm and Keleher were urban merchants from Albuquerque. Holt was a Farmington editor, Thomas Murphy was an experienced lawman whose career in Sierra County dated back to 1884. [26] Dr. Milligan, presumably, was not connected with agriculture, and his former associate in San Miguel politics, T.B. Mills, was a businessman interested in mine speculation. Mills' absence from the territorial executive committee provides additional proof that his struggle for pre-eminence in the reorganized Populist movement was an uphill one.

Following the selection of the executive committee, Stamm took over the gavel from Evans. The Populist delegates then turned to the report of the committee on resolutions. Adoption of the Omaha platform of 1892 was recommended, including both the resolutions and planks. The preamble was enthusiastically endorsed, but with one modification. The call in the Omaha preamble for "'equal rights and equal privileges securely established for all the men and women in this country'" was substituted in the version presented to Spanish-speaking voters of the territory with a call for equality for "*all* living in this country." [27] The omission of the word "women" was an indication that the Populists of New Mexico were not indifferent to native sensitivities, despite the minor role assumed by Hispanos at the convention. Subordination of women was traditional in the thinking of New Mexico natives, and the Populists at the Albuquerque meeting had decided not to raise the question of women's rights in their official pronouncements. The rejection of a proposal for women's suffrage, which was submitted to the resolutions committee, was another sign of this commitment to a pragmatic course.

The committee offered its own resolutions to the convention along with the tough Omaha platform it endorsed. Responding favorably to the recommendations made by Mills in his call, the committee demanded that the federal government donate lands to the states and territories for irrigating purposes. It condemned military interference with civil authority in time of peace. The immediate admission of New Mexico was endorsed. Also, the delegates demanded that negotiations begin between "the United States and Latin American republics, and other bimetalic [sic] nations of the world, for reciprocity of the said nations for the interchange of their products." Reacting to Mills' recommendation to abolish the electoral college and have the president and vice president elected directly, the resolutions committee added to the list of those who should be elected by a direct vote the district judges, marshals, and postmasters. A deep distrust of local politics was evident throughout the report. A popular referendum for all laws passed by the territorial legislature was proposed, and a demand was made that all official fees collected be put *directly* into the "public treasury and all officials [be] paid a reasonable salary."

Although most of the committee's own resolutions reflected local concerns, several of them elaborated on national Populist declarations. The call for abolishing national banks, contained in the 1891 Cincinnati platform and the Omaha resolutions of that year, was repeated, as was the demand in the

Omaha platform for the creation of postal-savings banks. In addition, the plank from the Omaha platform insisting upon a national currency, "safe, sound, and flexible, issued by the general government only" was endorsed. There was, however, one modification: "no money [should] be issued that is not a full legal tender for every debt." Undoubtedly with the upcoming November elections in mind, the committee elaborated on another 1892 Omaha resolve. It endorsed the call for "fair and liberal" pensions to ex-Union soldiers and sailors, but added dependents to the list of pension recipients. Finally, rebuffing a proposal which would have committed the Populist convention to Henry George's single-tax doctrine, the committee submitted its handiwork to the convention. The report, ten resolutions in all, was endorsed by the convention along with the familiar Omaha platform. [28]

The nomination of a candidate for territorial delegate was the most important action taken by the Albuquerque convention, however. Stamm appeared to have an edge, the Albuquerque merchant having the firmest power base and his Bernalillo organization showing unusual determination. But Mills had as advantages his legislative experience and the success he enjoyed in his varied business ventures. Indeed the Mills image as a mining expert and business promoter could have had an adverse effect on his chances in a party which proclaimed its dedication to the common welfare. Recognizing this danger, Fred Holt made a point of glorifying the down-to-earth virtues of the former San Miguel leader. Describing Mills' ventures in the Cochiti mining district, Holt characterized the Populist leader as being just like any other hard-working sourdough. At Cochiti, he lived in a tent, often with temperatures fifteen below zero, yet continued to hammer away with his pick. When he arrived at the Albuquerque convention "fresh from camp with calloused hands," he greeted the members in his usual friendly fashion and showed a willingness to serve his party again. [29]

Mills and Stamm, as expected, were chosen by the delegates, the nominations being made around midnight on September 13. Press reports were conflicting, but Stamm was pictured by the *San Juan Times* as a reluctant candidate who tried to withdraw his name. Notwithstanding Stamm's alleged unwillingness, a ballot was taken on the two candidates. Mills, although he lacked the support of a loyal home delegation, won by a vote of 8 to 5. The tired delegates, described as being enthusiastic over their choice, then moved to make the nomination unanimous. [30] They were most eager to present to the electorate the image of a strong, united territorial party. The harmony of the new political movement, however, was questioned in the opposition press. One Albuquerque journal asserted that the Populist meeting was extremely dull, the only excitement occurring when Keleher and his allies insisted on backing Stamm against the victorious Mills. [31]

From an historical standpoint the most significant development at the convention was the one noted by the critical *Optic* of Las Vegas. The ten resolutions presented contained some of the important statements from the landmark Omaha platform. The clarion call for free silver, however, formally made by territorial Democrats as early as 1890, was *not* given such special consideration. The Populist convention "has not one word to say about free coinage, the most important principle the populists of Colorado have to work on," chided the Las Vegas newspaper. "Dodging the silver question, Col. T.B.M. | Mills], will not aid you among the miners and laboring classes." [32] Of course, the Populists of New Mexico were concerned about the ailing silver industry and aware of the importance connected with that industry's future — almost all politicians in the territory recognized the ramifications of the silver question by 1894. But the omission of a special statement at Albuquerque weakens the case of those historians who dismiss Rocky Mountain Populism as simply a case of silverism. New Mexico Populists were definitely multi-issue oriented; indeed, if their Albuquerque platform was at all sincere, more so than their Democratic and Republican rivals.

The selection of Mills to carry the Populist banner in the race for territorial delegate produced a flurry of editorial comment. Mills was a "model candidate for the pops, having favored every new cranky issue for several years," carped the *Daily Citizen* of Albuquerque. [33] The Republican paper did admit, however, that the Populist candidate was aggressive, and stronger than his party. "Col. T.B. Mills of Cochiti will probably make a better fight than any other man the representatives of his political faith could put up." [34] The *Albuquerque Democrat,* a crosstown rival, asserted that the "only bad thing about the populists in New Mexico is their candidate for delegate to congress." [35] In Las Vegas, a Spanish-language newspaper published by Felix Martinez and edited by newspaperman William H. Manderfield's rebellious son, H. Enrique Salazar, [36] could find nothing complimentary to say about the former San Miguel legislator. *La Voz del Pueblo* dismissed Mills as an unpopular man who could only be described as "crackbrained." [37] The *Optic* was just as cruel. It pictured Mills as an unsuccessful politician in quest of a "fat office, as there are no more world pickings just now." [38]

The attitude of Holt's *San Juan Times,* of course, was entirely different. Mills was presented to the voters as a champion of the people. The *New Mexico Nugget,* a newly established weekly in Albuquerque, was equally enthusiastic. Edited by C. Ed Stivers, the *Nugget,* which had become the official territorial voice of the People's party, was described by the *San Juan Times* as typographically first class. It is a good "clean family paper." Because of its "rapidly increasing circulation," the existence of the *Nugget* was interpreted as a sign that a "new party has come into |the] territory to stay." [39] In Populist campaign literature the handsome Mills, as expected, was lauded as a super legislator, an eloquent speaker, and a progressive citizen. He was a man deserving of the support and votes of the workers and producers. Those who believe in free coinage and who are tired of the "old corrupt parties" now have a friend. The "Colonel" will listen to the little people and will "exercise his influence in favor of the masses and against the monopolies of the East." [40]

As the Democrats had heretofore enjoyed much of the support of the protest element in New Mexico, there was speculation about the impact of Mills' candidacy on Democratic prospects in November. The partisan *Daily Citizen* elatedly reported that the Populists were continually gaining new recruits from the Democratic party. [41] The Albuquerque *Morning Democrat* had to admit that the Democrats in the territory were in danger. Calling Mills a "two for five" candidate, it conceded that the Populist standard-bearer would probably draw two Republican votes for every five Democratic votes he was able to attract. [42]

Because the governor, secretary, and other major officials were appointed by the federal government under the territorial system, the office of territorial delegate was the most important elective one for the Populists. If the Populists were to exercise any local influence, however, they had to achieve successes in the county and legislative races. Aware of the importance of local contests, the Populists made an impressive bid in Sierra County. There, a complete slate was assembled with a candidate for the Territorial Council, three for the lower house, and nominees for county commissioner, probate judge, probate clerk, sheriff, assessor, treasurer, coroner, surveyor, and county superintendent. [43] San Juan Populists had also assembled an imposing ticket. At a September 8 meeting in La Plata, in which Dr. McFarland was elected chairman of the county central committee, the size and enthusiasm of the gathering were so heartening to Fred Holt that he remaked editorially in the *Times* that "those who have been wont to consider the Populist movement as being premature or childish had better adjust their glasses and fall into line or 'get off the grass'." [44]

On September 22, a large county convention was held in San Juan. The Saturday meeting was well attended, and a committee on resolutions was selected. Lou W. Coe, cousin of the Lincoln Farmers' Alliance leader, Jasper Coe, was chosen as one of the three committee members. The 1892 Omaha platform was reaffirmed, and that important electoral reform, the Australian secret ballot, was advocated "without marks of any kind." But local issues were not ignored. Among the other resolutions adopted was one calling for strict governmental economy on both county and territorial levels. The convention delegates also called for the establishment of only one school commissioner for San Juan instead of three and the distribution of unused tax money among the people of the county. [45]

The impact of the growing Populist movement in San Juan was having a profound effect on the two major parties. Attendance at Democratic meetings was slim as a result of Populist defections, and there were frequent reports of disharmony at Republican gatherings. San Juan Democrats were alleged to have named three ''open and avowed'' Populists as their party committeemen. One of them, Walter von Buddenbrock, was serving on the executive committee of the local People's party at the time of selection. [46] Although the source of this information was the admittedly biased *San Juan Times,* it was evident that the party was organizing on the grass-roots level. Precinct meetings were often held in schools, symbolically close to the people, and the basis of representation was one delegate for every twenty votes cast by members of ''both old parties at the last election.'' This system provided maximum representation for the advocates of the self-styled common man's party. [47]

The Populists also made their expected electoral bid in Bernalillo County. As early as August 25 there was speculation that the Bernalillo Populists would ignore pleas for union with the Democrats and nominate a straight ticket. [48] Democrats, however, were hopeful. They met on September 13, and quietly adjourned without naming a county slate. The surprising move, according to one newspaper, was part of a plan to ''gobble up the populists by a fusion movement.'' [49] On September 21 the *New Mexico Nugget* announced that there would be a delegate convention held in the Wheelock and Stamm Building, or Stamm's hall as the official Populist organ called it. The October 2 gathering would ''put a full county ticket in nomination.'' [50]

The political course of the Populists was not so smooth in other counties, however. In San Miguel, the re-creation of a powerful People's party seemed stymied by Martinez, notwithstanding some unfounded optimism that the Populists would repeat their resounding victories of the two previous elections. [51] Felix Martinez, dropping all pretense of being a Populist in 1894, was manipulating that political coalition called the Union party, and planning to attend the territorial Democratic convention in Las Cruces with a delegation of handpicked political allies.[52] The *Albuquerque Democrat* later called Martinez's strategy, which was designed to prevent a Republican comeback, ''The San Miguel Plan.'' [53]

When the Democrats convened in Las Cruces on September 17, Joseph, the five-term delegate, was a natural front runner to succeed himself. Although his popularity was on the decline and many prominent Democrats considered him weak, Joseph's prospects were given a boost by the withdrawal of Francisco A. Manzanares, an ex-delegate and successful Las Vegas businessman. [54] Interestingly enough, Manzanares' voluntary withdrawal from the delegate's race in 1884 gave Joseph his first opportunity to run for the office. [55] Joseph's stock was further bolstered when Manzanares advised his friends to support the veteran incumbent. Some opposition did develop, though, on the opening day of the convention when delegates from Bernalillo County met with Albert Bacon Fall and several delegates from the south and decided to back a second bid by Harvey B. Fergusson. [56] According to George Curry, Fergusson was defeated by only a handful of votes. [57] Contemporary press reports, however, claim that he withdrew his name, thus making the nomination of Joseph unanimous. [58]

The Democrats' convention resolutions stressed silver above all other questions. Regarding free silver as the "foremost" issue in the 1894 election, the Las Cruces convention declared "in favor of free and unlimited coinage of silver at a ratio of 16 to 1, as it existed prior to demonetization by the republican party in 1873." [59] Territorial Republicans, of course, could not allow this partisan resolution to stand without rebuttal. When they assembled in Socorro later in the week, they characterized Grover Cleveland as the "arch-enemy of silver coinage, and the chief supporter in this country of the mono-metallic creditor class of Europe." Although attacking those responsible for the "Crime of '73," the Republicans concentrated on the repeal of the Sherman Silver Purchase Act, which occurred during Democrat Cleveland's administration.

The tariff again became one of the favorite issues of New Mexico Republicans in 1894. Claiming that the New Mexico wool industry had been "almost entirely destroyed," the Socorro delegates reaffirmed their conviction that the protective tariff was the one essential safeguard for the large sheep-raising enterprise of the territory. The reduction of the lead tariff also was condemned, Governor Thornton, a Cleveland appointee, being rebuked for his alleged advocacy of both free wool and free lead. [60]

Antonio Joseph, however, received the giant's share of criticism from the Republicans. His ten-year failure to deliver on his pledge to win statehood was censured. He was pictured as opposing free public schools for New Mexico. [61] As the territory's sole voice in Congress, he received the blame for all of the unpopular actions of the Cleveland administration that adversely affected New Mexico. Such decisions by the national administration as the abandonment of old Fort Marcy in Santa Fe worked to his disadvantage. The speculation that the government would return Geronimo and his "horde of Apache murderers" to neighboring Arizona was also mentioned by the Republicans in their Socorro platform [62] in order to discredit Joseph.

The most significant difference between this campaign and Joseph's previous ones, however, was the attack on him from the territory's political left. The incumbent delegate had enjoyed the support of New Mexico's protest elements for years. Consequently, the Populist *New Mexico Nugget* really caught the native leader off guard when it labeled him a landgrabber, a charge to which he had been curiously immune during his long tenure. According to the *Nugget*, Joseph had shamefully obtained confirmation to a land grant by getting naive residents in Taos County to sign a petition, which he represented as being for the construction of a public road. The petition was actually a land deed for himself, one which Joseph hastily recorded in the county courthouse. [63]

Joseph would also have to face opposition from a number of strong potential candidates in his unprecedented sixth bid for office. The Republicans, when they assembled at Socorro, had several good candidates from which to choose. Two frustrating ballots taken by them on September 21 resulted in a standoff between J.A. Ancheta, Miguel A. Otero, and J. Francisco Chaves. Before the third ballot could be taken, however, T.W. Heman nominated Catron in a well-timed two-minute speech. The impact of the nomination proved decisive. Delegations began to switch to the familiar old leader, and he was finally declared the unanimous choice of the convention. [64]

Although Catron had been defeated by Joseph two years earlier, his prospects in 1894 seemed bright. He was "at the peak of his power and prestige as a lawyer, wealthy landowner and dominant leader in the Republican party," to quote one prominent Democrat. [65] The issues were also in his favor. Cleveland's stand against silver coinage had hurt Western Democrats. The consistent Republican position on tariff protection for wool and lead still had voter appeal. Moreover, the Republicans had no intention of allowing their rivals to forget that their party was in power when the Depression of 1893 began. [66] Joseph's own failures helped Catron in this race. The durable officeholder was no longer able to command reassuring support, and his failure to gain admission for New Mexico destroyed one of his reliable campaign issues. Finally, there was that new and most distinctive dimension of the 1894 race: the Populist bid for power. Led by the People's candidate for delegate, T.B. Mills, the Populists were determined to make major electoral inroads into the more progressive elements of Joseph's support. The ramifications of this newest threat to the territorial Democrats were carefully watched by all politicians during the busy autumn of 1894.

8

THE 1894 CAMPAIGN

The leadership of the People's party decided to present to the voters of New Mexico the same comprehensive program of reform in the 1894 election that the national Populists campaigned on two years earlier. Silver coinage was to be an important issue. It was not, however, to push "out the others," leaving them "smashed on the ground" like the eggs destroyed by the cow-bird in Henry Demarest Lloyd's famous 1896 analogy. The justification for organizing the scattered Populists in San Miguel, Bernalillo, and other counties into one unified territorial party was effectively presented by Stamm. Speaking as chairman of the Territorial Central Committee of the People's Party, the Populist leader indicted the two major parties and the economic system of the nation in a manner reminiscent of Ignatius Donnelly. He insisted in a published address [1] that if both parties were honest, there would be no need to organize a new party. But the Republican and Democratic parties had become instruments for "class laws pure and simple." The result was the rise of pauperism and crime on the one hand and the amassing of great fortunes on the other. The law in America had become an obstacle to social progress, since it was being interpreted in such a way as to be against the masses and in favor of the classes, creating "a snobbishness, [an] idle aristocracy of great wealth."

Stamm continually alluded to the contrast in wealth between the producers, the nation's farming and laboring people, and the non-producers, the capitalists and businessmen. Why should millions of human beings toil desperately 312 days of the year for the "sole purpose" of eeking out an existence? Reiterating a point made by Henry George in *Progress and Poverty*, Stamm also asked how there could be want and misery in a nation "so favored by national resources." The answer to these questions was obvious to him: "sixty per cent of the goods of labor [go] to one twentieth of one per cent of our population, four-fifths of these who have never in their lives done a complete day's work."

The system of government was responsible for this inequality, in Stamm's opinion, and the two major parties had to shoulder the blame. Because of the manipulation of the two parties by "unscrupulous leaders," these organizations had become the ''machinery'' used by the petty politicians to gain selfish ends and the avaricious to accumulate riches. The honest, hard-working people had no choice but to turn away from their old parties and identify with a political organization that would represent them. That party, according to Stamm, was the People's party. Recognizing the difficulty of changing old voting habits, he admitted that the abandonment of traditional party loyalties was not easy. With the country in such desperate circumstances, though, rank-and-file Republicans and Democrats were urged to consider whether their parties deserved ''one more chance.'' Stamm also refused to regard parties as sacred. The fact that the Populists of today were the Democrats and Republicans of yesterday was proof that, if the People's party ever became ''corrupt beyond redemption,'' it too would be displaced.

Stamm recognized the overriding importance of silver to the economy of New Mexico. But he also saw the controversial metal as a major solution to the nation's money problem. It was the demand for an increase in the amount of ''circulating medium'' that brought the People's party into existence. Silver coinage, however, was just one way of reversing the deflationary trend that had beaten down farm prices and appreciated rural debts. The supply of all kinds of currency should be increased, Stamm insisted. Interpreting the current economic crisis in terms of the quantity theory of money, he asserted that ''all financial authorities agree that prices advance as the volume of money is increased.'' If the government would undertake a serious program of currency expansion, the depressed economy of the nation would begin its slow recovery.

The ramifications of unlimited silver coinage for the Territory of New Mexico were not underestimated by Stamm, despite his concern about the national currency situation. ''We all know that the free and unlimited coinage of silver at 16 to 1 would give New Mexico a standing that she will never achieve without it.'' But Republicans and Democrats in the territory also made noisy assertions that they favored free silver! Stamm's response to statements that the silver issue was non-partisan was to point out that ''a delegate — or a representative and two senators — from New Mexico do not make up the Congress of the United States.'' The Eastern wings of both national parties were, as editor Fred Holt phrased it in the *San Juan Times,* dominated by ''golden calf worshippers.'' [2] How effective can a handful of Western Democratic or Republican silverites be in a Congress dominated by old-line party men conservative on the money question? Only the Populists could be trusted in Stamm's opinion. Currency expansion was almost their *raison d'etre.*

100

The Depression of 1893 was regarded by Western Populists as providing an opportunity to discredit the system. Stamm saw the depression and the issues related to it as furnishing his party with a storehouse of political ammunition. The image of the Democratic party under Cleveland had been tarnished in the West by the president's insistence that the Sherman Silver Purchase Act be repealed. His method of handling the so-called gold crisis also made his party controversial. But neither was the Republican party to escape Stamm's wrath. Both political organizations "have held control of this beautiful republic for thirty years, and the ruin which they have brought the masses is simply without precedent." The demonetization of silver in 1873 and the high McKinley tariff were cited by Stamm as examples. As for the Depression of 1893, it was "well known that the panic had started six months prior to the election of Mr. Cleveland." Harrison's secretary of the treasury, Charles Foster, was "very anxious to trade bonds for buying the gold that was rapidly going to Europe." This action was proof to Stamm that the Harrison administration was aware of the decline in the national gold reserve even before the depression began. Since conservatives in both parties blamed the depression on the gold flow to Europe, Foster's actions also incriminated his party.

The purpose of Stamm's address was to win converts to Populism, as well as to explain the party's stand on important issues.

> If we want silver to be restored to its old position; if we want money in abundance in order to look for jobs; if we believe that it would be beneficial that our mines be worked to their greatest capacity; if we want *acequies* for irrigation and railroads built; if we want to give remunerative employment to each unemployed person in this country; in [reality], if we want to see New Mexico prosper, we should, by way of our votes, help place the People's party in power.

Recognizing the ridicule already used to discredit Populists and the vulnerability of their controversial stands, Stamm strove to embolden the faint-hearted and the hesitant.

> Do not hold back for fear of being rediculed [*sic*]; do not lend more help to our enemies because some particular portion of the People's party platform does not please you; remember, it is impossible to write up a platform that will please 12 million voters in all respects.[3]

Stamm's blunt stand on issues was echoed by other Populist leaders in New Mexico. Fred Holt, the editor of the *San Juan Times,* warned his readers that millionaires are multiplying at an "accelerated rate at one end of the line, while paupers, tramps and vagabonds are increasing more rapidly than at any period of our history, at the other." [4] Holt, too, interpreted the country's economic strife in terms of a class struggle. The little people in America were arrayed against the monopolies, and the government was shamelessly serving the latter. There was, however, one hopeful fact. The judiciary might continue to serve monopoly power in countless ways, but it can never "issue an injunction or restraining order prohibiting men from . . . voting the Populist ticket. This much freedom is left us at least." [5]

An executive committee of the People's party in Grant County underscored the sentiments of both Stamm and Holt. Taking a more optimistic tack, the Grant Populists stated that they had an "abiding faith that the masses, gathering wisdom from experience, will unite to achieve victory over the corrupt politicians, the incompetent officials, the selfish financiers, the venal legislators and extortionist employers," whose rule today is the curse of the nation. "Upon this declaration of principles we invite the co-operation of the voters of Grant County and New Mexico." [6] Even *La Voz del Pueblo,* published by the turncoat Populist, Felix Martinez, saw the conflict which was developing in America's industrial society. The "worker is awake and proposes to make his rights be respected by the monopolists." [7]

Prominent in Populist newspaper editorials and campaign speeches was that pronounced anti-monopolism which had permeated the entire third-party movement. As a leading cause of agrarian reform nationally, it was also a major reason for social protest in the territory. Historically, cattle and land monopolies had been the chief villains in New Mexico. But the land-grabbers and cattle kings were not to be the major targets of the Populists in 1894. Perhaps the willingness of territorial Democrats to champion anti-monopolism in New Mexico accounted for this change in Populist strategy. Whatever the reason, the results were noteworthy. Although the Populist *New Mexico Nugget* harassed Joseph for land-grabbing, [8] more fundamental national issues dominated the party's efforts in the election.

The *San Juan Times,* for instance, indirectly endorsed governmental ownership of the railroads. It refuted the familiar charge that "public improvements, government railroads, canals and telegraph[s]" were forms of irresponsible socialism. [9] It also reprinted an article from the *American Non Conformist* showing how the State of Georgia was able to take over the Northwestern railroad, which had been "abandoned by the owners as worthless," and operate it and guarantee its bonds, turning a profit over to the state treasury of $12,000. The point of the article was obvious. "Let the government take the whole lot of them and do likewise." [10] Even editor Fred Holt was reluctant to attack the railroads with too much intensity, though. The relative newness of railroad corporations in the life of the territory was one cause for his moderation; the first tracks did not reach New Mexico until 1879. The need for rail transportation was another. In San Juan County railroads had not yet arrived. But transportation was needed to move the produce of the county's irrigated valleys to the silver camps and other communities of western Colorado. The *Times* was put in the embarrassing position of mildly endorsing government ownership of railroads and, at the same time, promoting needed private railroad construction in the county. Its pages consistently carried advertisements about the passenger service of the Atlantic and Pacific, Santa Fe, and Denver and Rio Grande railroads. [11]

The two major parties also came in for criticism, as part of the stress on national issues in 1894. "We declare that both the republican and democratic parties of today are dominated by individuals who are indifferent to public welfare, and who use their respective party organizations only for private ends," declared the Populists of Grant County. [12] Is there a man in San Juan County who is not, body and soul, opposed to trusts? queried the *Times.* Why, then, should anyone continue to vote for the "old two tickets"? Aware of the better anti-monopoly record of New Mexico's Democrats, Holt was especially severe with the national Democratic party. "Has not [the] record of the democratic congress, senate . . . and house, cabinet and president clearly shown to every sensible man that the democratic party is simply bought, owned, controlled and worked solely and entirely in the interests of trusts, sugar, coal, Pullman, whiskey and what not[?]" The outspoken editor concluded, however, by asking if the "preceding republican administration" was any better. [13]

Many disciples of Populism in New Mexico took an even broader approach to the money question than Stamm took in his published address. The Grant Populists warned of the powerful spokesmen for Wall Street and the "professional money changers" who were manipulating the currency system to "aid the creditor at the cost of the debtor." [14] Holt expressed his belief that free coinage was just one way to bring about currency reform. He also believed in greenback expansion. "Thirty years ago [during the Civil War] our public servants issued greenbacks to pay men for killing each other; but now when we talk of issuing money" for the construction of public improvements and the building of government-owned railroads and communication facilities, "it is socialism pure and simple." [15] Holt's *San Juan Times* supported a proposal made on August 3 by Senator William A. Peffer, the Kansas Populist, to appropriate $500,000 for the secretary of agriculture to use for the construction of reservoirs for the storage of water in semi-arid states. A companion bill in the lower house called for the reservoirs to be built on tillable lands west of the 90th meridian, which would logically include the Territory of New Mexico. An amendment to one of these measures, calling for the employment of 100,000 men for four months to be paid in ''full legal tender greenbacks, crisp and new, as the soldiers were paid,'' was regarded as the ''most sensible and imperatively demanded'' piece of legislation that the Congress could enact. ''But the bankers and bond brokers will not allow the the starving people to be thus saved and the country made habitable.'' [16]

Although Holt advocated greenback expansion, he was intense in his opposition to another kind of soft money, national bank notes. ''On the sixth of November,'' the editor wrote, referring to the impending election, ''you have a chance to prove that you are opposed to paying interest to national bank bankers for the use of your money, saving millions of dollars to the people and destroying a national curse. You can prove it by voting a straight Populist ticket.'' [17]

The expansion of the nation's currency was of prime importance to the more ideologically committed Populist. He not only wanted to create a market for the territory's silver industry, but he also believed that such expansion would bring about a long overdue price rise, reduce the debt on individuals, and lift the small ''producer'' out of his state of degradation. The unlimited coinage of gold and silver alone would not accomplish these objectives. ''If you want industrial freedom[,] vote with the only party which [is] against contraction and a 'specie basis' promise to pay.'' [18] The reference was, of course, to the People's party. Faith that Populists, if given control of the government, would inflate the currency with fiat money as well as silver and create some sort of agrarian paradise was strong. ''If you want more money, lower rate of interest, better prices for wheat, corn, cattle, hogs and labor everywhere, work, talk and vote for the populist ticket and elect no man who is not in favor of monetary and industrial reform.'' [19]

Silver coinage, of course, was the most attractive way of bringing about currency expansion in the Territory of New Mexico. Politicians of all persuasions in the silver-producing West sensed the importance of silver. Its significance would continue to grow as the impact of the repeal of the Sherman Silver Purchase Act and the panic of 1893 became more profoundly felt. A Denver attorney wrote Catron, who had been straddling the silver issue for months, that he would not be displeased with Catron's success, provided he was sound on the silver question. ''Coloradoans are all cranks on that question, and democrats and republicans unite at least on that issue.'' [20] The economy of New Mexico was not so dependent upon silver as was Colorado's, but the enthusiasm for unlimited coinage in New Mexico's silver-rich neighbor to the north was spreading southward in 1894.

The *San Juan Times,* critical of the way the nation's economic system was being manhandled by the two old parties, tied the demonetization of silver in 1873 to the drop in prices that followed and the indifference to this development on the part of plutocratic officeholders. Before demonetization 35,000 bushels of wheat or 350,000 pounds of cotton equalled the annual pay of the president of the United States, "while today he receives the equivalent of 100,000 bushels of wheat or 1,000,000 pounds of cotton, and the same proportion applies to all other fixed salaries and incomes." [21] Not to be outdone by silver Democrats and silver Republicans, the Populist journal also attacked Eastern senators who opposed Arizona's admission because her enabling act contained a clause making silver legal tender for all debts. "In all probability these objectors are professed bimetallists of the Cleveland-Sherman stamp," it declared, including both Democrats and Republicans in its indictment. They saw no objection to giving gold legal tender "quality," but had doubts about Arizona's right to treat silver in the same fashion. Their position was unbending even though the Constitution, by implication, granted states the right to make both metals legal tender. [22]

Particularly uncomfortable to the old-line party men in New Mexico was the breakdown of congressional votes on free coinage that the Populist press loved to publicize. The *Times,* aware that such tabulations benefited the People's movement, published in its October 5 issue a recent House vote on silver coinage. In it twelve Republicans, one hundred Democrats and eleven Populists supported free silver, while 114 Republicans and 113 Democrats opposed it. Not one Populist vote was recorded against free coinage. The "People's party [is] the only national party demanding free and unlimited coinage at 16 to 1," it concluded. This vote, cast during the 53rd session of Congress, was published in at least three issues of the *Albuquerque Democrat.* [23] One hundred Democratic votes as compared to only twelve Republican in support of free silver, proclaimed the Democratic journal. The 113 negative Democratic votes were, of course, omitted in the published tabulation.

The continuing Depression of 1893 was exploited by territorial Populists other than the angry Stamm. The theme was a consistent one. The "panic" was the result of policies pursued by both parties; the Democrats were just unfortunate enough to be in office when the depression began. The remedy was new leadership, which, of course, meant Populist leadership. The change, however, was not to be accomplished through revolutionary means.

In the "war between capital and labor, now but begun," declared the Populist leaders of Grant County, "our sympathies are with labor, but we believe that ballots are more effective than bullets, and the acts of lawlessness done by supporters of any cause react to the hurt of the cause." [24]

Another Populist stand supported by territorial leaders was the opposition of the national movement to alien landownership. Although restrictions on foreigners buying land in the territories had been imposed by Congress as early as 1887, there was still considerable apprehension. Much of the concern was no doubt a result of the activities of the Maxwell Company in Colfax County. A speech by the chairman of the state central committee of the People's party in Colorado was published approvingly in the *San Juan Times.* Sixty-two million acres of the total national domain were owned by aliens, the Populist leader asserted, along with 173 million in the hands of railroad owners and 21 million held by speculators, leaving less than 336 million for the rest of the people. Our public lands have been passing into the hands of "foreign syndicates," and much that is held on a fee simple basis by "our people" is covered by a mortgage indebtedness that is almost as certain as a clear deed. [25]

The attitude of New Mexicans toward alien landownership was by no means unanimous, though. Forbidding aliens to own land could slow the development of the territory. Thus, once again the desire for reform was pitted against local economic motivation. The *Las Vegas Daily Optic* called restrictions on alien ownership by government a "short-sighted policy [that] has cost New Mexico dearly." Aliens, the Republican journal explained, have helped to develop the resources of the territory. The money taken from New Mexico by aliens is small compared to that paid by them for labor and transportation and that received locally in the form of taxes and insurance. [26]

As to whether New Mexico Populists were anti-intellectual or nativistic — charges made against them by historians such as Richard Hofstadter — the evidence is scanty and, therefore, inconclusive. The *San Juan Times* did reprint an attack against the well-educated legal profession, which first appeared in the radical journal, the *Wealth Maker.* "Lawyers are very rarely men of unbending principle. For money they will clear the guilty and convict the innocent. They are professional liars and moral law breakers." [27] The role of New Mexico attorneys in so-called land-grabbing enterprises had conditioned many New Mexicans, in addition to Holt, to accept this blanket indictment of the legal fraternity. But lawyers, notwithstanding the presence of some questionable individuals, were among the important leaders of any frontier state or territory. Many were cultural as well as political leaders. The profession in New Mexico included all types, from the incorruptible Harvey

Fergusson to the controversial Catron. Thus, the bitterness of this published attack was not really justified. Holt's apparent willingness to put all attorneys into one category may have been due to the absence of prominent lawyers in the New Mexico People's party. As a matter of fact, not one reference to a Populist lawyer could be found in the sources consulted.

A more direct attack on the better educated was found in the Declaration of Principles enunciated by the Populist leaders of Grant County. [28] "Our laws would be better if fewer 'talented' men had to do with making them. The demand of the hour is for an infusion of hard sense." In a statement reminiscent of Democrats of Andrew Jackson's day, the Grant Populists declared their belief in the rotation of offices, "especially in such offices as are to be filled in New Mexico, where no prior training or special qualifications are required other than those possessed by hundreds of our humblest citizens." A bias against the young was also revealed. "We hold it necessary to select as legislators courageous men of recognized integrity, and who have reached the years of discretion, rather than irresponsible seekers after place, or 'promising' young aspirants of unformed character." Fortunately, these statements, revealing such deep suspicions toward anyone with talent or creativity, were moderated by a little good sense. "We maintain that men entrusted with public office are the servants and not the masters of the people. That, being once in place, they should conscientiously do the work for which they are paid, instead of devoting half their time and all their so-called talents securing a third term."

In assessing the extent of anti-intellectualism among New Mexico Populists, one is confronted with some dilemmas. First, the view of the Grant County leaders toward the better educated and the young may not be representative of the rank and file in New Mexico. Secondly, distrust of the educated was not uncommon in frontier America, if Turner and other historians are correct. Also, New Mexico's unusual ethnic composition should be considered. Native New Mexicans had their own culture and language, unfortunately accorded little respect by many Anglos. The Roman Catholic Church, which had long enjoyed a virtual monopoly over the spiritual life of these Hispanos, had resisted the efforts of Anglos to encroach upon its control of education. As Anglo-supported public education was regarded as a threat to the influence of the Church, clerics and believers alike frequently opposed organized learning under public auspices. Obviously, such an attitude could create another source of anti-intellectualism in the territory.

The view of the New Mexico native toward public education was also conditioned by the fact that in a state-supported school system he might have to learn in another tongue. Even so, some Hispanos — one suspects they were a minority at this time — promoted the opportunities provided by a public-supported educational program. Felix Martinez, whose brief commitment to Populism was admittedly questionable, was a supporter of better education for his people. "The future advantage for the native-American race of our territory," *La Voz del Pueblo* declared, "consists of a good and liberal education" for our youth. Insisting that this would be the "magic" for solving the difficulties faced by Spanish-speaking people, Martinez's journal boasted that the natural talents of the native New Mexicans were "generally very good." All that was needed was the kind of assistance that would allow the schools of the territory to reach the native Hispano, who was characterized as a "diamond in the rough." [29] Probably a more common attitude toward education in the territory was the one related in an anecdote by Miguel A. Otero. Referring to his friend Dr. John B. Pettijohn, who as a candidate for superintendent of schools in San Miguel County was the only Republican to lose during a particular election, Otero told of Pettijohn's reaction when the returns came in on election night. As the "educator" saw his vote drop in the northern part of the county, he remarked in disgust:

> I want to tell you how this happened, and I wish further to state that it was taking mean advantage of me. While I was electioneering down in the southern part of the county, the Democrats started the story up north that if I were elected, I would require all my teachers to be able to read and write, and before I could get back up there to deny this villainous political libel, they beat me. [30]

So, if the Populists were anti-intellectual, they were not alone. Many Hispanos and Anglos in the territory, both Democrats and Republicans, shared this bias with those Populists who were so inclined.

As for the charge of nativism leveled against the Populists by some historians, the record of the New Mexico party appears more respectable. No derogatory remarks against the foreign born have been found among the writings and speeches of Populists during the 1894 campaign; nor were any anti-semitic comments uncovered. There were hostile remarks about foreign creditors in connection with the country's economic development, including the currency situation, but no bitter references to Anglo-Jewish bankers or to foreign subjects living in New Mexico. The drain of money to Europe, however, did disturb the *San Juan Times*, which demanded an early end to American borrowing abroad. For over forty years, declared the *Times*, we Americans have been forced to look across the Atlantic for the money needed to "develop and operate all the vast industries of this nation, paying in interest billions of dollars of money, the cream of labor and the products of labor of this nation, until we are squeezed dry and deprived of all ability to raise even interest [any] longer.'' If we must borrow, the newspaper continued, we should ''borrow only American money and pay all interest to ourselves, who are the government.'' 31 The conviction also was expressed that if we, the people, had borrowed ''all the money from the United States that we are now borrowing from foreign capitalists, paying interests in the same to our government, we would need no other revenue and have millions of surplus every year.'' 32 Such remarks were obviously nationalistic rather than nativistic.

The issue of anti-Catholicism was injected into the campaign of 1894 by Democrats. The *Albuquerque Democrat* on October 12 quoted W.B. Childers, an Albuquerque attorney and Democratic leader, to the effect that the Colorado Republicans were saturated with the attitudes of the A.P.A. from ''head to foot.'' The reference was to the American Protective Association, an anti-Catholic and nativist organization. The association had also taken root in the territory, the *Democrat* warned. ''In New Mexico the operations of this unscrupulous organization [were] not conducted as openly as in Colorado for reasons too apparent to need explanation.'' The journal also claimed that one of its employees was solicited to join in Socorro.

The A.P.A. had moved westward from the Mississippi Valley, where it had originated. It began to develop support in the Rocky Mountain West sometime after 1890. A branch was established in Cheyenne in 1891, but because of its secrecy it attracted little attention until January, 1893, when its influence helped elect a Republican mayor. One of the reasons for its growth in southeastern Wyoming was the presence of approximately 4,000 Catholic railroad workers of foreign background. Their employment during the hard times that followed the 1893 panic was resented by less well-to-do native Americans. 33 Activities of the A.P.A. were also evident in Denver, Colorado, where a branch of the anti-Catholic order was established in May of 1892. In Wyoming and throughout much of the West the organization found its most congenial home in the Republican party. The effort to smear other political parties by associating them with the American Protective Association, however, was too effective a political device to be overlooked. In Denver, for instance, a priest named Father Malone charged the Populists with having A.P.A. members within their ranks. Making the accusation to help the Democrats, the priest hit a responsive chord. The *Rocky Mountain News* of Denver insisted that no Populist could be a member of the A.P.A., and was commended for this assurance by the state Populist organ, the *Coming Crisis*. 34

The existence of a strong branch of the A.P.A. in Spanish-speaking, Roman Catholic New Mexico would be most unlikely. Even so, Catron received a questionnaire from a nativist source, probably the American Protective Association or a group associated with it, demanding his "prompt response." Specifically, the Republican candidate was asked to reveal his stand on such issues as separation of church and state, free public education, more stringent immigration laws, and the readjustment of appointive federal offices to benefit native Americans. Catron, who had many friends and political allies among Hispano leaders in the territory, ignored this arrogant demand. [35]

Catron knew that a favorable response to such a questionnaire would have been an act of political suicide. Other Republican leaders also knew enough to be wary of any possible association with the A.P.A. or any other organization of this ilk. But Democrats, aware of Republican connections with the A.P.A. elsewhere, tried to associate Republicans with the anti-Catholic group whenever they could during the 1894 election. A pamphlet in Spanish was circulated during the campaign with these headlines: "The American Protective Association! An Anti-Catholic Society! Supported by Republicans!" Comparing the A.P.A. with the Know Nothings of the 1850's, the pamphlet accused such national Republican leaders as Levi P. Morton and Thomas B. Reed of being equivocal or worse about the nativist organization. Senator Edward O. Wolcott, Republican from Colorado, was charged with having A.P.A. leanings. Influential Republican Senator Orville H. Platt of Connecticut was accused of opposing the admission of New Mexico, because he feared it would become a Catholic state. "Who can believe a party [Republican] that favors an anti-Catholic society?" The published appeal concluded with a plea that New Mexico voters re-elect Antonio Joseph, the native candidate and nominal Catholic, as delegate. [36]

The Populists of New Mexico seemingly were not vulnerable to the charge of nativism or A.P.A.ism during the 1894 election. The best tactics that the Republicans or Democrats could use against them were either to ignore or ridicule them. The first approach is evident to anyone perusing the press for news of this election. Populist items were usually small ones relegated to the back pages. The second technique, to mock them, was also obvious. "Ridicule is the only method so far adopted by the opposition," Holt declared in his newspaper. [37]

As for substantive election issues, the two that seemed most harmful to Populist prospects were the alleged Populist extravagance in spending public funds, a national issue, and the statehood question, a local one. Capitalizing on the first, the *Albuquerque Democrat,* apprehensive about the effect that the Populist bid would have on the chances of the Democrats, accused

Populists in the United States Congress of supporting appropriation bills that would amount to half a billion dollars "or about twenty times as much as the national debt." Listing several Populist money bills designed to cope with the adverse effects of the depression and the other weaknesses of the economic system, the *Democrat* concluded that the "pop party is too expensive a luxury to afford just yet." [38]

On the second issue, the admission of New Mexico, the Populists had little to offer territorial voters. With only three members in the United States Senate and less than a dozen in the House, they were in the weakest position to promise decisive action on statehood. The Democrats could probably present the best case with their control of the presidency and the lower house of Congress. But Delegate Joseph's repeated failures to win admission had weakened his party's position on this issue. The incumbent delegate, according to the Republican *Daily Citizen* of Albuquerque, had even resorted to blackmail in order to win votes. Asserting that congressional Democrats were going to make the admission of the territory a matter of barter, exchanging statehood for New Mexican votes, Joseph warned his constituents that statehood was contingent upon his re-election. The threat was a "cold-blooded" one, he admitted, but the Washington situation warranted it. [39]

Having little leverage on the popular statehood issue, the territorial Populists tried to minimize its importance. The "two old parties" talk about admission, they maintained, when they should be talking about the depression. The need to help businesses and relieve "the suffering masses from want and distress " was considered more important at this time. The past performance of both parties in the statehood struggle also invited a more direct attack. All that former Republican Territorial Delegate Stephen B. Elkins, a vocal statehood proponent, had ever done during his two terms was to turn his office into a real estate enterprise and a place to get private land grants confirmed, the *San Juan Times* editorialized. Thus, the "land-grabbing" issue was cleverly injected into the statehood question. Finally, to strengthen the Populists on the statehood issue, there were the predictions of a Democratic disaster during the November election. These assertions were accompanied by Populist bravado concerning the party's expectations. Populism "will prevail west of the Mississippi to the Pacific this coming election," declared the *Times,* "and the majority of representatives in the west will be 'middle-of-the-road' and to be in sympathy with them will be in the interests of New Mexico politics." Statehood boosters take notice! [40]

Another major issue of the 1894 campaign was the perennial controversy over the tariff. Because wool had been put on the free list, territorial Democrats, as low-tariff advocates, were again forced to go on the defensive. The tariff question put the candidates of the People's party, also, in a vulnerable position. Populist ideology, if such a term legitimately can be used, was difficult to reconcile with the protective tariff. High tariffs usually shielded American monopolies from foreign competition. Territorial Populists remained strangely quiet on this issue, though. They probably did not want to alienate members of the livestock and mining industries any more than was necessary. An attack on the familiar expression, "the higher the tariff, the higher the wages," which originally appeared in a Colorado newspaper, was reprinted in the *San Juan Times.* "The tariff now averages nearly twice as high as it did in 1886, but the average wage of labor is not half so high, and millions of laborers can't get any work at any price. Please explain." [41] Surprisingly, this reprint was not accompanied by a warm endorsement of its sentiments in the pages of the *Times.*

Democrats, however, could not minimize the tariff question as the Populists attempted to do. Republicans in the territory seized the issue and used it with relish against their traditional foes. The *Las Vegas Daily Optic* was especially aggressive. It attacked the contention that wool had been placed on the free list because the removal of the tariff would cause greater consumption, "hence higher prices." Unprotected wool would only destroy the sheep industry which was the "nearest approach to agriculture" in the territory. The expenses of bringing wool from Australia were not one-fourth that of producing it in New Mexico. [42] The Republican *Evening Citizen* of Albuquerque reported that South America would flood the nation's market with cheap wool. An official of the Argentine government was quoted as predicting an increase in the amount of Argentine raw wool on both the European and American markets. [43] The wool issue was such a boon for Republicans in 1894 that anxious requests for literature attacking Democratic support of free wool were made by them in at least one county. [44] As for the silver industry, it had been "crushed by democratic legislation," first by demonetization and "afterward by placing [silver], together with all its combinations, upon the free list." Cattle raisers were adversely affected by tariff reduction too. Many of them felt compelled to drive beeves by the thousand to Old Mexico, where they could be fattened more cheaply before being sold on the inadequately protected American market. The remedy for all these woes, declared the *Optic,* was to go "solidly republican!" [45]

The Republican press also pictured territorial Democrats as striving to separate themselves from the " gold-bug" Cleveland administration. Joseph was reported as backing Cleveland's free wool tariff policy, but breaking with the "stuffed prophet" on the silver question. [46] According to a Catron supporter, Governor Thornton, a Cleveland appointee, and Harvey Fergusson traveled to Silver City to campaign for Joseph. The pair "harangued for two hours" in behalf of the five-term delegate. They also

112

attempted to woo back Democrats who had strayed into the Populist party. More significant were their statements denouncing Cleveland "and his silver policy in the hardest language." The president was accused of being a "traitor to the party, and his constituency." [47] In response to the divide-and-conquer strategy of the Republicans, Joseph's supporters reiterated time and time again their candidate's solid support of free coinage. The *Albuquerque Democrat* insisted that the miners of Bland, the Cochiti, and other mining districts of Bernalillo County would vote for Joseph, because they knew that he would protect their interests. Catron, on the other hand, would not receive their support. The miners knew that he was only concerned about the welfare of land-grant owners, the *Democrat* maintained. Moreover, he would not allow miners on his "Spanish grants" without having them pay a toll. Nor would these miners vote for Mills. If the Populist candidate were elected, he would not work against their interest, but such an outcome was impossible. "Hence every vote thrown away on Mills will help to elect Catron." [48]

With a Populist candidate in the delegate's race and third-party tickets in a number of counties, Republicans were elated and Democrats were depressed. Catron supporters no longer felt compelled to waste time answering such charges against their candidate as his questionable role in the Borrego-Chavez affair. [49] Even the Republican's extensive landholdings did not seem like such a great liability this time. Those who opposed New Mexico's land and cattle monopolies were divided between two spokesmen, Mills and Joseph, and territorial Republicans were eager to exploit the schism.

To promote this division most effectively the Catron people concentrated on those counties where agrarian protest and anti-monopolism began. The Populists had their greatest strength there, and would be most likely to detract from the Democratic vote in those counties. Mills mentioned several of the counties in an optimistic interview with the *New Mexican* near the end of the campaign. He predicted that he would carry one of them, his old home county of San Miguel. Silver-rich Grant and Sierra counties also would vote Populist, because of his party's stand on free coinage. Lincoln and Colfax, where chapters of the Farmers' Alliance had fought land and cattle monopolies so aggressively, were placed on his side, along with agricultural San Juan. As five of the six counties had been in Joseph's column in the last election, Mills was forced to deny that his candidacy was in the interest of Tom Catron. [50]

"The Pops are cutting the bottom out of the Democratic party in Lincoln county," reported the Republican Socorro *Chieftain*. [51] A supporter from Grant County wrote Catron that there were 140 Populists prepared to vote for Mills, 116 of whom were "pronounced democrats." [52] Even more optimistic was a report from Lincoln County. There a party worker declared that the Populists would poll 200 votes or more, "and their strength all comes from the Democrats." [53] Such assessments were typical of the reports that Catron was getting from swing counties or counties that had previously been for Joseph. In Dona Ana County, which Joseph carried in 1892 by 271 votes, a supporter wrote: "The Populists are from the Democrats mostly! 4 Dem[.] to 1 Rep[.] . . ." [54] Populist leaders in Grant County reported that Democrats were "so sore at their own party that they find it quite a relief to join the pops." [55]

In Colfax County a disenchanted Joseph backer predicted that, although the incumbent delegate would "carry most of the Mexicans," he would be beaten. One of the causes of his defeat in Colfax would be the activities of the Populists. They will "pull votes from the democrats more than the republicans." [56] *La Voz del Pueblo* of San Miguel County attempted to reverse the trend against their candidate. "Long live Joseph, the friend of people of New Mexico and the representative most loyal to the interests of our territory." The longtime delegate was represented as being the best guaranty of restored prosperity for the territory and the one man who could secure New Mexico's admission to the Union. [57]

In San Juan County, where the *San Juan Times* was predicting Mills' victory in the territory over both Catron and Joseph by "not less than 500 votes," [58] Joseph's prospects appeared dim. He had carried the county two years earlier by sixty-six votes, but with the *Times* backing the Populist cause he could no longer count on support from the protest elements in San Juan. Also, in another setback, the *Index* in Aztec, the county seat, announced that it would support all Democrats but Joseph. [59] A campaign trip to the county by Joseph was reported as a failure by one delighted Catron backer, while another supporter predicted that the Republican candidate would do much better in San Juan County than he did in 1892. [60]

Although the Populists were active in 1894, not all of them were committed as thoroughly to the cause as were Stamm and Holt. There were some who were unwilling to vote for their party's nominee for delegate or even support the moderately progressive Joseph. F.A. Blake, one of the founders of the San Miguel party in 1888, was one of these. He went so far as to congratulate Catron on his nomination. "I think some effective work can be done to aid you in this county," he said of San Miguel. He also attempted to arrange a meeting in Las Vegas with the Republican candidate. [61] Because Catron was the antithesis of almost everything that was Populist, Blake's actions were those of either a disgruntled person or an opportunistic one. His bitterness toward Martinez is understandable. Perhaps Mills also deserved some of his wrath, for he may have cooperated with Martinez to deprive Blake of a Populist nomination to the Territorial Council in 1892. But to turn to Catron to spite these two is opportunism of the rankest sort.

In another defection, the Populist organization of Union County, as a body, endorsed Catron's candidacy. Made up largely of Hispanos who were formerly Democrats, the party met in Clayton on September 29, and voted to fuse with the Republicans through a joint county ticket. [62] The Catron lieutenant most responsible for this arrangement was Lewis C. Fort, an attorney from East Las Vegas who had served prominently in the Territorial Council during the Twenty-eighth session. [63] Fort had traveled to Clayton before the county Populist convention to meet with such influential Populists as Emiterio Gallegos, Mateo Lujan, Saturnio Pinard, and Francisco Gallegos, all members of the party's central committee. His efforts met with surprising success. Writing to Catron afterwards, he boasted of the enthusiasm he encountered and urged him to fix a date when he could come to Union County to speak to the new converts. [64]

Fort's success in Union County was probably due to several factors. He was already popular in the new county, which was created on February 13, 1893. While he was district attorney of San Miguel in 1891, which then included much of Union County, he traveled to Clayton to take custody of a notorious killer who had murdered an old man in his sleep. As the accused man, whose name was Faulkner, made loud, abusive statements about Fort during the trial in Las Vegas, the prosecuting attorney became quite a local hero. [65] A more likely cause of Fort's success, however, was the support that his candidate had given to the recent creation of Union County. [66] Also, the veteran Republican's warm association with Spanish-speaking leaders in the northern part of the territory strengthened his position, while Democratic feuding in Union County weakened his opposition. [67]

As election day approached, Joseph was crusading on the proposition that only he could bring statehood. Catron and his supporters, on the other hand, were trying to convince the voters that Democrats as free traders would expose the territory's industries to ruinous competition if elected. Catron's eagerness to become New Mexico's lone voice in Congress made him responsive to any counsel that would help his cause. A proposal by Fort that he oppose the removal of the county seat of Colfax from Springer to Raton to win Democratic support was the type of suggestion that would strike a responsive chord in Catron. [68] As for Mills, he concealed his disappointment in the lack of enthusiasm for his candidacy by acting confident. Catron will lose Rio Arriba and Santa Fe counties and have a reduced majority in Valencia, he predicted, attempting to sound as convincing as possible. [69]

115

Election day saw a record number of people at the polls; but the voters of New Mexico were in no mood for a revolutionary change. They gave Mills only 1,835 votes, or 3.77 percent of the total. Catron, who won by receiving 51.30 percent of the vote, did not need Mills' divisive impact on the progressive segment of the electorate to score his victory. The 2,762-vote margin he garnered in his 18,113 to 15,351 triumph over Joseph exceeded the Democratic votes lost to Mills by almost a thousand. [70] Joseph apparently blamed his defeat on his failure to win admission. Republicans believed that their tariff stand and their candidate's strength in the northern counties had been most crucial in the outcome. [71] They also felt that they had effectively exploited the statehood issue. Banners bearing the inscription ''Vote for T.B. Catron and Statehood,'' for instance, appeared throughout Bernalillo County on election day. [72] Neither major party responded in any visible way during the campaign to Stamm's criticism. Nor did either acknowledge his gloomy critique of the social and economic ills of the country. The customary issues of local or territorial concern once again monopolized a New Mexico election.

The Populists did enjoy one gratifying success: they carried San Juan County. Holt's readers reacted positively to his Midwestern brand of agrarian Populism. They cast 233 votes for Mills, 225 for Joseph, and 165 for Catron. Mills, attracting normally Democratic voters, was second in Sierra County with 280 votes. He pushed Joseph's tally below Catron's, 254 votes to 453. The Populist candidate also did well in two counties which had been areas of early political and economic protest. In Lincoln, he gathered 213 ballots, although Joseph won the county from Catron, 555 votes to 520. In Colfax, Mills polled only 160 votes, but that was enough to prevent Joseph from winning the county. Catron edged his frustrated Democratic opponent there by a vote of 851 to 794. In Grant County, where the silver issue was in the forefront, 290 ballots were cast for Mills. Although this was a small vote compared to that cast for the two major candidates, it was large enough to make Joseph's 748 to 723 triumph over Catron a close one.

The Populist standard-bearer must have been disappointed by his showing in two counties. In San Miguel, birthplace of the new third-party movement, only 160 voters backed their former representative to the Territorial Council. Even so, the vote was large enough to deprive Joseph of a victory; he lost the county to Catron by a mere three votes. In Bernalillo, where the People's party became a full-fledged territorial party, Mills received only 210 ballots out of 4,368 cast. The fusion movement in Union County, however, caused Mills the greatest humiliation. He polled just one vote, although the strange alliance of Republicans and Populists failed to deliver the county to Catron. Joseph outpolled him by a count of 487 to 398.

116

Mills' prediction that Catron would lose Rio Arriba and Santa Fe counties did not materialize. The Republican won handily in Rio Arriba, polling 1,564 votes to Joseph's 1,340. Mills received only three votes in Rio Arriba in another embarrassment. In his home county of Santa Fe, Catron edged Joseph by a count of 1,517 to 1,485; Mills' 135 votes had deprived Joseph of victory in yet another county. Catron's impressive accumulation of votes in Bernalillo and Valencia counties insured the newly elected delegate that his margin of victory in the territory would be a comfortable one. [73]

Populists also were disappointed in the outcome of the legislative and local races. They evidently failed to place a representative in the newly elected Thirtieth Legislative Assembly. Even in San Juan County, where every Populist candidate on the county ticket won, their choice for a seat in the territorial House lost. [74] In local races the story was a little happier. County offices were picked up in several places, and in Bernalillo Populist support of the Democratic candidate for probate clerk accounted for the only Democratic success in a Republican landslide. [75] But their showing, on the whole, was most disappointing. In San Miguel County, for instance, both they and the Republicans lost to the Union party, ex-Populist Felix Martinez's formidable new political machine. [76]

The *Times* of San Juan County was dejected about both the territorial and national results. The defeat of Lafe Pence, the Colorado Populist who spoke at the party's first territorial convention at the beginning of the campaign, was regretfully noted. Democrat "Silver Dick" Bland's loss in Missouri was particularly distressing. It prompted Holt to call the 1894 election a "goldbug" victory. [77] Referring to his party as the "one silver party in the field," the frustrated editor concluded that "honest (?) money and hard times are what [the people] want. They have them!" [78] Fortunately for Holt he could proclaim that "San Juan county was saved." Attributing the victory in part to an increased vote, particularly in the "American" precincts, Holt pictured a large rooster on the front page of his newspaper as a sign that San Juan Populists had something to crow about. [79]

The final response of most New Mexico Democrats and Republicans to the Populist challenge of 1894 was still one of ridicule with some bitterness added. Many Democrats could not forgive the Populists for detracting from their vote. Mills was "nothing more than a dumb rooster to take votes away from the beloved son of the people, the Hon. Antonio Joseph," *La Voz de Pueblo* editorialized. San Juan County, the last stronghold of the People's party in New Mexico, also was derided by Martinez's scrappy newspaper as "San Juan of the Populists." [80] Republicans, on the other hand, were content to belittle Mills and his party. "Col. Mills has probably won a hat"

117

from us, remarked the *Evening Citizen* of Albuquerque. "The wager was that he would not get 1,000 votes in the territory." The Republican paper alluded to current talk about a possible merger of the Democratic and People's parties in Bernalillo County. "This is rough on the pops, but they are accustomed to calamities." [81] The impact of the election had undeniably had a calamitous effect upon the People's party. The stubborn political organization, however, was not ready to accommodate its critics by disappearing. It refused to fade into oblivion even though the citizens of New Mexico had not responded to its earth-shaking issues.

9

CONFUSION OVER FUSION

A remarkable unity on the question of free silver permeated the territory during the days that followed the 1894 election. When the newly elected Thirty-first Legislative Assembly convened in Santa Fe in December of 1894, there was exceptional bitterness generated by a struggle to control the lower House. On only one subject could most of the legislators agree: there should be free and unlimited silver coinage in the United States. But on little else was there agreement. With twelve Democrats and eleven Republicans elected to serve in the House, and one Republican seat in dispute, a power struggle was inevitable. If the Republican whose seat was in contention could be disqualified, the Democrats would gain control of the House. A strategy was developed to accomplish this purpose in the office of Felix Martinez, one of the Democrats elected to serve in the Thirty-first session. Another plan to disqualify two Republican members in the upper house [1] was also part of the overall Democratic strategy to "steal" control of the Thirty-first assembly. Fortunately for the conniving Democrats, Territorial Secretary Lorion Miller was also a Democrat. He cooperated by swearing into office those persons chosen by the Democratic strategists for the legislative seats in dispute. The result was a Republican bolt, leaving primarily a rump Democratic body to carry on the legislative work of the territory. [2]

Despite the preoccupation of the legislators with this struggle, they were able to draw up a joint memorial to Congress in which they urged free coinage. In it they condemned the "money changers, speculators, and national bankers, who [were] constantly striving to contract the volume and enhance the value of money, while depreciating the value of all property, cheapening labor, and making the payment of all debts a correspondingly greater burden." Although a rump body, the legislature spoke for the territory when it declared for a "bi-metallic standard of values" with silver on a par with gold at the 16 to 1 ratio. [3]

Bimetallism was an escalating sentiment throughout much of the nation in the mid-nineties. Its impact on New Mexico was such that it was the one question that could create a consensus among feuding politicians. In some respects, however, silver was losing its political attraction as a partisan issue. All parties, not to be outdone by their rivals, were eager to convince the voters of their greater devotion to free coinage. Silver as an issue was being neutralized. Perhaps it was because of this development that the Populists at their first territorial convention in Albuquerque in 1894 did not emphasize the coinage question with a special resolution. But with practically every silver mine closed down in New Mexico as an aftereffect of the depression, even more people were turning to free silver as a solution to the nation's problems. Free coinage would bring prices up and help debtors pay their debts. And, of course, in New Mexico there was the additional advantage: unlimited coinage would restore the market for a major territorial industry. As the commanding issue, the monomania of silverism (to quote Professor Hofstadter in another context) was enveloping the mountain West with a greater urgency than ever before.

Populists, who had always stood for free silver, were to feel this new sense of immediacy. In New Mexico, the territory's most successful Populist newspaper reflected the new concern generated by the silver crisis. The *San Juan Times,* still edited by Fred E. Holt in the late spring of 1895, devoted increased attention to the nation's economic woes, including the crisis caused by demonetization. There remained in Holt's mind a lingering concern over the inequality of wealth in the United States. He informed his readers that, although America's aggregate wealth was the largest, she was in fourth place in per capita income. The *Times* continued its support of rural activism to better the farmer's economic position. It took the lead in the formation of a San Juan Fruit Growers Association to enable the farmers themselves to dictate prices rather than commission men in Durango, where most of the county's produce was sold. Unity is necessary and a man who ''refuses to join a movement of this necessary kind . . . opposes his fellows.'' [4] Although the journal still promoted San Juan County as an agrarian paradise, [5] it devoted much of its space to the hardships caused by the Depression of 1893. The panic had been cruel, it admitted, but it had brought an awareness to the American people of a need for revolutionary national policies; a ''change in the money laws, better municipal government, [were] questions before the country receiving earnest attention.'' [6] Increasingly, however, the pages of the *Times* became crowded with items about silver.

In the May 31 issue of the newspaper, for instance, ''Silver Dick'' Bland of Missouri was quoted in a Denver speech. According to Bland, the prices of wheat, cotton, oats, and hay in 1890 had shown a 40 percent decline since 1873, the year that silver was demonetized. [7] In the same issue, a silver conference in Salt Lake City to select delegates to the National Silver Convention in Memphis on June 13, 1895, was given sympathetic attention. [8]

The price of silver was listed in almost every issue of the *Times* as a reminder that the silver crisis remained the most serious one facing the country's "producers."

Advocates of free coinage in the Territory of New Mexico grew more numerous and outspoken. Many of the articulate silverites were from the Democratic party, which had been the first to declare unequivocally for free coinage. Joseph had been strong on this issue, particularly during his last two terms. Once describing himself as a "silver Democrat true and strong," he introduced free silver memorials from his constituents without hesitation. A more important Democratic exponent of free coinage was Harvey B. Fergusson. By the summer of 1896, politicians and newspaper editors were talking as if his nomination as Democratic candidate for delegate was a certainty. A persuasive stump speaker, he had been denied his party's designation twice, despite the support of a growing number of younger men. A truly progressive person, the forty-seven year old Fergusson would have been appealing to most modern liberals. The son of an Alabama slaveholder, he had denied his aristocratic heritage. Fergusson not only became a champion of farmers and working people, but he also showed a genuine sympathy for Blacks. He spoke in behalf of them at several celebrations marking Emancipation Day. [9] Coming to New Mexico in 1882, he eventually established a successful law partnership in Albuquerque [10] and became an early supporter of free silver.

Silver sentiment was strong among Republicans also. Catron used all his skill to straddle the issue. A conservative party regular, who was aware of the importance of the issue to those he represented, the delegate hoped his national party would take the kind of stand on silver New Mexicans could tolerate. The most prominent voice for bimetallism among the territory's politicians, however, was former Governor LeBaron Bradford Prince, an orthodox Republican on most questions and a vigorous promoter of free coinage. His convictions on the subject were not entirely due to unselfish motivations, however. Like many territorial leaders Prince was a speculator in mining enterprises who was disturbed by the collapse of the silver industry. Nor was restoration of silver a religion with him; gold holdings were listed among his numerous mining investments. He possessed three miles of the "best placer territory" in Colorado, extending from Floyd Hill to Idaho Springs. The nature of his holdings prompted the *Daily Populist* of Denver to headline a story about one of his visits to Colorado: "A Goldbug from Work, but Not from Principle." [11] The former governor was in reality a pragmatic silverite whose political views harmonized with his economic investments.

Striving to influence governmental policy and public opinion in favor of silver, Prince traveled to countless meetings and conferences to promote free coinage. He corresponded with as many men in government and business as he could. During the World's Columbian Exposition in Chicago, Prince chaired a committee appointed by the Trans-Mississippi Congress, of which he was a longtime member. The purpose of this committee was to arrange a "Silver Day" at the fair. [12] Sensing the importance of the 1896 election to the silver issue, Prince made numerous trips to the East to devise a political strategy that would aid his party's pro-silver forces. After visits in Philadelphia and New York City, in the summer of 1895, he wrote his associates about a so-called "Philadelphia program." This plan called for the control of the next Republican national convention by men sympathetic to free coinage. Philadelphia was the center of this movement for bimetallism, Prince insisted. There plans were being made to control the entire Pennsylvania delegation to the national convention and "fully half of [those] in about seven states in this vicinity." With the strength of the Western delegations added to the ranks of these Eastern proponents, there would be a "show of strength as would bring the South into line and control the convention." Prince asserted that money was available to implement this campaign strategy. A Pennsylvania manufacturer by the name of James Dobson, one of three big contributors in the Keystone State, was ready to make donations out of his ten-million-dollar fortune. [13]

Prince was also active in seeking a compromise with silver proponents in other countries. Along with the West's most prominent silver advocate, Republican Senator Henry Moore Teller of Colorado, the New Mexico leader endorsed a proposal published in *The Arena*, a pro-silver national magazine. It called for the coinage of silver at the 15½ to 1 ratio rather than the 16 to 1 ratio. "The ratio is the only one that could receive the concurrence of France and the other Latin Union countries." [14] A photograph of Prince which appeared with Teller's in *The Arena* was significant especially to New Mexicans, who often compared the former governor with the Coloradoan.

Questions of international cooperation were ticklish because they involved such controversial issues as trade relations and tariffs; Republicans were typically wary of issues of this kind. Suspicions were undoubtedly aroused by a petition circulated by Prince proposing a tariff to equalize costs of production so that the United States could trade with poorer silver-standard countries and not reduce the wages of American workers to the "level of Chinese coolies." The signatures of such eminent Westerners as Teller, Senator Edward O. Wolcott of Colorado, and Senator Francis E. Warren of Wyoming on the petition also caused alarm. [15] More threatening perhaps was the recommendation that the United States cut her tariffs for those nations which would keep their mints open to American silver. Montana Senator Thomas H. Carter, one of the petition's signers, attempted to reassure its critics that free coinage "coupled with free trade [could not] be successfully established and maintained by our government." He did insist, however, on greater trade with the poor silver nations of the world. [16] Significantly, England was pictured as the one great obstacle to progress in all these discussions about international monetary cooperation. One critic wrote that the world was willing to adopt bimetallism except for "one square mile in the city of London," the city's banking district. [17] Prince, like many other silverties, agreed.

Prince worked relentlessly in behalf of free coinage. He was active in organizing pro-silver people on a nonpartisan as well as a partisan basis. A proposed Trans-Montane League to advance bimetallism absorbed much of his attention. It was to be organized on a regional basis with separate Southern, Northern, and Western leagues. The new silver organization would be composed of state and territorial executive committees. One Republican, Democrat, and Populist would serve on each committee. County and precinct committees would also have a representative membership. Each member's $3 purchase of the silver tracts, *Coin's Financial School* and *The Dishonest Dollar,* would help defray costs of promoting the League and distributing the tracts. [18] Prince had written his own book on free coinage, *The Money Problem, or Bi-Metallism vs. a Single Gold Standard,* [19] which brought him considerable prominence.

On a more partisan basis, the ex-governor lobbied to get the Republican national committee to establish a Western headquarters, so that Western silverites could have better communications with national leaders and greater say in party policy. After the party's national convention in 1896, Prince accelerated his program to gain more influence for the West. In August he wrote to Republican leaders such as Warren and Frank Mondell of Wyoming, Wolcott of Colorado, and the party's new standard-bearer, William McKinley. [20]

Before the Republicans could convene in Saint Louis for their national convention, party leaders, particularly from the mountain West, had to devise a strategy to reconcile Eastern anti-bimetallism to the pro-silver views of their own constituents. Catron was determined to achieve such a reconciliation. While contemplating some compromise to placate hard-liners on both sides of the silver question, the portly delegate, who bore a physical resemblance to Grover Cleveland, attempted to calm the passions of his followers. Writing to his lieutenant, Miguel O. Otero, on March 5, 1896, he urged him to use his influence to prevent a free coinage resolution from being passed at the territorial convention for the selection of national delegates scheduled to meet in Albuquerque in about three weeks. Warning that a New Mexico statehood bill in the Senate would be jeopardized by such a resolution, Catron counseled his supporters to concentrate instead on the territory's admission, and the tariff issue. He also expressed his impatience with Westerners in Congress who were tacking free silver amendments on practically "every proposition" being considered. [21]

Otero's success in achieving moderation at the Albuquerque meeting pleased Catron. But the unsympathetic stand taken on silver by the Republican national convention greatly disturbed him. Although the money plank adopted by the Republicans at the Saint Louis gathering did advocate bimetallism through international agreement, it strongly disavowed unilateral free silver coinage. The party platform insisted that "the existing gold standard must be maintained." [22] The victory of gold forces at the June convention produced a dramatic bolt. Senator Teller, who had offered a substitute resolution calling for free silver, left the convention after its defeat. Accompanied by a handful of delegates, the proud Coloradoan led his band of Western silverites out of the convention hall amidst boos and jeers. Mark Hanna, a former bimetallist who had given in to the party's gold supporters in order to win the nomination for his candidate, William McKinley, looked with contempt upon the scene. When Senator Frank Cannon of Utah delivered the valedictory for the departing silverites, Hanna's gruff voice could be heard above the others shouting "Go! Go!" In the convention hall observing the departure sat the elated Herman E. Taubeneck, national chairman of the People's party, while in the reporters' section, walking across desk-tops to get a better view, was the outspoken silverite from Nebraska, William Jennings Bryan. [23] The first episode in the bitter Battle of the Standards was over.

Teller became an instantaneous hero among silverites because of his bolt. Populist leaders, who had scheduled their convention last in a move to gather all dissident silverites under their umbrella, gave serious consideration to Teller as their presidential standard-bearer. Westerners admired him, while Southern Populists, engaged in a struggle with Democrats for control of local politics, would probably find it easier to live with a Republican bolter than with some pro-silver Democrat. Taubeneck wrote Ignatius Donnelly, who had his own designs on the presidency, that the People's party should insist that the Democrats nominate Teller or run the risk of dividing the silver forces in the November election. [24]

In New Mexico, the Populist *San Juan Times* endorsed Teller four days before the national Democratic convention convened. In order to secure a "combination" of Democrats, Populists, and silver Republicans (the newspaper editorialized on July 3) it was necessary to gather around a man "whose peculiar qualifications adapt him to the essential differences of each party, in such a way as to bring [them] together on the main issue. Teller is the man who enjoys the necessary characteristics of patriotism, honesty, intensity of purpose." The inspiration for this recommendation for Teller was not solely Holt's. He had been replaced as chief editor by another person friendly to Populism, V.R.N. Greaves, who had returned to New Mexico from California sometime during the previous two years. [25] Holt, who was now assistant editor and manager of the *Times,* was probably a midroader in 1896, if his earlier editorial statements were truly indicative of his political views. Perhaps he had to defer to his superior in this strong editorial stand for Teller.

When the Democrats gathered in Chicago on July 7, "Silver Dick" Bland was the best known of the pro-silver Democratic candidates. But the debate of the Democrats over the money plank proved to be a heated one. It was evident from the start, however, that the odds on a free silver declaration were better than had been the case in Saint Louis. Bryan stole the convention from Teller, Bland, and other possible presidential contenders with his eloquent "Cross of Gold" speech. "You shall not press down upon the brow of labor this crown of thorns, you shall not crucify mankind upon a cross of gold." On the fifth ballot the delegates nominated the charismatic Bryan.

Populists throughout the country were apprehensive about the diametrically opposed positions taken by the two major parties on silver. Should they support Bryan and risk destroying the party, or should they nominate one of their own leaders and possibly contribute to a McKinley victory by dividing silver supporters? Stamm, who favored fusion with Democrats at home, probably wanted his national party to back Bryan and the Democrats. The Democratic platform, although it did not support all Populist reforms, advocated several important ones. In addition to free silver, there were planks calling for a graduated income tax and stricter federal control of the nation's railroads. The platform also denounced "government by injunction" and condemned Cleveland's intervention in the Pullman strike. [26] The president's action in that strike had been unpopular with many New Mexico Populists.

When the Populists convened for their national convention in Saint Louis in late July, the confusion was obvious. The election of temporary chairman became a test of strength between the fusionists, who favored Bryan, and the middle-of-the-roaders, who feared that a Bryan endorsement or nomination would spell an end to the party. The selection of Senator Marion Butler was regarded as a compromise. The young North Carolinian sympathized with the Southern viewpoint that the People's organization must at all costs be maintained as a separate party; at the same time, he favored Bryan's nomination over mere endorsement.

A platform, described by John Hicks as "long and typically Populistic," was adopted. Then, contrary to the wishes of the convention managers, the divided delegates decided on an unusual reversal in the order of party nominations: they took up the vice-presidential nomination first. They selected Tom Watson of Georgia instead of the official Democratic choice, Maine banker and shipbuilder Arthur M. Sewall. The delegates then nominated Bryan as their presidential candidate. [27]

The final episode in the selection of candidates for the election of 1896 occurred in early September at Indianapolis where angry Gold Democrats met. President Cleveland, disowned by most Democrats, was offered the presidential nomination by these bolters. His refusal caused the pro-gold *Albuquerque Daily Citizen* to headline a story: "The Stuffed Prophet of Reform Knows When He Has Enough." [28] William B. Childers, an influential Democrat and Albuquerque attorney, left his party for good when he attended the Indianapolis convention with J.W. Schofield to represent the goldites of the territory. [29] The Republican *Daily Citizen* noted that Idaho, Nevada, Utah, and Wyoming had no representatives at the convention and silver-rich Colorado had a "solid delegation of one." [30] It obviously sympathized with the Democratic bolters, however, calling them "real democrats" or "sound money democrats." [31] The Gold Democrats nominated two native Kentuckians to represent them, Senator John M. Palmer of Illinois for president and former Confederate General Simon Bolivar Buckner for vice president. [32] The *Daily Citizen,* sensing a serious split in the Democratic party, hopefully endorsed the *New York Herald's* estimate that the Palmer-Buckner slate would win 960,000 votes. [33]

Local politicians were perplexed by the actions taken in their national conventions. Equivocation was no longer possible. On the other hand, the fact that the battle lines were at last drawn appealed to those who felt strongly one way or the other about free silver. New Mexico Populists accepted Bryan's nomination without any great reservations. As for Bryan's two running mates, Watson and Sewall, New Mexicans did not have to be concerned. As a territory, New Mexico was not entitled to choose presidential or vice-presidential electors. The Battle of the Standards in the Territory of New Mexico would by constitutional arrangement revolve around the upcoming race for territorial delegate.

New Mexico Populists decided to schedule their territorial convention first — unlike their parent organization which, except for the Gold Democrats, had met last. The national strategy of the Populists — to welcome all unhappy silverites to their party after their national conventions — had failed because of the decisive Bryan victory at Chicago. Territorial Populists, aware of the silver sentiments of their Democratic counterparts, were not going to make the same mistake. Determined to be the first to take a firm hold of the silver issue, the party scheduled its convention for September 23 in Las Vegas. [34]

Some arrangement for fusion among the silverites in the territory appeared inevitable. The example of the national Populist organization and the local realities dictated such a move by territorial Populists. The strength of the midroaders in the New Mexico party had never been great. A unilateral bid for power with Mills as the candidate for delegate appeared unlikely, because of his poor showing in the 1894 election. As a matter of fact, Mills was supporting the unannounced candidacy of Republican Bradford Prince. The Populist leader, obviously placing the silver issue above all others, had decided to overlook Prince's known conservatism. He was working in the southern part of the territory to win for Prince a majority of the delegates to the Las Vegas convention. He obtained the consent of Populists in Sierra County to allow a Prince supporter by the name of J.D. Wagner to cast all the proxies of the county organization for the ex-governor. He made a similar arrangement with the Grant Populists, even though the man chosen to cast the Grant poxies was, like Wagner, no longer a county resident. Mills was also in close contact with prominent Populists in San Juan County, the only county he had carried in 1894. [35]

The other likely candidate for Populist support in 1896 was Democrat Harvey Fergusson. His selection would be more in harmony with Populist strategy elsewhere. A silverite, but also a reformer, Fergusson had the backing of Stamm, who was both the chairman of the Populist territorial committee and New Mexico's national committeeman. Stamm not only had to fight Prince's nomination but had to prevent a number of the party's bimetallists from migrating to the pro-silver Democratic party. Such defection in fact occurred at Albuquerque in mid-September: those who had met to select Bernalillo County's delegates to the Populist territorial convention resolved to disband the county party and join the silver Democrats. [36] Stamm was furious. He called another meeting at his store, where, following his "spirited" speech to the delegates, a complete slate was chosen to attend the Las Vegas gathering. Among them were Stamm and nine others, including Joseph T. Johnson, who chaired the meeting. "No instructions were given to the local delegates," the *Albuquerque Daily Citizen* reported, "leaving them at liberty to vote for either Col. T.B. Mills, M.P. Stamm, or any other gentleman who might be sprung upon the convention for [the] delegate honor." [37] The omission of the names of Fergusson or Prince by the "goldite" Albuquerque paper was probably intentional, as a fusion of territorial silver forces in any combination was a threat to Republican regulars.

127

By now the free coinage issue was sweeping the territory like a brush fire. Even before their territorial convention, Populists talked of joining with other silverites to win in November and show the nation where New Mexico stood on the coinage question. Despite Mills' manipulations in Sierra County in behalf of Prince, many Populists in that county spoke of fusing with silver Democrats on the local level, in order to put like-minded people into office. [38] One of the few exceptions to this all-for-silver approach was found in San Juan County. There pragmatic Democrats and Republicans discussed a possible combined county ticket to defeat the successful Populists. [39] But even in "San Juan of the Populists," it was conceded that most pro-silver Populists and Democrats would support the Democratic nominee for delegate or a Populist, if the midroaders were to prevail at Las Vegas.

The delegate's race in 1896 seemed more important than in 1894. The Democratic *Santa Fe New Mexican* was one of the newspapers taking the Populists more seriously. Acknowledging Mills' small vote in 1894, it asserted that the vote was so evenly distributed that year, and the strength of the two "principal parties" so equally divided, that the Populists in 1896 would probably hold the "balance of power in no less than nine counties, or just half the whole number." The Populist boast that they would double their vote in November was not discounted either. [40] The Republican *Daily Citizen* of Albuquerque also was concerned, particularly as rumors of fusion between Populists and Democrats became more numerous. "The populist who says he is satisifed with the kind of fusion he is getting would say anything," the *Daily Citizen* insisted in an effort to discourage Populists from fusing with Democrats. [41] Although Populist stock was on the rise throughout New Mexico, ridicule still found favor among hostile territorial newspapers. The *Citizen* continued to poke fun at the advocates of Populism. Alluding to the opening day of the Populist convention, September 24, it warned the Populists that on that day "several men will be hanged in Las Vegas, and it would not be good politics to mix the two attractions." [42]

Two strategies began to emerge as the time neared for the nominating conventions. Fergusson and his supporters launched a campaign to win both the Populist and Democratic designations for delegate. Simultaneously, Prince and his backers were working among sympathetic Populists and silver Republicans to win endorsements from the parties they represented. In Fergusson's case, as a reformer and solid favorite his prospects were bright.[43] Prince's chances for both nominations largely hinged upon whether Catron would decline a second term or whether he could be defeated by Prince at the Republican nominating convention scheduled for Las Vegas three days after the Populist convention.

Prince, using his national reputation as a silver advocate, had probably begun seeking Populist support as early as July. Undoubtedly he had communicated with Mills before that persuasive Populist traveled to the southern part of the territory in search of proxies for him. Another important contact was Arthur Boyle. A most unlikely candidate for a reform movement, Boyle, an Englishman by birth, was the son-in-law of William Blackmore, the Liverpool and London solicitor who had once speculated in New Mexican land grants on a grade scale. [44] Himself an agent for land companies and speculators, Boyle had been a remittance man and a former Republican. [45] His background as a railroad director and land developer, and as a former business associate of Catron, [46] symbolized all that New Mexico reformers had been fighting against since the late eighties. Although he had been involved in some public-spirited endeavors, such as donating five hundred dollars to Santa Fe's Tertio-Millennial Celebration of 1883, [47] Boyle's career was hardly characteristic of a professed Populist. Prince and Mills may have been men of property, but this newcomer from Santa Fe was almost the quintessence of the maligned New Mexico land-grabber.

Prince also was corresponding with silverites from his own party in an effort to take the nomination from the favored Catron. William H.H. Llewellyn, who later became one of Theodore Roosevelt's Rough Riders, wrote from Sierra County on August 15 that dissatisfaction with Catron among silver Republicans was substantial. Insisting that Catron's defeat was certain if he were renominated, Llewellyn wrote of the desire among his associates in the southern part of the territory to have a candidate ''not in opposition to anyone but a candidate open and above board that the opposition to Catron can have a common center of attraction.'' You are that candidate, he informed Prince. ''We all agree that we shall send delegates to the Convention for you.'' Llewellyn informed the ex-governor in the same letter that he had been in contact with Prince's old friend, T.D. Burns of Chama, urging him to secure delegates from such northern counties as Rio Arriba, Taos, San Juan, and perhaps Mora. Hoping to bolster Prince's confidence, Llewellyn maintained that Sierra and Grant counties would probably send Prince delegates to the Republican convention at Las Vegas when it convened on September 26. [48]

Prince's most militant ally, however, was his wife, the indomitable ''Governor Mary.'' In her efforts to help her husband, Mrs. Prince cornered one of Catron's closest allies, Max Frost. The embarrassed Frost was urged to support Prince and was asked to communicate on her husband's behalf with Edward L. Bartlett, a Santa Fe delegate whom Prince had appointed as solicitor general when he was governor. When Mrs. Prince later discovered that Catron had found out about her conversation with Frost, she was furious, accusing Frost of breaking a confidence. The ordinarily smooth Frost

129

responded with a letter which was both an apology and a denial. He insisted that he did not tell Catron or even the employees in his own law office about their conversation, and suggested that Mrs. Prince or her husband accompany him to ask Catron himself for verification. [49] The strategy of this aggressive lady had been most unwise. A confidant of Prince wrote him a week later warning him not to trust Frost or Bartlett. They are "your untiring enemies!" [50]

Reports reaching Prince from around the territory gave a mixed picture of his prospects. He was informed that he had a number of "old friends" on the Mora delegation to the Republican nominating convention. [51] A vigorous effort was being made in San Miguel County to elect a silver delegation that would back Prince. There was also a campaign in the county to win adoption of a resolution in support of the 1894 pro-silver Republican platform which Prince had helped to prepare. [52] A cheerful note from Socorro County told of the election of a full slate of silverites pledged to back him at Las Vegas. [53] Two weeks earlier, Rio Arriba Republicans, no doubt influenced by Prince's friend, Burns, elected a friendly delegation. [54] The action followed a declaration made on July 19 in a meeting in Rio Arriba chaired by Prince. Territorial Republicans, according to the declaration, should defy their national party by favoring free coinage, but should continue supporting the high Republican tariff, particularly as it applied to wool and lumber. [55]

Not all of the ex-governor's political correspondence was encouraging, however. In Grant County, where he expected support because of the plight of the silver industry, the picture was confused. A Prince backer wrote that of the four delegates elected to the territorial convention two were for Prince and one was for Catron. The fourth, C.M. Foraker, brother of former Ohio Governor Joseph B. Foraker, was uncommitted. They were, however, "all silver men" and would work for a strong silver resolution. [56] A letter from a supporter in Grant County to Catron interpreted the situation quite differently: Foraker was in Catron's camp, as were two other members of the delegation; only one delegate, Don H. Kedzie, might "be friendly to Prince." [57] On September 23, the *Albuquerque Daily Citizen* corroborated the latter evaluation, reporting that the "free coinage advocates" had failed to carry the Grant County Republican convention.

The prospects in Bernalillo County were even more bleak for Prince and his supporters. Pedro Perea and Solomon Luna, two powerful native leaders, favored Catron. It was also reported that the platform adopted by Republicans at Saint Louis would be "endorsed without reservation." One discouraged Prince supporter from the county predicted that Catron would be renominated, despite his "miserable record." In that event, Fergusson will

130

probably be elected, and " those of us who have property in Santa Fe will be ruined." [58] Bernard S. Rodey, a silverite from Albuquerque, wrote that the "Perea goldites" were opposing him. They had already managed to keep him and another Prince backer, Frank W. Clancy, off the delegation to the territorial convention. [59] But the victory of the gold forces in Bernalillo was not achieved without a cost. One Republican leader, Joseph E. Saint, described as a "very violent free silver man," bolted the party to campaign for the Democrats. [60]

But the most gloomy assessment of Prince's chances was the one offered by Frost, who obviously wanted to discourage the former governor. Writing to Prince on September 17, he predicted that the delegations to be selected shortly in Santa Fe, Mora, Taos, and Guadalupe counties would be pledged to Catron. Bernalillo had already elected representatives instructed to vote for Catron, while in Chaves County Republicans had chosen a delegation pledged to support the Saint Louis platform, an action Eddy and Lincoln Republicans were expected to take. Frost's assessments were apparently offered in good faith. With the exception of Socorro, which supported Prince, they proved to be accurate. Alarmed that there might be open strife at the Las Vegas convention over the silver question, Frost hoped to influence the only man who could stem the divisiveness — Prince. "I think this matter [silver coinage] should be settled in the committee on resolutions or in caucus," he suggested to the silver leader, "and should not be agitated openly after the caucus has decided."

The open secret that Prince was seeking both the Populist and Republican nominations was causing concern in the territory. The Republican *Albuquerque Daily Citizen* tried to dissuade the silver leader from pursuing this strategy. "There is yet time for Governor Prince to get inside the republican breastworks," it insisted on September 7. Four days later it dealt with an alarming rumor. "The democratic papers now claim ex-Governor Prince. No doubt this claim is similar to many others made — false in every respect." But by late September Prince's quiet Populist candidacy could no longer be discounted. "Governor Prince wrote the republican platform at Socorro two years ago. He may not do so next Saturday at Las Vegas." [61]

When the Populists met at Las Vegas, three days before the Republican convention there, tension was higher than it had been in 1894. Prince delegates, some of whom were recent converts to Populism, mingled with silver Republicans in the lobby working among the delegates for Prince's nomination. Their major argument was a persuasive one. Prince was already assured of the support of "six or seven republican delegations," [62] they insisted. If he won the Populist nomination, his selection by the Republican party would be guaranteed. All silverites would then be united behind their most prominent spokesman.

Active in this effort to stampede the Populist convention for Prince was the tireless T.B. Mills. The basis of representation for the convention was five delegates-at-large for each county and an additional delegate for every fifty votes "or fraction thereof" cast for Mills in 1894. Moreover, each county was entitled to cast its "full vote through one or more of its delegates present." [63] Mills, as a result of his trip through the south, had arranged to have one of his allies cast all the votes of Grant County. But a similar arrangement with Sierra County was in jeopardy because Wagner, Mills' ally in that county, was leaning toward Fergusson and the silver Democrats. [64] The most important Fergusson supporter at the convention, however, was Stamm. He held ten proxies for the Lincoln County Populists. The great distances to be traveled in the territory, and the low economic status of most Populists, tended to discourage attendance at the convention, but these factors were at the same time giving certain key figures enormous influence. Stamm, despite his preference for Fergusson, had no objection to a "straight 'middle-of-the-road' man," but he was determined to stop Prince's nomination at all costs.

The first order of convention business was to determine the legality of numerous proxies held by certain delegates, and the committee on credentials met for this purpose immediately following Chairman Stamm's 10 a.m. call to order. Shortly before the noon recess, Mills, probably representing his old home county of San Miguel, appeared before the credentials committee. He stated that a delegate from one of the northern counties was expected to arrive soon and asked the committee to accept the credentials of the latecomer when he arrived, which the committee readily agreed to do. When the delegates assembled that afternoon, the committee submitted its report. Before it could be acted upon Mills arose to read an August 31 letter from a San Juan Populist. The writer asserted that, not wishing to see the People's party "snuffed out" in his county, he would send Mills the San Juan proxies for him to cast, if no county representative could attend. Presumably the latecomer alluded to by Mills in the morning was from San Juan. As he had failed to arrive, Mills wanted permission to cast all the proxy votes from San Juan County.

Mills' request caused a furor. San Juan probably had the best Populist organization in the territory. It was the only county which supported Mills in 1894. It seemed most presumptuous for one man to assume he could represent the wishes of an entire county organization. Besides, as Stamm observed, the correspondent from San Juan was not the county chairman, nor could it be

132

ascertained whether he was even a county officer. The credentials committee refused Mills' request, but the convention body, probably responding to aggressive pressure from Prince's supporters, overruled the committee. Mills was thus given a major voice in the convention's deliberations.

Four men were nominated for the office of territorial delegate: Fergusson and Prince, the two frontrunners, and two hopefuls named Hadley and Robinson. During the seconding speeches for Prince, Arthur Boyle told the delegates that, if they nominated the former governor, the gold-bug Democrats would not put a candidate into the race but would support Prince instead. Such information was hardly "soothing to a genuine populist," observed Stamm. [65] On the first ballot Prince moved into the lead, polling 33 votes to Fergusson's 24 with Hadley and Robinson gaining ten apiece. As 39 votes were needed to win, Prince was only six votes shy. On the second ballot Prince slipped, losing ten votes to Hadley. Fergusson's and Robinson's strength remained the same. On the third ballot, however, Prince was victorious. Hadley withdrew, apparently urging his twenty backers to support the silver Republican. Prince's total was 43 votes, four more than necessary for his nomination. [66] Hadley was probably a stalking horse for the Prince forces. He may have been Walter Hadley, a Las Cruces Republican from the territory's troubled silver country and a member of the Territorial Council, although evidence could not be found to prove this. [67]

With Prince delegates in control the convention approved a typically tough Populist platform. Then, following the example of the Populist national convention, they declared for Bryan and Watson. Aware of their candidate's conservatism on matters other than silver, the delegates also took an extraordinary action. They passed a resolution stating that the silver Republican had been nominated without his solicitation and that he was not expected to endorse every plank in the platform. Thus, Prince was free "to follow his own convictions for the good of the territory." [68] Silverism had totally triumphed with the selection of Bradford Prince.

The platform adopted by the New Mexico Populists reveals the incongruous nature of the convention's action. Many of the so-called radical planks of 1894 were repeated, while other reform proposals were added. The delegates endorsed such reforms (most of which were in the 1896 national platform) as the free and unlimited coinage of silver and gold at the 16 to 1 ratio; a graduated income tax; a postal savings bank; government ownership of railroads and telegraphs; the election of the president, vice president, and senators of the United States by direct vote; the initiative and referendum; and the granting of liberal pensions to veterans. [69] They demanded that arid lands be granted to the territories in which they are located, and that there be an increase in the volume of money in circulation "commensurate" with the growth of the country's population. They also condemned any increase in the public interest-bearing debt and any military intervention in civil affairs during time of peace. Both of these proposals had appeared in the 1894 platform. The party's pro-labor bias was again reflected; the amending of immigrations laws to "exclude paupers and criminals," an old labor crusade, was advocated along with creation of a labor tribunal to adjust differences between employers and employees. In addition, public works projects for employment of the jobless were endorsed to cope with the lingering effects of the panic. [70]

To soften the disappointment of some Populists over Prince's selection, two planks were added. In them the nomination of Prince was justified as a way of harmonizing Jeffersonian Democracy with "unadulterated Lincoln Republicanism." The Republican party "in its infancy believed as the Populists do today," but it had since fallen under the control of monopolists. It now had but one aim, office, and one principle, gold. Directing their wrath at Prince's Republican rival, Catron, the delegates attacked the large territorial land grants held by private individuals, forgetting Prince's old association with the Santa Fe Ring and Mills' interest in land speculation. "Bona fide settlers on all public lands [should] be granted free homes, and that includes land grants." [71] Congress should pass laws so that honest mining claims on land grants can be "perfected," the platform insisted. Monopoly of and speculation in land should be forbidden, as land is the "common property of the people"; therefore, all "unearned grants of land" should be subject to forfeiture and be reclaimed by the government, and no portion of the public domain should be "hereafter granted except to actual settlers, continuous use being essential to tenure." But the strong position taken against land-grabbers in the platform was not extended to alien land-holders. This omission undoubtedly reflected the concern of many New Mexicans that prohibitions against alien landownership had slowed economic growth in the territory. [72]

Another concession to local sentiment involved the tariff question. A "sufficient and economically adjusted" tariff in the form of a specific tax, particularly on wool, hides, and sugar, was advocated. The existing tariff was denounced. Also catering to local concerns were planks calling for immediate statehood, elimination of the poll tax, preservation of local self-government, economy in government, and an end to the casual issuance of county and territorial warrants, which had been the cause of so many scandals in New Mexico. Symbolic of the nation's future course was a resolution in which the delegates, obviously representing local sentiment, expressed their sympathy for the Cuban people in their struggle against the Spanish. [73]

If the platform adopted by the convention was intended to placate the more orthodox Populists or potential midroaders it did not succeed. Stamm bolted the convention taking his supporters with him. He announced that, as territorial chairman and national committeeman, he would appeal Prince's nomination to Senator Marion Butler, who had succeeded Taubeneck as national chairman. Denouncing the ''funny'' politics in evidence at Las Vegas, Stamm insisted that Prince's designation, notwithstanding his position on silver, was an abandonment of party principles to ''the only enemy we have[,] the republican party.'' [74] Stamm's action, however, was futile in the face of such growing sentiment for free coinage. By 1896, silver had effectively forced all other issues out of the limelight in New Mexico. The Republican *Daily Citizen* of Albuquerque reported that, prior to Stamm's bolt, Thomas Keleher said he would ''rise up and endorse Prince'' if his old political ally in Bernalillo made good his threat to leave the convention. [75] The journal predicted even more trouble for the quarreling Populists. ''When Chairman Stamm hears from Boss Butler he may make certain populists in this territory quake in their knee joints.'' [76]

Democrats, disappointed that the Populists did not fuse with them, were also critical over Prince's designation. They resorted to sarcasm. ''It was very kind of the Pops to leave the bars down for Gov. Prince, so that he would not be expected to endorse 'every plank' in their platform.'' [77] Attempting to minimize the effects of the Populist decision, the *Santa Fe New Mexican* insisted that the ''cunning'' strategy would in ''no wise embarrass the Democrats this year.'' Rather the nomination of Bradford Prince would ''force a hot fight in Republican ranks.'' [78] But the Santa Fe paper had to acknowledge the shrewdness in the Populist strategy. The Populists have evidently gone into this campaign with a determination to make their votes count as against the methods pursued two years ago.'' [79]

In the short respite between the Populist and Republican conventions in Las Vegas, Prince received advice as to his future course. Some of it urged him to take the ''unsolicited'' Populist nomination regardless of what happened at the Republican meeting. F.A. Blake, still calling himself a Populist after his support of Tom Catron in 1894, wrote Prince on September 24, apologizing for having missed the Populist convention by one day. He begged Prince to take the nomination offered by the People's party. Your designation was

> very satisfactory to me and will be to many others among the rank and file of voters if you accept the nomination without refferance [sic] to what other political parties may do and go into the field as a candidate on the strength of this nomination. Wheather [sic] you are elected or not a political force would become organized and christalized [sic] that would soon become a powerful factor in shaping public affairs in the true interests of the great mass of the people of the territory. [80]

135

As the Republican convention approached there were indications of danger for the confident Prince forces. An avid Prince supporter, R.L. Baca, wrote him on September 25 that Bernalillo Republican Pedro Perea planned to confront Prince at the convention and demand that he tell the delegates whether he was a Populist or a Republican. Supporters of Catron had already convinced Baca that the incumbent delegate would be nominated on the first ballot and that Prince would have to "take [his] medicine." The efforts of Bartlett and Frost to become chairman and secretary, respectively, of the territorial central committee were also reported by Baca. He felt that the unprincipled nature of Prince's foes was proven when they tried to convince the Taos delegation that Catron was a loyal silverite as well as a protectionist.

Prince supporters, however, had already drawn "first blood" by winning the Populist nomination. Also, according to a telegram printed in the Albuquerque *Democrat,* the silver and gold forces at the Republican convention would be "evenly divided," giving Prince a good chance for a second nomination. [81] Catron, still unaware that the silver question had even submerged his pet issue, the high tariff, continued to hedge on free coinage. Boasting of his substitute for free silver — unlimited coinage of the American silver product and a prohibitive tariff on imported foreign silver bullion — Catron attempted to convince his followers that, because of the country's favorable balance of trade (averaging nearly fifty million a year) the silver sent to Europe for the purchase of goods would be returned with an "additional amount of fifty millions more, in order to purchase our staples." By this method the United States could take care of all its silver, especially if it "could abolish all currency under ten dollars except silver." [82] In the platform being prepared for Catron by Judge John R. McFie and Ralph E. Twitchell the candidate's proposed tariff on foreign silver was given strong backing. It was pointed out, for instance, that the government of Mexico was charging four cents for each silver dollar coined while the United States was doing it free of charge for Mexican silver owners. [83]

Most of the Republican delegates to the convention, however, were quite aware of the pressure being generated by the silver issue. They had moved ahead of Catron's qualified position on the free coinage of the American silver product. One report claimed that of the ninety-three delegates only fourteen were "outspoken" for Catron. Feeling he could not be re-elected, many of them filed into Catron's headquarters, "three out of four" urging him to withdraw because his prospects for victory in November were so poor. Catron responded with characteristic obstinance. "Some he cursed; others he threatened; others he cajoled. They all squirmed, and retired, promising to behave as best they could, 'under the circumstances.' " [84]

Whether or not the report of restiveness among Catron backers was correct, a majority of the delegates were party regulars who took their pre-convention pledges seriously. A test of strength occurred at the first session of the convention on Saturday, September 26, on the matter of electing a temporary chairman. Catron and the ''goldites'' backed Bartlett for the position. The Catron candidate thus had the support of the ''solid gold delegations'' from Bernalillo, Valencia, and San Miguel, and the pro-gold delegates from other counties. The balloting was close, but a majority of the ninety-three delegates voted for Bartlett. The decision left some forty zealous silver delegates disappointed and angry, a few even talking about a bolt. Catron's backers than installed Colonel J. Francisco Chaves as permanent chairman, while Prince delegates sat quietly in the hall looking ''glum.'' The fight for silver coinage, without any qualifications, was made, however, despite the two setbacks. W.E. ''Billy'' Martin and his fellow delegates from Socorro aggressively carried the battle for a free coinage resolution, but the necessary support was not forthcoming. According to the *New Mexican,* the delegations from the silver counties of Grant and Sierra ''flunked'' the test. [85] In the end Catron was nominated by acclamation. [86]

Democrats assembled three days later at Santa Fe with Fergusson's nomination almost a foregone conclusion. The Albuquerque lawyer had firmly established himself as his party's spokesman for free coinage. At the May meeting in Las Vegas to select delegates to the Democratic national convention, it was Fergusson and Fall who had proved their devotion to silver by unsuccessfully opposing an endorsement of Cleveland's pro-gold administration. A companion proposal to endorse the president's silver-leaning appointee, Governor Thornton, was also fought by Fergusson and Fall, because of Thornton's insistance that Cleveland's presidential performance receive convention approval. [87] Ten days before the territorial nominating convention met, Fergusson gave an able response in Silver City to a speech by Childers attacking free coinage. [88] On September 24, the Democrats of Santa Fe County took an action regarded by many party members as symbolic of what would happen at their territorial meeting. Santa Fe County instructed all fifteen of its delegates to vote for Harvey Fergusson. [89]

When the Democrats assembled on September 30, the veteran Antonio Joseph was there, but not as a candidate: the five-term former delegate was to preside over the convention. He unified the delegates with ''one of the most powerful and timely speeches of his life.'' Praising William Jennings Bryan, who he asserted had given him a ''personal pledge'' to support statehood, Joseph called for the free and unlimited coinage of silver ''without waiting for the consent of any other nation.'' He scored ''Catronism'' and the actions of ''Thomas Borrego Catron.'' The convention responded with a strong plank in favor of bimetallism and the unanimous selection of Fergusson. [90]

As a result of the activities of the territorial conventions, there were three candidates for delegate from whom voters could choose, Catron, Fergusson and Prince. But Prince, a conservative Republican on everything but silver, was plainly troubled by the conflicting advice he was receiving. Most Republicans urged him to decline the Populist nomination. Llewellyn, however, asked the ex-governor to remain on the People's ticket until he could consult his friends to see if they felt he should stay and make a "fight to the finish." [91] The *Albuquerque Daily Citizen,* frankly worried, was doubtful as to Prince's course. "It is supposed that Governor Prince is laboriously working on his letter of acceptance of the populist nomination for delegate to congress." [92] But the Republican journal was still hopeful that Prince's old loyalties would prevail. It rejected, for instance, an assertion made by a Denver newspaper that Prince was no more of a Republican than Senator Teller. "This is not so. Governor Prince has not bolted his party as did Mr. Teller." [93]

Prince had another problem. His failure to leave the Republican party after it endorsed the Catron substitute for free coinage was being severely criticized by silverites. An editorial in the Las Vegas *Examiner* upbraided him for remaining with his party after it had rejected him and his stand on free coinage. "Ex-Governor Prince can make himself famous and give himself a national reputation by embracing the example of Senator Teller." The Las Vegas paper urged Populist leaders to fuse with the Democrats in the territory, as the Democratic party was no longer the party of Grover Cleveland. Bryan and the silver Democrats, it insisted, had made the party worthy of Populist support. [94]

A week passed following Catron's nomination and Prince still had not publicly clarified his position. The decision, however, was not to be his. Prince received a letter from Santa Fe dated October 5 indicating that certain Populist leaders were talking about dropping him from the ticket. The leader in the effort was Elwyn T. Webber, owner of the Claire Hotel in Santa Fe and part owner of the Lincoln Lucky Gold and Silver Mine at San Pedro. [95] Webber, an enthusiastic bimetallist, had conferred at length in his hotel with Fergusson, who had arrived in Santa Fe on October 5. After conversations with other Populists, Webber apparently decided not to send Prince a formal notification of his nomination. It was feared that if Prince should decline, the territorial Populists would consider themselves spurned as a party. The Populist leaders decided instead to replace Prince with Fergusson as the new fusion candidate. A meeting was scheduled in Las Vegas by the party's territorial central committee to make the change. [96]

Prince's informant proved reliable, for on October 6 Webber and Boyle arrived with Fergusson for an afternoon meeting of the central committee.

Mills was present, along with another Las Vegan, Dr. Milligan. Other committee members in attendance were Wagner, the former Mills lieutenant from Sierra County; an Hispano named Herrera (it cannot be determined whether he was Juan Jose Herrera), and a Professor Giltner. The group passed three resolutions: one annulled that action of the territorial convention calling for the appointment of a special committee to notify Prince of his nomination; the second removed the silver Republican as the party's nominee, and the third designated Fergusson as the party's new candidate for delegate. [97]

An official manifesto justifying the committee's action was published three days later by the *Santa Fe New Mexican.* The removal of Prince was defended on the grounds that although the former governor was ''sound'' on money and had carried the free silver message to ''nearly every state in the Union,'' he had failed to leave his party after it had adopted the Catron substitute for free coinage. The Populists, the manifesto continued, had every reason to believe Prince when he stated to their convention that, if his views ''were not adopted in convention by his own party, he would follow the example of Senator Teller, by placing principle above party, and severing his connections with same, and placing himself at the head of the silver element of the territory.'' But Prince, as a delegate to his party's convention, had failed to condemn that body's endorsement of ''the gold standard.'' Therefore, Fergusson, who was in ''full sympathy with the principles of the People's party,'' ought to receive the nomination. Hoping for maximum Populist participation in the new strategy, the manifesto's framers expressed their belief that the new fusion effort with the Democrats should be extended to other elective races and be along ''equitable lines, in legislative and county affairs.'' [98]

Prince, obviously embarrassed over the whole affair, responded to the Populist manifesto in the same (October 9) issue of the *New Mexican* which carried it. Striving to sound magnanimous and hoping to minimize the importance of his removal, Prince insisted that no discourtesy was intended toward him at the hastily called Populist meeting. Rather, the Populist central committee ''simply took a short cut so as to put Fergusson, who was present, on their ticket without delay.'' The former governor maintained that it had been his purpose all along to decline the nomination; he had merely been awaiting his notification to formally, but reluctantly, refuse. The Populist central committee knew of his intention in late September, after the adjournment of the Republican convention. Prince told the committee members at that time that, although he was grateful for his selection, he could not be a member of one party and receive the nomination of another. When his formal notification failed to arrive after a week, Prince, according to his own testimony, communicated with a committee member on October 1, prior to leaving town on business, to inquire about the delay. He was shown two letters, obviously from prominent Populists, both of which urged him to make the race. An offer to raise generous campaign funds for him was included in one of them. The silverite also insisted that he wrote Mills on the same day, again giving his irrevocable decision to decline the Populist noimnation. Consequently, when Mills read Prince's letter at that October 6 meeting of the Populist central committee, there should have been no doubt about the ex-governor's future intentions. Knowing he would not be their candidate, Prince continued, the pragmatic Populists decided to remove him on the spot and replace him with Fergusson. "Out here people do not always stand on strict formality when it is in the way of practical result."

Despite the generous tone of Prince's published response, he was a man who placed great store on his dignity. He must have been humiliated by the unceremonious way in which he was removed from the Populist ticket. It is doubtful that the conservative, lifelong Republican would have left his party to join such a controversial body as the People's party, notwithstanding their common devotion to silver. Actually it was Prince's intention to win both the Populist and Republican nominations and, with the support of both parties, be elected as the territory's voice for silver in Washington. Personal ambition also motivated the former governor; he had been an unsuccessful candidate for delegate in 1884. [99] Prince, however, wanted the honor of rejecting the nomination for himself, which explains the strained tone of his effort to minimize the action of the Populist central committee. Now the unhappy silverite had lost the Republican nomination and had been removed as the Populist nominee in a unilateral action by the lowly People's party.

The press did not make Prince's discomfort any easier. Silverites expected the spurned leader to do what was best for silver, regardless. On the day he was replaced by Fergusson, the *Santa Fe Daily New Mexican* added to his embarrassment by giving him an unsolicited vote of confidence. Perhaps knowing through Fergusson that Prince was about to be removed, the Democratic journal was saying in effect that Prince was a true silverite "at heart" and would do nothing to jeopardize the cause of free coinage. The territory's most zealous bimetallist "knows just where he is 'at,' and when the time comes — it may be tomorrow — he will do the right thing." [100] The *San Juan Times,* although no longer a "radical" Populist journal expected even more of him. "If ex-governor Prince wishes to be consistent and to place himself on record as a patriot, he will not only support H.B. Fergusson, for delegate to congress, but he will get out of the territory, if possible, and work for the success of William Jennings Bryan. This is no time for an advocate of bimetallism and a professional champion of the people to remain silent." [101]

Despite all the confusion in the quest of silverites for an acceptable fusion candidate, it looked as though there would be just two candidates for delegate in the November race. But the Gold Democrats led by Childers, ignoring the hostile response to their cause in the territory, assembled in Albuquerque in mid-October for a party convention. They nominated a mining engineer, W.E. Dame of Cerrillos, speaker of the territorial House during the past session, as their candidate for delegate. The Democratic and Populist press unmercifully attacked this tiny band of goldites, only eleven in number, who felt so strongly about the issue that they nominated a single-standard man. Dame's attitude, as expressed in his defiant acceptance speech, did not help much either. ''I am a good enough American to have voted for Thomas B. Catron, rather than H.B. Fergusson, who is a greater anarchist than W.J. Bryan.'' The *New Mexican* was determined to discredit the new movement. It accused two of the Gold Democrats at the Albuquerque convention of having had their expenses paid by Republicans. Dame and two other convention delegates had also shown their corruptibility by accepting free railroad passes. [102] The *San Juan Times,* on the other hand, saw some humor in the affair. ''It was a howling farce with W.B. Childers as the leading laugh provoker.'' [103]

The weeks prior to the November 3 election were feverish ones, Fergusson and Catron in the center of the campaign arena leaving Dame almost isolated from the public dialogue. Prince's future role was in doubt, although the pressure on him to be another Teller and bolt his party was severe. Fergusson enjoyed an important edge with his unequivocal silver stand, while Catron was compelled to promote his dubious substitute for free coinage. How the two major candidates would handle the silver question in the days to come would be crucial, such was the nature of what historians would later call the Western silver crusade.

141

10

"THE SILVER CRAZE"

The autumn days remaining in the campaign of 1896 were marked by an even greater emphasis on the importance of free coinage. Nervous New Mexico Republicans called the growing preoccupation with the money question the "silver craze" or the "free silver craze." Max Frost, discouraged with his candidate's prospects in the silver counties of southwestern New Mexico, quoted a Silver City resident as saying "Catron had better do all or most of his work in the Mexican counties as the mining counties cannot be changed because of the silver craze." [1] A member of the Republican central committee of San Juan County wrote Catron that farmers in the irrigated valleys of the county were "thoroughly imbued with the silver craze, and to a fanatical extent." [2] M.W. Mills, after the balloting on November 3 but before the final count was made, observed that the Anglo towns in the territory were against Catron for a number of reasons, but the major obstacle to his success was the "Silver craze," which was destroying his chances for another term. [3]

Although the silver issue probably had some bearing on every electoral contest in the territory, it was to have its most profound effect on the election for territorial delegate. R.E. Twitchell, who helped to frame the Republican platform with its controversial Catron substitute for free coinage, recognized the relevance of the silver question to the Catron-Fergusson race — that the attitude of the New Mexico voter toward free coinage would significantly influence his choice for delegate. Hoping to stem the intensity of the silver craze, the Las Vegas Republican, in an address "To the Wage-Earners of This Territory," warned that unlimited silver coinage would result in a spiraling inflation which would cut the wage earner's income in half. It was important, therefore, to elect a delegate such as Catron, who would oppose bimetallism without at least the minimal safeguard of an international agreement. "It is true that a vote for delegate does not signify a great deal in the politics of the nation," Twitchell admitted, "but the vote which you will cast in November will be taken by the nation at large as a sample of the vote which you would cast were you permitted a voice in the nation's councils." [4]

The importance of the silver craze was accentuated by the fusion movements occurring between many of the county Populist and Democratic parties. Even before Fergusson and the Populist central committee had agreed that their parties should fuse along ''equitable lines'' in county and legislative races, Populists and Democrats in Sierra County were already organizing for a joint campaign. On September 24 the Sierra Populists, in a meeting at Hillsboro presided over by J.D. Bone of the mining camp of Chloride, showed their independence by condemning those Populists who had supported Prince at the territorial convention. Stamm's bolt, which occurred the day before the group met, was enthusiastically endorsed.

Hewing closely to more orthodox Populist politics, the Sierra Populists referred to the common people as ''producers'' and labeled the current crisis as an inevitable result of the ''crime of 1873 — the demonetization of silver.'' The delegates at the Hillsboro gathering also resolved that, ''as our Democratic brothers are struggling with us for identical issues resulting equally well for all,'' the Populists of Sierra should join forces with the Democrats and put together a ticket that will ''satisfy all silver men no matter of what party affiliation.'' Bryan and his controversial running mate, Sewall, were endorsed without hestitation. The popular Nebraskan was lauded as a ''fearless knight.'' [5]

Sometime on that same day the Populists and Democrats of Sierra County met in joint convention and fused, calling themselves Silver Democrats. The Democratic rooster was adopted as their emblem. A slate of candidates was chosen with at least three seasoned Populist politicians on the ticket. Robert West, who ran as a Populist for county treasurer in 1894, was nominated for county commissioner of the second district. Julian Chavez, commissioner candidate two years earlier, was their choice for probate judge, while Andrew Kelley, a candidate for assessor in 1894, was again nominated for that position. [6]

In Santa Fe County the Populists apparently fielded their own candidates under the customary party label, but Fergusson was put at the head of the ticket and almost half of the candidates were known to be Democrats. Arthur Boyle was nominated for the Territorial Council to oppose Republican Charles A. Spiess, Catron's law partner, and another attorney, Democrat A.B. Renehan.[7] Catron lieutenant Edward L. Bartlett did not seem concerned about the combined ticket offered by the Santa Fe Populists. ''We think it will help us,'' he wrote Catron. [8] An equally disdainful attitude toward Populists was expressed by a Catron supporter in a letter assessing the delegate's prospects in Bernalillo County. Alluding to the nomination of a Populist named Carroll, the correspondent, S. E. Aldrich, a trader from Round Rock in the Navajo

Indian reservation, asserted that Carroll's selection would strengthen the Republican party and "hurt the whole Democratic Ticket, including Mr. Fergusson." [9]

But in some counties fusion was taken as a serious threat by Republicans. The *New Mexican* stated that "Catronists" in San Miguel had offered to give the Populists two spots on the Republican county ticket, if they would withdraw their support of Fergusson. [10] Frustrated because the People's party, which later reorganized as the Union party, had controlled county politics for six years, Republicans were determined to win in San Miguel. Their convention to elect delegates to the territorial gathering was described as the largest of its kind ever held in the county. But they incurred serious liabilities by their support of the McKinley and Hobart ticket and their endorsement of the pro-gold Saint Louis platform. [11] Consequently, the Populists refused the offer and joined with the Union and Democratic parties, and "silver advocates" of all parties, to field an impressive ticket. It included as candidates for the Territorial Council James S. Duncan, a Las Vegas banker and owner of the community's Opera House, and Placido (Patsy) Sandoval, a well-to-do farmer. [12] Because of the large representation of the county, Catron was concerned about the outcome. He contributed no less than a thousand dollars to the San Miguel campaign, much of it probably coming from his personal resources. [13]

In Union County, where Populists merged with Republicans in 1894 to support Catron, a complete reversal occurred. The People's party joined with the Democratic party in a fusion arrangement, in which all candidates were reportedly doing better financially than their Republican counterparts. "I do not think a couple of hundred dollars can be spent to better advantage than in Union," wrote Frost, urging Catron to find campaign funds somewhere for his supporters in Union County. [14] Even the Hispanos, with whom Catron had always been popular, were joining the Populist-Democratic alliance. The secretary of the party central committee in Union County stated that all the native inhabitants, except the families of the large Gallegos clan, were joining the coalition. "In some precincts fusion seems very popular and in others[,] because of his [Fergusson's] free trade views[,] it's the contrary." [15]

In "San Juan of the Populists" the county organization was still formidable, despite its failure to send delegates to Las Vegas for the party's territorial convention. In late September, the People's party nominated a full slate of candidates for county office. It later agreed, however, to fuse with the Democrats for the legislative contests and to support Fergusson in the delegate's race. An interesting feature of the straight ticket offered by the county Populists was that half of the candidates were Hispanos. If nativism existed among the San Juan Populists, they did not let it interfere with their pursuit of practical politics. [16] For the Territorial Council, the Populists endorsed the popular Democrat, Antonio Joseph, and William Locke, both of whom would represent the district incorporating San Juan and Rio Arriba counties if elected. For the House, Juan Jaquez and Felix Garcia, two candidates listed as Populists by the *San Juan Times,* received the support of the San Juan People's organization. [17]

The energetic county party in San Juan prompted the *San Juan Times,* no longer a Populist newspaper, to remark that the People's party was still a "vigorous and undiminished quantity in San Juan county." [18] The reasons for its continued success were effective organization and an electorate highly susceptible to agrarian Populism. Even so, silver, as elsewhere throughout the territory, was a commanding issue; much of the food produced in the county was marketed in the silver camps of southern Colorado. [19]

One advantage the San Juan Populists lacked in 1896 was the support of a partisan newspaperman such as Fred Holt. An experienced journalist, C. Ed Stivers, formerly of the Durango *Herald,* had bought control of the *San Juan Times* from Greaves, Holt's successor as editor. Although Stivers was once editor of the *New Mexico Nugget,* official Populist organ in 1894, and was a bimetallist and supporter of the 1896 Democratic platform, he proudly proclaimed his independence when he assumed control of the *Times* in mid-October. I am "'entirely free from political shackles locally,'" he editorialized on October 16. To prove his sincerity, he supported a silver Republican for the lower House, a Democrat for sheriff, and a Populist for county clerk. [20] The hostile attitude of the new editor toward any hard-line Populist doctrine was unmistakable. Commenting on that favorite of the party's midroaders, Tom Watson, the official choice of the People's party for vice president, Stivers was disdainful. "Let's see: Watson, Watson — who is Watson, anyway? There must be a man by that name – or was it a thing?"[21]

The shift of the *San Juan Times* from a journal concerned with a multitude of reforms to one concentrating on silver was symbolic of a political transformation occurring throughout the nation. The dominance of the free coinage issue in New Mexico in 1896 was dramatized by the forceful stands taken in behalf of bimetallism by territorial newspapers. The pro-silver *New Mexican* reported that the *Optic,* the Chloride *Black Range,* and the Las Cruces *Rio Grande Republican,* "all staunch, tried and true Republican newspapers in past years have repudiated Candidate Catron and his crowd." [22]

146

Although Catron had faults, this switch by Republican journals can only be explained by Catron's unwillingness to take a straightforward stand in favor of free coinage. The free and unlimited coinage of silver as a panacea for the social and economic ills of the day had captured the imagination of more voters than Catron realized. The *San Juan Times* opined that 45 of every 50 San Juan men were for free coinage, and that all silver supporters in the county would cast their ballots for Fergusson. [23] The Silver City *Eagle* insisted that more than eighty percent of the voters in the territory favored free silver, its only concern being that not all pro-silver citizens would support Fergusson, because of the misguided belief that the Republican party "will, eventually, in some way or the other come to the rescue of silver." [24]

One territorial journal that withstood the pressures unleashed by the silver craze was the *Albuquerque Daily Citizen.* Edited by Thomas Hughes, a veteran newspaperman, the *Citizen* continued to criticize the impatient proponents of free silver. Unlimited silver coinage would close every mine in New Mexico, it insisted, because silver miners in the United States could not compete with underpaid silver miners from Mexico. The miners of Leadville, Colorado, have refused to work for $2.50 a day in gold, even though Mexican miners were willing to accept only 50 cents a day in their own money. [25]

Hughes, who was also a candidate for the Territorial Council, admitted that the unlimited purchase of silver by the United States Treasury would raise the price, but with "no new demand for silver in Europe" its value would again decline. [26] Attacks on the coinage of the American silver product, Catron's substitute for free silver, were answered in kind. "The democrats give away their case when they assert that the free coinage of the American product of silver is not practical and cannot be kept at a parity with gold, as republicans insist must be done. If the American product cannot be kept at parity with gold, how do the unlimited coinage advocates expect to square their talk." [27] An offer by the pro-silver editor of the Denver *Republican* to purchase a million silver dollars at 90 cents apiece was ridiculed by Hughes, who pointed out that by law the government must redeem in gold all outstanding money, including silver dollars. If a policy calling for the free and unlimited coinage of silver were inaugurated, however, this same offer could not be made, for no one could afford to pay 90 cents for a 53-cent silver dollar. [28]

For its opposition to free coinage, the *Daily Citizen* was severely criticized. The *Las Vegas Daily Optic* accused the Albuquerque paper of betraying bimetallism and the people of silver-producing New Mexico. It, too, could have won the accolades of the Republican federal officeseekers of the territory by supporting the national party in 1896, the *Optic* declared, but it preferred to have the "honest support of the people at large than the applause of a few politicians.'' [29] The *Citizen* promptly responded by charging the *Optic* with ''political harlotry,'' asserting that the Las Vegas journal had a record of selling its support to the highest bidder — that in mid-September the *Optic* had offered to support Catron for $500 and when it did not succeed in ''bleeding the Republican nominee'' threw its support to Fergusson. [30] Russell Kistler, Republican editor of the Las Vegas daily, was known to be a man with a serious drinking problem and often in need of funds to keep his newspaper alive. He apparently had sold his support to the Democrats in 1880 and 1886. [31] Considering the importance of the silver issue in New Mexico, his conversion to Democratic politics in 1896 suggests reasons other than personal, however. But his endorsement of Fergusson in early October did mark a reversal of the stand he took in March, when he characterized anyone who would desert the Republican ranks in 1896 as an ''enemy to his party and the Territory.'' [32]

The impact of the silver craze was the indisputable major factor in the campaign of 1896, and territorial journalists besides Kistler were swept along by its force. Issues that had dominated past campaigns were subordinated, although not necessarily forgotten. Antimonopolism, which had absorbed the energies of Alliancemen in the late eighties and Populists in the early nineties, was almost obscured as an issue by the conflict between silver advocates and ''goldites.'' The *New Mexican* tried to revive the issue by reminding its readers that the greed of trusts had led to Harrison's ''overwhelming'' defeat in 1892, and yet in 1896 ''hundreds of trusts still oppress the American people.'' Candidate Bryan could be counted on to change this, the Santa Fe journal editorialized. [33]

The *San Juan Times,* about a month before the campaign began, pointed with alarm to the large number of railroads falling into the hands of European capitalists. Sixty percent of the stocks and bonds of the Pennsylvania Railroad were owned by Europeans; English investors controlled the Great Northern. And, of special interest to New Mexicans because of the Dutch-owned Maxwell Grant, was the reported ownership of the Illinois Central by Dutch investors. According to the *Times,* the annual ''money demand'' on the United States by European investors, plus the tourist dollars flowing to Europe, amounted to 400 million dollars. Even the threat of alien-controlled monopoly power, however, was tied to the money question. These Europeans were demanding payment in gold, the *Times* asserted, thus aggravating the serious deflationary trend caused by the shortage of money. [34] Only unlimited silver coinage could reverse the downward course of price levels that had plagued the country during the nineties.

The heated dialogue between silverites and gold bugs was carried in pamphlets, leaflets, and campaign brochures as well as in newspapers. To cope with the strength of the free coinage forces in New Mexico, who controlled a majority of the territorial newspapers, a pamphlet was circulated entitled "To American Bread-Winners[:] A Word on Wages in Silver Countries." In it, the familiar argument that wages paid in silver countries were lower than elsewhere was repeated, and Democrats were accused of using the coinage controversy to sidetrack the tariff question. [35] The fusion of Populist and Democratic silverites was critically dealt with in a pamphlet entitled "A Populist Humbug." [36] Silverites responded by circulating the little book on the money question written by Prince. [37] And ten thousand copies of a pro-silver speech that Prince had made at the Trans-Mississippi Commercial Congress were distributed by the Young Men's Bimetallic Club of Durango. [38]

Prince, still embarrassed by his tiff with the Populists, elected to play a relatively quiet role for the remainder of the campaign. [39] Always aware of future political prospects, however, he was careful to repair any damage done to his career. He sent his pro-silver booklet to Bryan, to maintain his silver connections, [40] and a letter to Mark Hanna complimenting him for his management of McKinley's campaign. [41] Both actions were an effort to recover any favor he might have lost as a result of his controversial involvement with Populism.

As for the two major candidates in the campaign, Catron and Fergusson, they were compelled to campaign vigorously throughout New Mexico to clarify their views on the money question. The Gold Democrats recognized themselves as part of a futile protest, so that Dame could afford to expound his unpopular views on free coinage; Catron on the other hand, who wanted another term, could not allow charges of "gold bug" to go unanswered. A letter signed by Saint, the silver Republican from Bernalillo, and seventeen other members of Catron's party was symbolic of the troubles Catron faced. These Republican bolters denounced the territorial party for taking dictation from Eastern politicians, condemned the platform with its Catron substitute for free silver, and assailed party leaders for not standing up for silver as Senator Teller had done. [42]

Aware that the opposition was drawing no distinction between the Catron substitute and the gold standard, the proprietor of the *Silver City Enterprise,* a Catron supporter, printed a private letter written by the worried incumbent which showed that he was not against silver coinage *per se.* The letter had a good effect, and extra issues of the *Enterprise* were circulated. [43] Catron's substitute, calling for the coinage of the American silver product, continued to cause confusion, however. One backer from the mining district of Bland begged Catron to make a campaign visit to explain his views on silver to 102 bewildered registered Republicans. [44]

Even silverite Harvey B. Fergusson, with both the Populist and Democratic nominations, was not immune to criticism. He was accused of being an approving delegate to the Democratic national convention of 1892, which nominated gold bug Grover Cleveland. The *New Mexican* denied that their candidate was a hypocrite, claiming that he was defeated as a candidate for delegate that year because of his uncompromising views on free silver. [45]

As loyal New Mexico Republicans could not compete with Fergusson and other fusion candidates in the debate over free silver, they tried to bring to the forefront other campaign issues. They found in the fusion of Democrats with those radical ''socialistic'' Populists the one issue emotional or irrational enough to cope with the silver craze — the law-and-order issue. Prior to Fergusson's ''popocratic'' nomination, the *San Marcial Bee* accused the Albuquerque Democrat of ''going about the territory making 'Crime of '73' speeches and exhorting the workingmen to become anarchists and socialists.'' Fergusson was labeled a ''demagogue of the first water,'' who had as his principal objective the sowing of the seeds of discord among the classes of people in New Mexico. [46] ''A vote for Catron is a vote for law and order in New Mexico,'' editorialized the *Raton Range*. [47] The Catron campaign is the only one concerned with law and order, echoed the *Rincon Weekly.* [48]

The Republicans also attempted a revival of the tariff issue. The *Albuquerque Daily Citizen* on September 22 had hoped to set the tone for the campaign when it scored the Democrats for removing the tariff on wool. The move, it stated, had almost destroyed New Mexico's ''greatest[,] most diversified interest.'' But his campaign issue, which had worked so well two years earlier, failed to arouse the electorate in 1896.

The dilemma of the Republican party in 1896 was that it either advanced the wrong issues or was successfully characterized as a bankrupt party. The perennial statehood question, for instance, an issue that Republicans had some success with in the past, was better exploited by Democrats in 1896. Bryan's views regarding the admission of New Mexico, included in his letter accepting the Democratic nomination, became known as his letter was reprinted in several issues of the *Santa Fe Daily New Mexican.* ''New Mexico and Arizona are entitled to statehood and their early admission is demanded by their material and political interests.'' [49] Associating almost every campaign issue with the money question, the confident Santa Fe journal insisted that ''with a free-coinage senate, [neither] Catron nor any other goldite can ever secure statehood.'' [50] Even the alleged anti-Catholicism of the Republican party, first used against Republicans in 1894, was joined with the silver issue. Goldites were accused of having hired a man to travel between Raton and San Marcial to organize lodges of the American Protective Association, in order to defeat Bryan and free silver. [51]

Catron's controversial career, not unexpectedly, again became an election issue. [52] Compared to the frantic debate over silver, though, the dialogue regarding Catron's shortcomings commanded only minor attention. One local issue that put his reputation squarely on the block was the furor over the legality of the Brice-Coler bonds. These bonds had been sold to finance railroad building in Santa Fe and Grant counties. Characterizing them as fraudulent, the *Santa Fe Daily New Mexican* accused Catron of betraying his constituents by using his influence to get Congress to validate the bonds. Joseph as delegate had refused to help the Brice-Coler bondholders, even though he was offered a commission of twenty-five percent of the face value of the securities if he could get them validated. But Catron, according to the *New Mexican,* had worked in behalf of the bondholders, who were determined to collect the money from Santa Fe and Grant counties they insisted was owed them. The delegate supported their efforts, even though he knew that "fully half" of the taxable property in Santa Fe County would be confiscated if the Brice-Coler bonds were legalized. The value of these railroad bonds, plus accrued interest, amounted to $750,000 "in round numbers," and the *New Mexican* feared that their validation would drive all forms of movable property out of the county. [53]

Editorial comment on Catron's alleged effort to validate the Brice-Coler bonds brought the only anti-semitic slur into public print that this writer has uncovered. The *Sante Fe Daily New Mexican* accused Catron, as a part of his effort to help the bondholders, of selling out to a "syndicate of Wall Street Shylocks." [54] The use of the term "Shylock," it should be noted, appeared in a Democratic, not a Populist, journal.

It is perhaps appropriate to mention here that the only other anti-semitic references noted by this writer were in Republican Bradford Prince's private collection of letters and papers. An unfriendly reference to the Rothschilds, for instance, was discovered in a report on the pro-silver Trans-Montane League, in which the former governor had shown such a great interest. Alluding to the alleged purchase of pro-silver newspapers by gold backers determined to silence the opposition, the report stated that the "only 'free press' the Rothschilds have left to the people east of the Mississippi" was the small daily newspaper. Another reference to the Jewish banking family appeared in an issue of the *Intelligencer Post* of Seattle published some eight months after the 1896 election. In it the Rothschilds were accused of having tried "time and again" to buy the famous gold-producing Homestake Mine of South Dakota. [55] Although Prince was an ardent silverite, these unfriendly references in his personal papers to the pro-gold Rothschilds obviously cannot be taken as an indication of anti-semitism on his part.

As the November 3 election day approached, Fergusson and Catron escalated their campaigns. The united Democrats and Populists had grown increasingly confident, because of popular acceptance of their free coinage stand. The press was full of optimistic reports on fusion movements involving Democrats and Populists in neighboring states such as Colorado, Wyoming, and Montana. Even the pro-gold Republican journal, the *Albuquerque Daily Citizen,* carried stories emphasizing the unity of silver forces in the Rocky Mountain West. [56] To keep territorial Populists involved in the joint effort, the *San Juan Times* quoted from an address delivered by Ignatius Donnelly, in which Bryan was lauded as having "proven himself one of the great men of the century — if not all time." The choice of both the Populists and Democrats was favorably compared with Washington, Jefferson, Jackson, and Lincoln. Donnelly characterized Bryan as being a "profound thinker, a logician, a born statesman." [57] In the face of such enthusiasm New Mexico Republicans grew discouraged. A Catron supporter later wrote that the Democrats in Grant County had spent ten times as much money as the Republicans on the strength of their confidence in a Bryan victory. They labored "like Turks, thinking of keeping or getting Federal offices under Bryan." [58]

The campaign Bryan waged was one of the most exciting ever conducted by a presidential hopeful. The tireless Nebraskan traveled through two dozen states and delivered over 600 speeches. An estimated five million people heard his voice — more than any candidate until the advent of radio and television. His message was favorably received in the mining states of the West, where the silver craze probably reached its greatest intensity. And his words were reassuring to debtor farmers of the South and the Midwest. In the East, however, where most of the electoral votes were, his words were turned against him by the well-financed supporters of William McKinley. To the industrial East, currency inflation with its rising food prices did not have the appeal it had in the agricultural West and South. It was not difficult to convince most workers and businessmen that free silver would destroy the country's credit system and probably wreck the national economy. As a matter of fact, when the ballots were counted east of the Mississippi and north of the Mason-Dixon line, it was discovered that Bryan failed to carry a single New England county and even lost Democratic New York City. He was defeated, moreover, in states like Wisconsin and Illinois, where the incidence of farm ownership was higher. Although the persuasive Bryan won more votes than any previous presidential candidate, he lost by 600,000 ballots to McKinley, who did his electioneering on his front porch in Canton, Ohio. [59]

But in rural America, in Populist strongholds and in areas where farm tenancy was most prevalent, the Democratic standard-bearer won impressive majorities. In the deep South his pluralities were overwhelming in every state but Georgia, where McKinley's vote deficit of 34,141 out of 156,332 votes cast was the closest he came to making a respectable showing. The vote in the upper South was closer, but the silver Democrat, with his fusion support, was triumphant everywhere except for the border states of Kentucky and Maryland. In the wheat belt, the Nebraskan carried his home state and Kansas and South Dakota. He lost to McKinley, however, in Minnesota and North Dakota. His margin of victory in the mountain states was as decisive as it was in the deep South. In Colorado, he won by a vote of 161,153 to 26,271. In Montana, his total was 32,043 out of 42,537 ballots cast. Bryan's margins in Idaho and Nevada were almost 4 to 1. Even in Wyoming, a Republican state with practically no silver, he was able to gain a narrow victory. [60]

In the three Western territories the trend toward Bryan and free silver could be read in local election returns. Although ineligible to cast their votes in the presidential election, territorial citizens expressed themselves on the coinage question by the votes they cast for delegate. In Oklahoma Territory, for instance, a coalition of silver Democrats and Populists elected a farmer, Joseph Yancy Callahan, who ran on a Free Silver ticket. [61] In Arizona, the popular Democrat, Marcus A. Smith, defeated his Republican opponent, A.J. Doran, by 1,975 votes. The colorful Populist, William O. ''Buckey'' O'Neil, however, garnered 3,895 ballots in his second bid for this office. He received only 195 votes less than the defeated Republican. [62] Totaling the votes of Smith and O'Neil provides an accurate gauge of silver sentiment in the mineral-rich territory.

New Mexico was no exception to the pro-silver sweep in the territories. Harvey B. Fergusson vanquished Catron by a vote of 18,947 to 17,017, while Dame, out of step with the voters, received only 66 ballots. [63] The impact of the silver craze on the outcome was evident. Catron had overwhelmed Joseph two years earlier by a margin of 2,762. The 3.77 percent of the vote earned by Mills, of course, largely accounted for the size of Catron's electoral advantage in 1894. [64]

Fergusson did particularly well in those counties where protest had begun in the late eighties. In Lincoln County, early stronghold of the Farmers' Alliance, he defeated his Republican rival 769 votes to 464. In Chaves County, which had been separated from Lincoln County for seven years, he won by a 4 to 1 margin, a ratio almost duplicated in another county severed from Lincoln, Eddy. [65] A Lincoln attorney attributed Catron's small vote to the fact that the Populists of the county were against him and the legislative ticket fielded by his party, and that some Republicans from the mining precincts around White Oaks and Nogal "went for Fergusson." [66] In Colfax County, where resentment against the Maxwell land monopoly still smoldered, Fergusson polled 1,272 votes to Catron's 660. The vote in Union County, partitioned from Colfax, was closer, but with the merger of Populists and silver Democrats Fergusson was able to best his rival by 149 ballots. In the cradle of Populism, San Miguel County, the vote was exceedingly close, 2,334 to 2,332 in favor of Fergusson. Angry charges and counter charges of vote fraud resounded. [67] Nevertheless, Democrats and Populists, cooperating under the Union banner, had carried the county, and the two Union candidates for the Territorial Council, Duncan and Sandoval, had won. In San Juan County, Fergusson, benefiting from strong fusion support, was victorious with 445 votes to 125.

Fergusson's sweep of the silver counties was just as impressive. In Sierra County the fusion movement succeeded as the Albuquerque Democrat won by a margin of 667 to 188. [68] A Catron supporter from Hillsboro attributed the "unheard of majority for Fergusson" to the large Democratic campaign expenditures and the irresistable silver craze. [69] Catron was buried by an avalanche of votes in Grant County, also, the Republican incumbent receiving only 455 votes out of 1,862 cast. One Catron backer, Fred A. Anderson of Rincon, shouted fraud: "There *was not a legal ballot cast in Grant county at the recent election,* and . . . the *Democrat ballots* of Dona Ana and Socorro counties were [also] illegal." [70]

As expected Catron made his best showing in those counties with a large Hispano vote. He edged Fergusson in Rio Arriba County by 208 votes. And in powerful J. Francisco Chaves' bailiwick, Valencia County, he won in the customary Republican landslide. Catron polled 1,410 votes out of 1,820 cast. The defeated incumbent also carried Bernalillo, the only county to surpass San Miguel in votes cast. The 2,669 to 2,049 victory achieved in Fergusson's home county [71] was largely due to the sympathetic Spanish-speaking community there. Much like a native *patron,* Catron had helped many Hispano leaders during his long career in New Mexico, and his support and friendship were rewarded in 1896. There apparently was some anti-free coinage sentiment in the county, also. Dame received 23 of his 66 votes in Bernalillo. [72] More important, Thomas Hughes, editor of the *Albuquerque Daily Citizen,* was elected to the Territorial Council, [73] despite his support of the gold standard. County Hispanos apparently were not as sensitive to the money question as their emotional Anglo neighbors.

Catron's candidacy was fated for two surprises in supposedly safe Hispano districts in northern New Mexico, however. Taos and Santa Fe counties went for Fergusson by narrow margins. Fergusson's 1,641 to 1,584 triumph in

Santa Fe county [74] was attributable in part to the aggressive pro-silver editorializing of the *Santa Fe Daily New Mexican* and Catron's unpopular association with the Brice-Coler affair.

In the legislative and county races there was considerable ticket splitting. The Democrats lost the territorial House of Representatives, which they had controlled under such controversial circumstances for the past two years. Republicans and Democrats, some of the latter running on fusion tickets, competed in some heated races with each party winning six seats in the Territorial Council. Perhaps in response to the silver craze, when the Republicans organized the House they selected the staunchly pro-silver Llewellyn as speaker. [75] In the Council, longtime Democratic leader Antonio Joseph was elected president. According to the Council Journal, Joseph won a "majority of all votes cast" in a contest against J. Francisco Chaves. [76] George Curry, however, who served on that body as a Democrat, asserted that a "mutual agreement" had been worked out between Republicans and Democrats to select Joseph by a unanimous ballot in recognition of the Taos Democrat's ten years of service as territorial delegate. [77] One safe assumption that can be made about the outcome of the election was that many Republican candidates in 1896 were able to separate themselves from Catron and his controversial silver substitute in the minds of the New Mexico voters.

Fusion tickets apparently did well in the 1896 race, because they were usually put together in counties where the free coinage issue was strongest. [78] Populists, on the whole, were successful when they cooperated with Democrats. When they did not, the results were often disastrous. In Santa Fe County, for instance, Populist newcomer Arthur Boyle was buried in his unilateral bid for the Council, receiving only twenty votes. The People's party candidates for sheriff and school superintendent in Santa Fe, John T. Forsha and F.C. Buell, respectively, received 24 and 14 votes apiece. [79] An exception to the rule occurred in San Juan County, where the Populists, making a separate bid on the county level, won every office but two; [80] the legislative candidates they supported in cooperation with the Democrats were also successful. Joseph and Locke were elected to the Council — the one-time delegate, as already noted, as presiding officer. And Juan Jaquez and Felix Garcia were chosen to the House by "respectable pluralities." [81]

The defeat of Bryan and free silver on the national level had a calming effect on the voters of New Mexico. Some of them accepted it with a subdued bitterness, a few with relief, others with resignation. One Silver City Republican, for whom Prince had campaigned in 1896, looked upon the coinage issue as settled. "It is as dead as slavery or the Southern Confederacy. The Gettysburg has been fought, some skirmishing . . . by the populists may be indulged in, but the same result will be reached at Appomatox." [82]

The defeat of free silver was regarded by T.B. Mills with a sad quiescence. Expressing relief that the disappointing campaign was over, he hoped for more "prosperous times" throughout the country. He did not, however, feel that the gold standard would bring them about. The one-time Populist candidate for delegate showed himself to be a consensus man in the end. If it turned out that he was mistaken about the gold standard, he would admit it. Mills also expressed a wish that free silver men would "throw no obstacles in the way in Congress to antagonize the policy of the Republican party." [83] Shortly after the election this unusual Populist moved to New York City to become a broker. [84]

A rather typical view of the 1896 election as it affected a developing frontier territory was expressed by the *San Juan Times.* Editorializing on McKinley's matchless opportunities to become a statesman, the newspaper, nevertheless, balanced its hopes with realism. It is "rather too much to hope that after the trusts and the money changers worked so hard for his election that McKinley will refuse to do their bidding, but his acts will be closely watched." Wanting to calm anxieties in reform-minded New Mexico, a territory which had spawned protest movements and supported free coinage, the *Times* urged its readers to give the president-elect a chance. If, perchance, it does occur that "his sympathies are with the people, then the people will be with him." The Farmington journal then turned to a crucial question for an underdeveloped territory — railroad building. "If the election of Mr. McKinley proves a confidence restorative as the Republicans have claimed it would, then there should be no trouble for the D.&R.G [Denver and Rio Grande Railroad] company to secure adequate eastern capital for the purpose of building the San Juan county branch, and this road should be completed from Durango to Farmington within the next twelve months." [85] In a territory concerned with growth and dependent upon outside capital for it, what chance did the allegedly radical People's party have for success now that its best issue, free silver, had been defeated?

11

THE TWILIGHT OF POPULISM

The doctrines of dissent, which had attracted widespread support in New Mexico, were to reap a bitter harvest following the defeat of Bryan in 1896. The past eight years, which saw the anti-monopolism of the late eighties give way to the silver crusade of the nineties, were to affect New Mexico's image in an adverse way. Eastern distrust of the Western states and territories was one of the fruits of the bitter campaign of 1896. New Mexico's territorial status made her especially vulnerable to the hostility of conservative Easterners and their spokesmen in Congress. Her large Spanish-speaking, Roman Catholic community had already given her an uncomfortable uniqueness. But the territory's exuberant identification with such doctrines of Western ''radicalism'' as free silver had prejudiced her position more than she realized.

Unhappy Tom Catron, while serving as the territory's lame-duck delegate, was made aware of the resentment provoked by New Mexico's controversial course of recent years. On December 10, 1896, while attempting to amend an 1887 law which forbade alien ownership in the territories, he was humiliated by Congressman William P. Hepburn of Iowa. Catron wanted the non-ownership provision repealed, because, as the territory's most prominent ''land-grabber,'' he had land to sell to wealthy foreigners. A growing number of territorial citizens, moreover, including Populists, could see that prohibition against aliens was slowing growth in New Mexico and other territories. Hepburn asked Catron if his amendment was not really contrary to the fundamental principles of Populism, which opposed the acquisition of American land by aliens. Was he not going against ''his party'' and the people of the territory in proposing such a change? The surprised Catron, whose identification with Populism was ironic, insisted that all political parties in New Mexico supported this amendment. He included Populists in this category, whom he estimated to number about ''500 or 600, or 1,000 or 1,200,'' a necessarily rough guess because of the feverish party switching during the 1896 election.

But Hepburn did not intend to let Catron escape his wrath or that of other House Republicans, who by late December were still responding emotionally to the recent Battle of the Standards. Amidst loud applause Hepburn continued to attack the territory through its helpless representative:

> Oh, while they [New Mexicans] were upholding Populism as understood in the rest of the United States and the people where I live understand it, these gentlemen were sneaking away from the effects of Populism by attempting to modify it in their platform in their own locality, yet they voted for the party.

He went on to say it was his intention to make the people of New Mexico aware that they cannot grow under Populism:

> I want them further to be taught that they can not modify the general doctrines of Populism as they are understood in the whole country by the adoption of a little resolution that they sneak into their local platform and then vote for the Populist party upon the general platform. [1]

Catron got his amendment through Congress, but Hepburn's public association of New Mexico with the Populist movement must have been galling to him.

If the conservative Catron was to have trouble with Congress because of New Mexico's erring ways, his successor, Harvey B. Fergusson, the silverite and fusionist, was really in for difficulties. A capable reformer, the new delegate was, in the words of historian Howard R. Lamar, a "fitting symbol of New Mexico's first serious identification with national problems." [2]
Largely because of the respect he could command, Fergusson was able to get through Congress one of the most significant pieces of legislation relevant to New Mexico, the Fergusson Act. This new law allowed the territory to receive, before admission, two sections of land in each township for educational purposes, plus an additional 50,000 acres. Although the act was supposed to prepare New Mexico for admission, Fergusson encountered the customary opposition, much of it no doubt due to his close identification with Populist politics and free coinage. The delegate persisted, however, also introducing two unsuccessful statehood bills.

Fergusson sensed the country's new political situation when he took his seat in March, 1897. In his maiden speech before Congress, he asked for wool protection for New Mexico, a favorite demand of territorial Republicans. [3]
His success in getting a specific duty on wool instead of an *ad valorem* one [4] earned him the gratitude of his Republican opponents, but did not diminish their determination to defeat him in the event he sought re-election in 1898.

The activities of the territorial legislature, which convened on January 18, 1897, also reflected the new political realities that followed Bryan's defeat. Legislative action during the previous eight years, of course, had not been marked by exceptional zeal for reform. The subordination of local authority to the Congress, which could set aside territorial laws, made most territorial bodies, including New Mexico's legislature, comparatively cautious. The inability of Democrats, or Democrats and Populists in coalition, to control both houses was another factor responsible for the tepid legislation enacted in New Mexico during this period. In the one legislative session that the Democrats did control, the Thirty-first, which they were accused of "stealing," major accomplishments were obviously foredoomed. Consequently, even if the country had chosen Bryan in 1896, there was little likelihood that truly significant reform legislation would have been enacted. With McKinley's triumph, then, prospects were greatly lessened that the divided legislators who met in Santa Fe in January of 1897 for the Thirty-second session would seriously consider such populistic proposals as the regulation of freight rates or the guarantee of monthly wage payments to laborers — bills introduced at an earlier session by Mills and Ancheta. Nor could these lawmakers, in view of New Mexico's political climate and her inferior territorial status, be expected to pursue the aggressive course of another Rocky Mountain legislative body, the Montana state legislature, which concurrently was enacting a number of mine safety laws and defiantly memorializing Congress to enact into law such Populist goals as the direct election of United States senators and the creation of postal savings banks. [5]

The major concern of the Thirty-second session was the economic development of the territory. Typical of its legislation were two laws: one to encourage railroad construction by exempting new roads from taxation for six years from their date of completion, and a law to authorize the use of convict labor to rebuild the capitol in Santa Fe (destroyed by fire on May 12, 1892); further, an 1884 law was amended to improve the effectiveness of the territorial Bureau of Immigration. One important deviation from the emphasis on economic development was a law to allow the owners of community grants, such as the Las Vegas grant, to incorporate. Accordingly, grant residents could through a corporate board of trustees, eject intruders by initiating legal suits — but they could also be sued themselves.[6] Perhaps the most modern piece of legislation enacted required fines up to one hundred dollars and a maximum jail term of sixty days for anyone caught polluting territorial streams and lakes with dead animal carcasses.[7]

The mood of the months that followed in New Mexico underscored the cautious direction taken by the Thirty-second assembly. When the territorial Republicans met in Albuquerque on October 1, 1898, for their nominating convention, a relaxed feeling was evident. In his keynote remarks George W. Pritchard spoke in behalf of the protective tariff as confidently as Republicans had before the overwhelming silver craze. Citing the $8,500,000 estimated loss by the Wool Growers' Association for the year ending June 30, 1898, Pritchard argued that this loss to sheep raisers was comparable to fifty dollars taken from each man, woman, and child in New Mexico. Protection was essential. ''There is no section in the whole country that receives more benefit from the protective tariff . . . than the people of New Mexico.'' Pritchard blamed the wool industry's plight on Democratic opposition to the tariff. He upbraided Democrats for the Depression of 1893, also, when ''children cried for bread'' and there was no employment. ''How many would like to return to those good old democratic days?''

A harmony prevailed at the 1898 territorial convention in contrast to the divisiveness of 1896. Prince was not a candidate for delegate. He rejected an endorsement by the Rio Arriba Republicans at their county convention in Tierra Amarilla and chose instead to support one of the two major candidates for the position, Maximiliano Luna or Pedro Perea. Catron also removed himself from consideration, agreeing to support either of the two Hispano leaders. In a friendly contest, Perea, a man whom Catron could manipulate, won handily over Luna. [8] A strongly unified effort on the part of territorial Republicans was thus assured for the 1898 campaign.

Democrats shared with their Republican counterparts this awareness that the old issues were back in vogue. Meeting in Deming, in a convention which the hostile *Albuquerque Daily Citizen* called a ''slim and cut and dried affair,'' they renominated Fergusson as their candidate for territorial delegate. His selection created pandemonium. Delegates stood on chairs and shouted themselves hoarse. [9] The party platform, however, was conventional; no populistic programs were advocated for the 1898 campaign. Protection of wool, home rule, statehood, and universal education were among the planks adopted, ''well known republican measures,'' taunted the *Citizen*. [10]

In the comparatively calm contest that followed the conventions, the revival of traditional party issues was just as evident. Fergusson's boast that he won a specific duty on wool for the territory was challenged by Republicans, who claimed that wealthy Republican sheepowner Solomon Luna was the one most responsible for the wool tariff. It was Luna who traveled to Washington to get his party's leadership to listen to the ''able republican arguments'' being offered by Fergusson. His intervention made the crucial difference, the Republican press insisted. [11] Moreover, Luna's success was proof of the need for Republican representation from New Mexico, notwithstanding

Fergusson's good intentions. "Delegate Fergusson has made the best democratic delegate this territory has ever had," editorialized the *Citizen,* "but New Mexico needs a republican delegate at Washington to properly represent her interests at the national capital." [12]

The issue of nativism cropped up again, but this time the roles were reversed. Republicans rather than Democrats were the accusers. Having an Hispano as their candidate for delegate, the Republicans attacked Fergusson, despite his known sympathy for native New Mexicans. Fergusson's campaign managers were accused of using the race or ethnic issue against Perea in order to win the undivided support of the "so-called American voters." [13] Determined to label Democrats as racists or race mongers, the *Albuquerque Daily Citizen* recalled that when the Republican party nominated Colonel J.W. Dwyer as their candidate for delegate in 1886, Democratic leaders boasted that he was "a Texas cowboy [who] killed a Mexican every morning before breakfast." [14]

Nativism was a pseudo issue in New Mexico. Many Anglos were prejudiced, feeling that their Spanish-speaking Roman Catholic neighbors were not one hundred percent Americans. But with Hispano voters in the majority, criticizing a candidate's native background in a major territorial race would be suicidal. As for such prejudice among territorial Populists, no evidence has been uncovered to associate them with nativism. There was the racist remark of J.E. Sligh (see page 16) against Blacks and Spanish-speaking people of mixed blood, but there is no proof that the Lincoln County Alliance editor ever became a Populist. Like so many New Mexico reform leaders, Sligh dropped from public view as abruptly as he rose to prominence. Populist organizations in San Miguel, San Juan, and Union counties, as a matter of fact, put many Hispanos in positions of prominence. Native participation also was evident in the Republican and Democratic organizations — witness the importance of Joseph, Luna, and the one-time Populist Felix Martinez in the activities of the two major parties. Consequently, nativism would be a dangerous political strategy for any territorial party.

A new dimension was injected into the 1898 campaign which had little to do with the political dialogue of the past few years. The Spanish-American War, fought during that year, helped to dispel some of the accumulated bitterness of frustrated reformers of the previous decade. Political parties in New Mexico, as elsewhere, supported the "splendid little war." Harvey Fergusson spoke for his supporters as well as his foes when he gave vocal support for the war in the halls of Congress. His boast that New Mexico met its full quota of volunteers for the famed Rough Riders before a majority of the states had responded was greeted with enthusiasm in the House. [15]

It was the Republican party, however, that benefited most from the popular struggle. Theodore Roosevelt utilized the fame he had gained as a Rough Rider colonel to make a successful bid for the New York governorship in 1898. The charisma of this exciting new leader was transferred to many of his comrades-in-arms. Rough Rider Major Alexander O. Brodie, for instance, was the Republican candidate for territorial delegate in Arizona. [16] In New Mexico, Captain George Curry, a Democrat with some Populist sympathies, switched parties to be of the same political persuasion as Roosevelt. [17] Other Rough Riders on the Republican ticket in New Mexico in 1898 were former silver Republican leader Llewellyn (who was a particular favorite of Roosevelt), Frederick Muller, and Maximiliano Luna. All three of these men served as captains of the famed cowboy cavalry. [18]

Republican identification with the popular war was strong, being regarded as an asset by Republican campaigners in the autumn election. Democrats, on the other hand, had image problems. Their support of the war gained for them the approval of most of the New Mexico electorate, but their critical stand on the proposed annexation of the Philippines weakened that approval. The *Albuquerque Daily Citizen,* quick to recognize a good issue, predicted that the Democratic leaders of the nation would fight the annexation of the Philippines. Democrats, it maintained, object to "everything tending to extend the influence and prosperity of the great republic." [19]

One factor that would not be prominent in the 1898 campaign was the Populist issue. Fergusson's fusion candidacy two years earlier had made him vulnerable to Republican charges of anarchism and socialism. The once vocal third party was almost forgotten in this election except in San Juan County. The Republican *Citizen* was premature when it announced on October 19 that: "The populist party has ceased to exist in New Mexico"; [20] even so, few traces of independent Populist activity could be found outside of "San Juan of the Populists."

There were fusion movements in 1898, but they were not initiated to accomodate the Populists nor blunt their challenge. In Bernalillo County, for instance, Democrats fused with those Republicans who opposed Perea and his county machine. The Democrats agreed not to choose their own candidates in return for a pledge made by maverick Republicans to support Fergusson. [21] In San Miguel, former Populists again joined with Democrats and unhappy Republicans to field candidates under the Union party banner. "Boss" Felix Martinez was still the undisputed leader of this coalition. Changing times, however, had affected the Union party, too. Regular San Miguel Republicans were more hopeful about success in 1898 than they had been for some time.

The Republican press pictured the Union party's membership as being a weird assortment of "democrats, silverites, populists and sorehead republicans." It insisted that San Miguel County had "suffered enough from white cap misrule." [22]

Only in San Juan County did an active, independent Populist organization persist. After four years of political dominance, however, the San Juan People's party felt uneasy about its prospects. The most successful territorial Populist organization was threatened in 1898 by a fusion ticket of Democrats and Republicans. The *San Juan Times* of Farmington, once the party's most articulate newspaper voice, was now in unfriendly hands. The new editors, R.C. Prewitt and Charles E. Starr, who replaced the ex-Populist Stivers, were outspokenly anti-Populist. As Democrats, they supported the fusion ticket, accusing the People's party of trying to "resurrect old dead issues." [23] Anti-monopolism, free silver, opposition to alien landownership were no longer pertinent issues, in their opinion. While Stivers had supported Populist William McRae, the well-liked incumbent county clerk, Prewitt and Starr backed McRae's opponent, Charles V. Stafford. The three Populist county commissioners, John Real, J.E. Manzaneres and P.M. Solomon, also were opposed. San Juan Populists must have yearned for those days when Fred Holt was editor of the *Times*.

In a rather unusual experience for territorial Populists, the San Juan party had to pay the price of those who govern. They were criticized for their mismanagement of public affairs. The charge of ring rule, a familiar one in New Mexico, was also leveled at them. "A vote for Arrington, Gilmore and Jaquez," the *Times* said of the three fusion candidates for county commissioner, "is a vote to down the Populist ring." [24] The term "Aztec ring" was used to describe the San Juan County Populist organization, indicating that there were regional rivalries within the large county. The *Times* asserted that the bosses in the county seat of Aztec had selected five of the candidates on the Populist ticket, thus ignoring the lower end of the county. [25]

The *San Juan Times* was unremitting in its faultfinding of Populist candidates. When Manzaneres was removed as one of the Populist candidates for county commissioner in order to replace Ramon Labato, the incumbent Populist probate judge who had withdrawn from the race, the *Times* took the opportunity to ridicule the entire ticket. The scramble of Populist officeholders necessited by Labato's withdrawal had caused confusion. Manzaneres, for instance, had to be replaced as commissioner candidate by a man named Coe, probably Lou Coe of the Lincoln County family that produced the Alliance leader, "Jap" Coe. Warning the "dear Pops" that a rotation of their candidates would not work, the journal queried whether a "crossover" involving McCrea, the county clerk, and another Populist candidate for county commissioner, P.M. Solomon, would not be the next momentous step. [26]

With territorial Democrats also on the defensive in 1898, an air of confidence permeated the ranks of Republicans on election day. Their optimism was not unfounded. Fergusson, who had easily bested Catron in 1896, was decisively beaten by Perea, who polled 18,722 votes to Fergusson's 16,659. The results of the legislative races were even more disastrous for the Democrats; they won only seven seats as compared to the Republicans' twenty-nine. [27] In San Juan County the Populists were humiliated as every candidate of the opposing fusion ticket was elected. "Populism will be no more in San Juan County[,] Forever," crowed the *San Juan Times,* [28] celebrating the twilight of the political movement. Nationally, the Democrats were defeated, Republicans winning 185 House seats in the new Fifty-sixth Congress to the Democrat's 163. The Republican party increased its majority in the Senate by six. Populist strength dwindled to nine seats in the lower house, a sharp drop from the previous Congress. [29]

A county-by-county perusal of the votes cast in New Mexico's delegate election revealed, however, that Democratic strength remained in those counties where protest had a long tradition. The Democratic incumbent, for instance, carried Lincoln County, where the *Nogal Nugget* once challenged cattle monopolists. He was also victorious in adjacent Chaves and Eddy counties. The influx of Southerners into these three southeastern counties doubtlessly accounted for much of the Democratic influence, but the persistence of anti-monopoly sentiment cannot be discounted. Democratic strength remained a major element in Colfax County, also, Fergusson easily winning there by a vote of 1,181 to 727. If bitterness over the Maxwell land monopoly was a factor in Colfax, it did not extend into another county where the grant was located, Union. There, Perea gained a 23-vote margin from the approximately one thousand ballots cast. [30] Fergusson was victorious, however, in San Juan County. He won conclusively, 450 votes to 182, even though the Populists who supported him in 1896 were all defeated. Democratic endurance in those counties where reform was of importance provides proof that the party continued to serve the reform-minded voters of New Mexico as a more viable alternative for change and improvement than the smaller People's party.

Fergusson won in the silver counties of the territory, notwithstanding the diminishing importance of the coinage of silver. His triumph in Grant County was impressive, polling 1,215 votes to 668. [31] The Republican press consoled the party faithful, pointing to the 400-vote increase in Republican strength in an area dotted with decaying silver camps in 1898. [32] Sierra County was also carried by Fergusson, but the decline of Democratic strength in Sierra was even more evident than in Grant County. [33] It was not the Democratic decline in the silver counties, however, that accounted for the Republican victories of 1898 so much as the restoration of Republican support in the Spanish-speaking counties of northern New Mexico. Santa Fe and Taos counties were back in the Republican column, Perea carrying Santa Fe by 434 votes and Taos by 81. The expected Republican landslide in Valencia County occurred, Perea winning an unprecedented 1,689 to 45 victory. Perea's feud with his fellow Bernalillo Republican, Mariano S. Otero, did not stem the Republican resurgence in his home county. Despite the fusion of malcontent Republicans and Democrats, Fergusson again lost Bernalillo, his votes totaling 184 less than in 1896. [34]

The biggest Republican success was in San Miguel County, where Felix Martinez's Union party was defeated. The entire local Republican ticket was elected by small majorities [35] and Perea carried the county by a comfortable 2,401 to 2,193 vote. [36] San Miguel Republicans were overjoyed. "The occupation of Boss Martinez at Las Vegas appears to be gone," proclaimed a happy headline. Although eight years had elapsed since the White Caps had infiltrated the Knights of Labor, Republican opposition was still directed toward these night riders. "People of San Miguel should rejoice over [the] downfall of the White Cap gang," the *Albuquerque Daily Citizen* crowed. [37] The bitterness generated by protest in San Miguel was dying slowly.

The decisive Republican victory prompted the chairman and the secretary of the party's territorial committee, J.S. Clark and Max Frost, to issue an arrogant statement on November 11: "The democratic and populist parties, the unionists and fusionists are practically dead." [38] In the case of the Democrats, the two Republican leaders were wrong. The Democrats would return to contest actively for power, although the next twelve to fourteen years would be difficult for them. As for the predicted end to fusion activity, New Mexico politics remained personal and fragmented; both characteristics promoted fusionism. But the proclaimed demise of Populism and Unionism proved prophetic. The Union party disintegrated shortly after its defeat. Martinez moved to El Paso, where he had begun to speculate in real estate in 1897. [39] The convincing defeat of the People's organization in San Juan County ended political activity on the part of Populists in New Mexico. After their decade of politicking, beginning with the formation of the germ party in San Miguel in 1888, the Populists had disappeared as a force in territorial politics.

Although much of its reform program would survive and be promoted by Progressives during the twentieth century, the national People's party also was in a fatal decline. In Kansas, regarded as the heartland of Midwestern Populism, the Populists were defeated; even "Sockless" Jerry Simpson lost his congressional seat in the seventh district. [40] The people of Kansas should rejoice over the defeat of the "pestiferous populist party," suggested the *Albuquerque Daily Citizen*. "Colorado is now the craziest political state in the union, Kansas having recovered from its populist lunacy." [41]

Assistant Secretary of the Interior Thomas Ryan, campaigning in his home state of Kansas for the Republican party, echoed the *Citizen's* belief that Populism was dead in Kansas. Insisting that most Populists had moved to the Republican party in the 1898, he predicted that a majority of them would stay. "The rest may keep up a semblance of an organization or drift into the democratic camp, but Populism as a force in politics has, I believe, passed away." Ryan's analysis of his party's success in Kansas could be applied to the nation. He emphasized the popularity of President McKinley, and he lauded the "splendid manners" of his fellow Republican campaigners, a boast of dubious significance. More important was his admission that the return of prosperity had done the most to help his party and damage the Populist cause. "Prosperity has discredited populistic arguments," [42] was his simple but pithy comment.

12

NEW MEXICO POPULISM
IN RETROSPECT

In contemplating the decade of Populist activity in New Mexico from the party's origins as a protest organization in San Miguel County in 1888 to its last electoral effort in San Juan County in 1898, one is struck by the party's greater successes in certain counties than by its overall performance throughout the territory. This tendency to be more successful on the local level is illustrated by the electoral victories of the People's party in San Miguel, particularly important because San Miguel and Bernalillo were the two most populous counties in New Mexico during the nineties. In harmony with the burgeoning strength of the Populist movement in the wheat-raising Midwestern plains to the east, the People's party of San Miguel seized power in the county in 1890. It sent a strong delegation to the territorial legislature. The group included such leaders as Theodore B. Mills, who became the Populist candidate for territorial delegate in 1894, and Pablo Herrera, the White Cap leader whose secret native organization infiltrated this first legitimate People's party in the territory. The silver counties of southwestern New Mexico comprised another area where the Populist movement demonstrated its local might. The upsurge of political strength there occurred just prior to or during the so-called "silver craze" which gripped the mountain states and territories of the West during the mid-nineties. The most durable Populist organization of all, however, was the one located in agricultural San Juan County. This party, operating in the classical Midwestern tradition of agrarian protest, was able to thrive from its capture of all county offices in 1894 until its demise in 1898. Moreover, it was not upstaged by the Democratic party, as was the case in Lincoln and Colfax counties, where active chapters of the Farmers' Alliance resisted the threats posed by the cattle or land monopolies.

Above the local or regional level, however, the impact of the People's party was not so strong. In 1894, for instance, when the Populists made a bid for the office of territorial delegate — the one elective office under the territorial system for which all qualified electors were permitted the vote — the outcome was a disappointment. Candidate Mills' tally of 1,853 votes, less than four percent of the total, was most discouraging to the former San Miguel legislator. Even so, he did carry San Juan County, called by hostile Democrats "San Juan of the Populists." But he fared badly in San Miguel, where he had lived before his move to Bernalillo County. In Sierra County he outpolled Antonio Joseph, the unsuccessful Democratic incumbent; his success in this silver-producing county, however, was tempered by the fact that both he and Joseph lost it to Republican Thomas B. Catron, who was elected that year by a vote greater than the combined votes of Mills and Joseph.

Notwithstanding the poor showing of the territorial People's party in the delegate election of 1894, the year 1896 was regarded with apprehension by both major parties because of the expected increase in electoral strength of the undaunted New Mexico Populists. One Democratic journal observed nervously, on the eve of the Populist territorial convention in 1896, that in 1894 Republican and Democratic strength was so evenly divided in nine counties that any appreciable increase in Populist strength could have determined which of the two major parties would control the territory. With predictions that the People's party would double [1] its vote in 1896, the Democratic party, ordinarily the chief beneficiary of New Mexico's reform sentiment, was particularly anxious. But the Republican party could not afford to ignore the strength of Populism either. On the basis of voting potential alone, 1896, the year of the Battle of the Standards, was the year of the Populist party's greatest importance on the territorial level. The party was solid on silver, the most consequential criterion for New Mexico voters in 1896. It was also the most natural political home for the protest elements of the territory. Consequently, the People's party served as a balancer in territorial politics prior to the 1896 election. Both Republicans and Democrats were eager to fuse with it, despite its poor performance in 1894. The eventual alliance of the Populists with the Democrats in support of Harvey B. Fergusson, the fusion candidate for territorial delegate, following the Populists' on-again off-again courtship with Republican L. Bradford Prince, was the most logical move for the party's ambitious leaders.

The two delegate elections in New Mexico in which Populists participated were difficult ones for the members of the struggling party. In 1894, their unilateral effort was either ignored or ridiculed by most of the territorial press. In 1896, the Populists faced the same painful decision that their national party faced in Saint Louis. Should they fuse and eventually die or not fuse and damage the prospects of New Mexico's able counterpart of William Jennings Bryan, Harvey Fergusson?

An insight into both of these delegate elections is provided by T.B. Mills. In a long letter to Prince written on October 13, 1896, [2] Mills revealed some of the inner workings of his party. The purpose of the letter was to give Mills an opportunity to apologize to Prince for his party's failure to send him a formal notification of his nomination as territorial delegate so he could gracefully decline. Prince, who could be regarded as New Mexico's counterpart of the nation's leading silver Republican, Henry Moore Teller of Colorado, had lost interest in the Populist nomination when he failed to win the Republican designation for that office from Catron. Mills admitted that he and Webber and Boyle, two other members of the Populist territorial central committee, did receive letters from Prince indicating that he would not accept the Populist nomination. Mills also had to admit that he reluctantly wrote the public manifesto explaining his party's reasons for replacing Prince with Fergusson. He insisted, however, that he opposed the insensitive and casual way in which the matter was handled, but was afraid to defy the committee members who were determined to remove Prince even before he received the formal notification of his nomination.

If Mills was anything, he was not timid or diffident. His failure to speak against a committee action he disapproved of was not characteristic of the vocal Populist leader. Only an extraordinary reason could explain his unusual conduct, and this was revealed in his letter to Prince. Mills had been under a cloud of suspicion for several weeks prior to sending this letter. He had, according to his own account, been unfairly accused by some fellow Populists, after he announced for Prince, of being a willing pawn of Prince's Republican rival, Thomas Catron. The secret alliance between Mills and Catron was allegedly two years old, going back to the delegate election of 1894. Conjecture as to the basis for this serious charge against Mills leads to an irresistible temptation to speculate. Catron, of course, would benefit from any divisiveness in the Populist party; division among any of the silver forces in New Mexico would be to his benefit. Prince's nomination as the Populist candidate for territorial delegate would fragment the strength of the silverites, if Fergusson, a staunch silverite, were the Democrat's nominee. Prince's designation by the Populists would also alienate the more conservative Republicans at the Republican territorial convention, which was scheduled to meet three days later. Their alienation could guarantee Catron's renomination in 1896.

More intriguing speculation involves Mills' motivation for working in behalf of the conservative Catron. To explain his motives Mills' detractors go back to a Democratic charge made in 1894 that he received $5,000 from Catron to encourage him to run as delegate on the Populist ticket. Such a candidacy would divide the Democrats by luring the reform element of the party to Mills' Populist standard, thus assuring Catron's victory. Mills, of course, denied the charge, insisting that he never received a cent from Catron. "I paid every dolar [sic] of the expense . . . of conducting the Campaign, for the people's party," he asserted in his letter to Prince. Mills declared that he personally assumed all the expenses of the party's central committee, the rent for the hall in Albuquerque where he was nominated in 1894, and the printing of election tickets in many of the counties of the territory. As proof of his integrity he boasted of an unpaid note for campaign expenses in one of the banks in his old hometown of Las Vegas.

Mills also stated in his letter to Prince that had he received $5,000 from Catron in 1894, he would have increased his vote threefold. Assuming for a moment that his prediction was accurate, such an increase would have meant that one out of nine voters in the territory would have cast a Populist ballot. A vote of this dimension would have far exceeded the less than four percent of the vote that was actually cast for the Populist candidate. If Mills' estimate were correct, he would have received a greater percentage of the vote in New Mexico in 1894 than did Populist presidential candidate James B. Weaver nationally in 1892. Mills would have polled about fifty percent more than Weaver, which was the approximate percentage increase of the national Populist vote in 1894 over 1892.[3] More important, though, the threefold increase in the Populist vote in 1894 would have put the party in a far superior bargaining position during the nominating conventions preceding the 1896 campaign. Undoubtedly the Populist role in any kind of fusion arrangement would have been more prominent had there been such a vote increase.

All this speculation, of course, is based upon the accuracy of Mills' prediction, which is questionable. Although New Mexico Populism was an under-financed operation, the results attributed by the Populist leader to the addition of an extra $5,000 in campaign funds seem exaggerated. There is, however, reason to believe that a better-financed Populist campaign in 1894 would have brought about some increase in Mills' vote total. There was, after all, a backlog of frustration and insecurity in the territory, much of it caused by the threats of land-grabbers and cattle barons, of bankers anxious to collect on their loans, and of old-line politicians willing to serve all these interests.

Mills concentrated much of his letter to Prince on denying the accusation that he had been purchased by Tom Catron for $5,000. What disturbed Mills the most was the reluctance of Catron and his associates to repudiate the charge and thus help to vindicate him. He attempted to be philosophical about the matter, however. I have been "too long in politics, to every deny, or admit, any charges, which might be made, as I know full well it would only make matters worse." As for the charge that he had supported Prince's Populist nomination as a way of helping Catron and of paying off his debt to the Republican, Mills assured Prince that he had campaigned for him because he honestly thought of him as a winner. "You with your record, both on the silver question, and the tariff, which is paramount with many in New Mexico, your election would have been certain, regardless of the ticket on which you were running." The Populist leader predicted that, if Prince had stayed in the race as the Populist standard-bearer in 1896, he would have taken two-thirds of Catron's expected Republican vote and perhaps one-half of the Democratic vote for Harvey Fergusson, who "has no personal strength, but the [Democrats] merely vote for him in preference to Catron." [4]

As Mills' integrity is brought into question by these charges, an analysis of them is essential, particularly because of the evidence of opportunism found among a number of territorial Populists. The most serious of the charges, of course, involved alleged payment of $5,000 by Catron to encourage Mills to run as delegate in 1894. If this accusation is true, incidentally, it would not be the only instance in which a Western Populist compromised himself for a price. In Wyoming, for example, Republicans under the leadership of Senator Francis E. Warren subsidized a Populist ticket in 1896 comprised of midroaders who resented a fusion arrangement made with the Democrats by some of their party leaders. One of the middle-of-the-road Populists, William Brown, a candidate for Congress, accepted donations and free railroad passes from the Republicans to help him make the race. [5] But Mills appears to be a different person altogether. He was not poor and his ego was, in this writer's opinion, large enough to discourage him from such dishonest political behavior. He knew Catron, serving with him in the Territorial Council in the early nineties. There is no evidence, however, that the two men were close. Moreover, if Mills' Populist commitment was at all sincere, they were ideologically poles apart. There is another factor that should be considered, too. Prince and Catron were strong rivals within the Republican party during the mid-nineties. For Mills to have achieved an intimacy with both men at this time would be improbable.

Mills' support of Prince as his party's candidate for delegate in 1896, however, is a different matter. The Populist leader was conspicuous for his advocacy of rail regulation and an expanded public education program and ran on a complete Populist platform in 1894. His support of the conservative Prince over the populistic Fergusson in 1896, therefore, does compromise his expressed convictions as a reformer. Their strong mutual devotion to free silver might explain the Mills-Prince alliance, but, as both men were involved in mining speculation, it also brings into question their real motives. In the final analysis, T.B. Mills appears to be more in the tradition of the Western empire builder, notwithstanding his vocal support of the underdog. His political ambitions, his interest in land grants and in mining and real estate developments, and his participation in the stock brokerage business after his departure from New Mexico do not conjure in one's mind the picture of an angry Populist stump speaker.

Opportunism, as has already been implied, was not unique to Mills; other Populist leaders were guilty of having baser motives. Prince's fellow Santa Fean, Arthur Boyle, was a most atypical Populist. Son-in-law of the famous English land speculator, William Blackmore, he had been associated with many land-grabbing enterprises in the territory. Boyle's affiliation with the People's party was unquestionably his response to the "silver craze." His lack of dedication to the Populist cause was revealed at the 1896 Populist territorial central committee meeting in Las Vegas, where Prince was replaced by Fergusson as the party's choice for territorial delegate. Boyle insisted then that Prince be sent a formal notification of his nomination even though he knew that the former governor would decline the offer and embarrass Boyle's newly adopted People's party. Elwin T. Webber, chairman of the Populist territorial central committee in 1896, was also essentially a free-silver reformer, being part owner of the Lincoln Lucky Gold and Silver Mine at San Pedro. The Santa Fe hotelkeeper, however, was less a speculator and man of property than Mills or Boyle.

Political as well as economic opportunism was common among the Populist leadership in New Mexico. Felix Martinez, the most prominent Hispano in the movement, joined the emerging San Miguel People's party in 1890 in order to advance his own career. After the electoral triumph of his new party in 1890, he worked to weld a strong alliance between Populists and Democrats in the newly elected territorial legislature. He ultimately succeeded in destroying the identity and independence of the San Miguel Populists by 1892. Grateful for his support, territorial Democrats recommended Martinez to President Cleveland as their candidate for United States marshal after the 1892 political campaign. But the opportunistic Martinez would not succumb to any party discipline, Populist or Democratic. He later became the key organizer for another party he knew he could dominate, the Union party, a coalition of discontented Republicans and Democrats and bewildered Populists. Following the defeat of his Union party in 1898, Martinez, a real estate developer who was also interested in land grants,6 moved to El Paso to continue his real estate promotions in that city.

Even less principled than Martinez was F.A. Blake, the Las Vegas newspaperman, who, along with some idealistic Knights, founded the San Miguel People's party in 1888. When Blake and his collaborators among the

172

Knights of Labor were eased out of their positions of party leadership in 1892 by Martinez, Blake bolted, bitterly attacking his former party associates in the press. Then, in 1894, his true commitment to Populism was revealed by his apparently open support of Thomas Catron, long the antithesis of reform in New Mexico. Blake's action was more reprehensible than the actions of the Populist leaders in Union County, who also supported Catron that year. These leaders, being practically all Hispanos, did not understand Anglo politics as well as Blake and were also susceptible to the influence that a powerful *patron* such as Catron could exercise. Blake's creditability as a Populist was also damaged by his support of Prince's short-lived fusion candidacy in 1896.

But not all the Populist leaders in New Mexico were motivated solely by political ambition or compromised by land or mining interests. National committeeman M.P. Stamm, the forthright merchant from Albuquerque, stood squarely on the national Populist platform of 1892. His opposition to Prince's nomination as delegate in 1896 was so unequivocal that he immediately protested it to Marion Butler, the party's national chairman. Moreover, his backing of Fergusson at the Las Vegas convention was most consistent with his political principles. The Albuquerque Democrat supported many of the major planks in the Populist platform, while Prince supported only the demand for free silver.

Equally dedicated to Populist principles was Fred E. Holt, editor of the *San Juan Times* of Farmington. A believer in all the planks of the Omaha platform, Holt was insistent that the Populist platform provided the only solution for the ills of the nation. The tenor of his editorial attacks on monopolies and the deflationary fiscal policies of the government and the attitude he maintained toward many of the nation's capitalistic values reveal in him an alienation that historians such as Norman Pollack see in much of the Populist movement. 7 Whether Holt remained a dedicated Populist after 1895 is not known. He was replaced as editor of the *Times* and apparently slipped into oblivion. If his past actions are any indication, however, Holt does not seem the type to back away from his convictions as did C. Ed Stivers, the editor of the official Populist organ, the *New Mexico Nugget,* who assumed the role of a political independent during his brief editorship of the *San Juan Times* in 1896.

One aspect of the People's party leadership, apparently not unusual, was the small number of ordinary farmers, stockgrazers, and silver prospectors in positions of prominence. The Herrera brothers and some San Miguel leaders were among the exceptions. The dearth of farmers among the party's elite has been noted in other sections of the country by Hicks and Hofstadter. It should not be too surprising, therefore, that few people in agriculture were important in the New Mexico party. But the absence of full-time silver miners as leaders is noteworthy. Of course, Mills, Boyle, and Webber had mining investments, Mills even doing some prospecting, but none of these men could be considered sourdoughs.

Professor Hofstadter has classified Populist leaders as a "ragged elite of professional men, rural editors, third party veterans, and professional reformers." [8] He was correct about the importance of rural or small-town editors as far as New Mexico was concerned. Holt, Blake and Stivers were prime examples. Whether Sligh, editor of the Farmers' Alliance organ in Lincoln County, the *Nogal Nugget,* ever became a Populist cannot be determined. If he did, yet another example of an influential Populist editor could be presented. As for third-party veterans and professional reformers, no evidence of their prominence has been found. Mills and Boyle were former Republicans, Martinez was an ex-Democrat, and Stamm, Holt, and Stivers were probably one-time Democrats, although their party allegiances cannot be confirmed. Oddly enough, no professional men were in positions of prominence, unless one broadens that term to include businessmen such as real estate developers or merchants. T.B. Mills, for instance, was so competent in mining laws and technology that he authored a book on mining, a feat which would place him in the category of a professional man in the eyes of many persons today. By far the most unusual aspect of the territory's Populist leadership, however, was the absence of a lawyer among the highest levels of the party hierarchy. [9] Prince and Fergusson, both of whom were fusionist candidates for varying periods in 1896, were attorneys, but, despite their Populist support, they were never party members.

The pronounced opportunism of several of the more prominent Populists in New Mexico brings into question not only the integrity of the People's party but the sincerity of much of its rank and file. It is usually assumed that the workers or voters of a party have not thought through the goals of their political organization as carefully as have their leaders. Often lacking a coherent philosophy or understanding, many ordinary party members can only be said to share certain social, political, and economic attitudes with those chosen to guide them. If this is so, perhaps the tough platforms adopted at the 1894 and 1896 territory-wide conventions for the People's party were not entirely representative of the convictions of a majority of the party members. The enthusiastic endorsement of the Omaha platform at the 1894 meeting may have been no more than a ritualistic ceremony, one which might be expected of any branch of the national People's party during an election year. Perhaps the other demands made at that meeting, such as the abolition of national banks and the direct election of all officials from the postmaster to the president, were really of concern to only a few of the Populists in the territory.

By the same token, just as ordinary party workers and voters lack the understanding and dedication of their leaders, they also lack the opportunities for self-advancement and political profit presented to their party chiefs. A Populist campaign worker in San Miguel, for instance, had less to gain, personally, in the electoral campaigns of that county than did the calculating Felix Martinez. A silver prospector from Sierra County could never be put into the same category as Mills or Boyle, party leaders motivated as much by land and mining investments as by political convictions. Opportunism, in short, was less a factor among the rank and file than it was among the party leadership.

One quality that leaders and followers in the party did share was a high degree of individualism. This frontier trait was as much shared by territorial Populists as the social and economic convictions that brought them together under the same political umbrella. New Mexico with its underdeveloped land and mineral resources was well suited to the buoyant attitude of frontier people so effectively described by Frederick Jackson Turner in his essays. Even the depression of the nineties failed to discourage a number of citizens whose hopes for the future remained grandiose. But sagging beef prices, interest rates that were higher than in Kansas, and aggressive land-grabbing began to make their effect. Finally the collapse of the silver industry destroyed that old confidence and sense of hopeful anticipation. With the gradual erosion of those opportunities that had caused optimism, optimism itself fell victim. Consequently, a new political organization, one less willing to compromise, such as the People's party, began to take on an allure for the newly dispossessed. Although condemned as radical or ridiculed as impractical, the party was perceived by many, especially those in economic trouble, as the one organization willing to articulate the grievances of the less fortunate. Populism in New Mexico was in a very real sense a product of the fears and insecurities of a number of the territory's citizens. In many cases these popular anxieties went back to the late eighties when threats were posed by local monopolies. Reaction to these threats ultimately took the form of a pragmatic protest effort rather than an extreme or doctrinaire movement, as some of the detractors of Populism in New Mexico had claimed it to be.

Proof of this long-standing protest orientation in New Mexico can be found by perusing the Populist territorial platforms of 1894 and 1896. At the 1894 Albuquerque meeting, for instance, delegates demanded that public arid lands be turned over to the states and territories so they could be opened for settlement. Undoubtedly this demand was one way frustrated Populists could bring attention to the immense number of acres in New Mexico falling into the hands of land-grabbers. In the 1896 platform they became more specific, insisting that small settlers be granted free homes on all public lands, including lands claimed by grant owners or other claimants. Land was the "common property of the people," and these New Mexico Populists hoped to implement this concept when they further insisted that mining claims, even on land grants, be recognized. The Populists also wanted to protest the so-called plutocracy that governed the territory through the two irresponsive major parties. So great was their disenchantment with Republican and Democratic officeholders that at their 1894 convention they demanded all fees be paid directly into the public treasury before the revenue derived from them was distributed in salaries to territorial officials. They also insisted that all laws passed by the territorial legislature be referred to the people. New Mexico Populists, moreover, wanted to protest national conditions, particularly the deflationary fiscal policies of the federal government, as the adverse effects of tight money were reflected in high interest rates in New Mexico. And, of course, they supported the clarion call of all Populists for a national currency, "safe, sound and flexible."

Populists in New Mexico were much like those Kansas Populists described by Walter T.K. Nugent in his study refuting Populist nativism. Territorial Populists, like their Kansas counterparts, were dedicated to "democratic republicanism and economic democracy." [10] They were pragmatic, true, but they were absolutely determined to make the American system work the way it should. Although their sense of purpose was probably modified by a streak of frontier individualism, they were unwilling to compromise on those factors which made it impossible for the system to function properly, such as monopolism, the antithesis of economic democracy; high credit rates; and unresponsive politics.

As frontier products, Populists were hesitant to attack the railroads so necessary to them or to risk a decline in economic development by condemning alien landownership; nevertheless, Populists were to call for changes far more basic than their Republican or Democratic counterparts. The San Juan County party is a good example of a political organization caught between a desire for growth and an urge to reform. Coming from a predominantly agricultural county, San Juan Populists shared the philosophy of traditional agrarian protest politics as practiced in the Midwest and the South. Consequently, they took forceful stands on a variety of issues involving agriculture. At the same time, the party's most relentless spokesman, Editor Fred Holt of the *San Juan Times,* was careful not to alienate completely prospective railroad builders in his county.

The People's party of New Mexico, in summation, was a pragmatic, multi-issue oriented protest party speaking out on the major political, social and economic questions of the day. It was not solely preoccupied with free silver, as Richard Hofstadter and many other historians of mountain-states Populism have contended or implied. By 1896, silver admittedly had become the dominant issue in New Mexico, but during the previous eight years of the party's life free coinage was one of a number of issues motivating the faithful. The failure of territorial Populists to include a silver plank in the 1894 platform is proof that the sum total of Populism in New Mexico was not silverism. The omission of an unequivocal demand for free coinage, when other planks of the national Omaha platform were reiterated, did not go unnoticed in the territorial press. The Republican Las Vegas Daily Optic, for instance, accused candidate Mills and his party of trying to dodge the silver issue in 1894. [11]

The issues that initially sparked New Mexico Populism were primarily problems indigenous to the territory. As an example, protest against a so-called cattle monopoly in Lincoln County produced a vocal farmers' movement associated with the Southern Farmers' Alliance. At least some Populist votes were harvested from this Alliance activity of the late eighties, although the sympathetic Democrats in Lincoln County got most of them. Also, a land monopoly, the Maxwell Land Grant and Railroad Company, sparked protest in Colfax County, resulting in several more militant Alliance chapters. In San Miguel County, protest took another form. Because of the threat to the Las Vegas Community Grant posed by Anglo encroachments and a determination by Anglos to fence those portions of the communal grant they claimed, the local assemblies of the Knights of Labor joined with alarmed Hispanos, including night-riding White Caps, to organize the first legitimate People's party in the territory. In San Juan County, where the most successful Populist organization in the territory dominated local politics for four years, the protest was against the low prices and high interest rates hurting farmers. San Juan Populists were also most sensitive to the silver issue, as the major market for the county's farmers was southwestern Colorado, where the numerous silver camps went into decline during the nineties. The silver craze, however, was more widespread in the southwestern corner of the territory, giving Populism a good foothold in such depressed silver counties as Sierra.

One factor that accounts for the electoral disappointments of the territorial Populists was the determination of Democrats in New Mexico to syphon protest votes into their own electoral column. In both Lincoln and Colfax counties it was the Democrats who spearheaded the opposition against monopolistic cattle barons and land-grabbers. In San Miguel, it was the ex-Democrat Felix Martinez who terminated the dominance of the People's party in the politics of that county. On the territorial level it was the five-term Democratic delegate, Antonio Joseph, who, although himself guilty of land-grabbing, was able to convince voters that he too was a reformer and an opponent of land and cattle monopolies. Joseph's uncompromising stand in behalf of silver coinage persuaded a substantial portion of the New Mexico electorate that his party provided a more comfortable alternative to reform than the People's party. Only in San Juan County could a hard-line Populist organization resist the appeal of the alert, silver-thumping Democrats.

With few triumphs to its credit one might legitimately question the significance of Populism in New Mexico. One assumption that seems reasonable to make is that the territorial People's party nudged the Democratic party to the left on both local and national questions. Both parties were aiming their political rhetoric at the same electorate to a certain extent, although the Democrats appealed to a much broader spectrum of political opinion. Even so, the straightforward reform platforms of the People's party were bound to make territorial Democrats more candid in their criticisms of the inequities and ills of the economic system during the nineties. But the significance of the movement can be established on a more empirical level. The eagerness with which silverites in both major parties tried to court the People's party in 1896 through some fusion arrangement, for example, is indicative of a feeling throughout the territory that the Populists were capable of swinging the balance of control in New Mexico one way or another. The charges leveled against T.B. Mills during the 1894 and 1896 elections by incensed Democrats or Populists that he sold himself to Republican Thomas Catron is proof that many New Mexicans believed that a separate Populist electoral bid would split the progressive-minded vote in the territory and insure a Republican victory. More important in terms of the movement's significance is the evidence that there was an indigenous reform spirit in New Mexico responding to territorial problems, such as local monopoly, before the collapsed silver industry thrust the territory into the troubled national arena. Moreover, the People's party was unquestionably the most representative of this new spirit, despite a Democratic receptivity toward demands for change.

A major question arising from this study is whether Populist movements in other states and territories of the mountain West were similar to those of New Mexico. No significant evidence has been found of strong nativistic or anti-semitic tendencies among the New Mexico Populists. In view of the territory's large Spanish-speaking, Roman Catholic population, nativism would, of course, have been politically unwise, even admitting the prevalence of an Anglo bias. How does the New Mexico Populist movement compare with those in the more culturally homogeneous mountain states and territories?

The study of Populist leadership in New Mexico has revealed few farmers and even fewer silver prospectors in important capacities. Was this true in those mountain states where Populism has not been adequately studied? Although tempered by the usual concerns of a developing frontier territory, the New Mexico Populists advocated a variety of controversial reforms and demonstrated a fervency for questions indigenous to the territory. Did other Populist organizations in the region crusade against local monopolies and in favor of changes in the social and economic system of the nation before the cascading silver craze destroyed the vitality of other reform issues in 1896? New Mexico Populism was not a one-issue movement; was it typical, or unique, in this regard among the Rocky Mountain states and territories, and throughout the West during the nineties? Perhaps the development of Populism elsewhere in the mountain West, rather than being a simple story of silver from beginning to end, was fully as complex as the story that unfolded in the Territory of New Mexico.

BIBLIOGRAPHICAL ESSAY

Lost causes throughout history have often left but scanty records. Moreover, contemporary descriptions and evaluations of such causes have frequently been biased against them. New Mexico Populism fits somewhat unevenly into both of these categories. Records of the movement are not plentiful, but certainly the research undertaken in this study was less frustrating than similar research might have been into a movement of the remote past as, for example, a religious heresy of the early Christian era. As for the accounts of the Populist effort left by contemporaries in the territory, they were largely prejudiced against the movement. But here, too, there were mitigating circumstances. The People's party and the protest movements that preceded it had their newspaper voices. Also, some politicos from both major parties, in an effort to attract the Populist vote, often rendered a rather balanced judgment of the movement. Their descriptions of territorial Populism were at least tolerant in tone. Consequently, with patient probing and the exercise of some historical imagination it was possible to reconstruct the development of a largely forgotten political movement. Added to the satisfaction the historian always derives from recovering the past was the opportunity presented in this study for a comparison of New Mexico Populism with Populism elsewhere.

MANUSCRIPTS

The most valuable collection utilized in this study was the L. Bradford Prince Papers found in the State Records Center and Archives in Santa Fe. Although not a Populist, Prince was a silverite and for a time the fusion candidate for the People's party in 1896. His collection of letters, newspaper clippings, and campaign material is the best private source of information about the White Cap movement in San Miguel County. It also provides valuable data about the activities of silverites in New Mexico and throughout the nation, and the delegate elections of 1894 and 1896 in which Populists were involved. In his collection are important letters from Populist leaders, such as F.A. Blake, co-founder of the first legitimate People's party in New Mexico, and Theodore B. Mills, the Populist candidate for territorial delegate in 1894. The lengthy October 13, 1896, letter from Mills to Prince found in the Prince Papers was the most revealing single source used in this study. The

181

extensive Thomas B. Catron Papers, located in the Special Collections Division of the University of New Mexico Library in Albuquerque, were also invaluable. They helped me to reconstruct many of the events in the 1894 and 1896 elections. As the Republican candidate for territorial delegate in those two electoral races — he won the first and lost the second — Catron received many letters dealing with the activities of all party members, including Populists. Also consulted at the University of New Mexico library were the Marion Dargan Papers, ordinarily helpful for territorial history but yielding little about Populism. The T.B. Mills Collection at the New Mexico Highlands University library in Las Vegas is disappointing in one way and satisfying in another. There are no personal papers of the prominent Populist in this collection except for a business ledger. There is, however, a large accumulation of trade journals and obscure territorial newspapers; the latter were essential in recovering information about the almost forgotten Farmers' Alliance movements in Lincoln, Dona Ana, and Colfax counties. Two other private collections consulted were the Andrieus A. Jones and Eugene A. Fiske papers, both kept at the State Records Center and Archives. Unfortunately, in these collections there is little of value about the Populist movement in New Mexico.

OFFICIAL RECORDS

The well-organized official records located at the State Records Center and Archives in Santa Fe were especially useful in helping me assess the impact of Populism on the legislative process in the territory. The published *Acts of the Legislative Assembly of the Territory of New Mexico* for the Thirtieth, Thirty-first, and Thirty-second sessions were helpful, as were the *Proceedings of the House of Representatives of the Territory of New Mexico,* the *Proceedings of the Legislative Council of the Territory of New Mexico,* and the *Acts of the Legislative Assembly of New Mexico* for the Twenty-eighth Session and the *Proceedings of the Legislative Council of the Territory of New Mexico* for the Twenty-ninth Session. The unpublished Council and House journals for the Thirty-second Session were also used with profit. For election statistics, the Records of the Office of Secretary of State, along with pertinent newspaper clippings from the Prince Papers, were excellent. The assessment roll for Lincoln County, 1889, was utilized to confirm the role of the Coe family in the Farmers' Alliance, and the assessment roll for Santa Fe County, 1896, was used in a similar way to identify Populist leader Arthur Boyle as English land investor William Blackmore's son-in-law.

DIRECTORIES AND ALMANACS

Because of the difficulties encountered in locating information about many of the Populist leaders in New Mexico, I consulted early business directories in the archives of the History Library of the Museum of New Mexico to determine at least the occupations of these leaders. Particularly helpful was the *Southern Pacific Coast Directory, 1888-9* (San Francisco), which provided occupational information about M.P. Stamm, Populist national committeeman in 1896, and Thomas F. Keleher. Both men were prominent in the movement, but no other background information about either could be found. Two other useful directories consulted at the Museum library were the *Business Directory of the Principal Towns of Central and Southern California, Arizona, New Mexico, Southern Colorado, etc., 1882-3* (Oakland), and the *Colorado, New Mexico, Utah, Nevada, Arizona and Wyoming Gazetteer and Business Directory, 1884.* Contemporary almanacs were also used, especially for election information of a statistical nature. Editions of *The Tribune Almanac* (New York) and *The World Almanac and Encyclopedia* (New York), copies of which are located at the University of Northern Colorado library at Greeley, were found to be valuable because of the county-by-county breakdown of some of the election returns.

NEWSPAPERS

The most helpful primary resource used in reconstructing the chronology of New Mexico Populism was the territorial newspaper. Usually information about the program and campaign activities of the People's party was not prominently featured, but it was there, nonetheless, for anyone willing to peruse carefully. Indispensable for facts about the anti-monopoly activities of the Farmers' Alliance are two newspapers in the Mills Collection, the *Nogal Nugget* and the *Raton Weekly Independent.* The *Santa Fe Sun,* from the same collection, was valuable in clarifying the relationship of the Knights of Labor and the White Caps of San Miguel County. An excellent source for news about the founding of the San Miguel People's party and the machinations of the party's unreliable leader, Felix Martinez, was the Republican paper, the *Las Vegas Daily Optic,* issues of which were found on microfilm at the University of New Mexico library. Another Republican newspaper, which became Democratic during the 1896 election because of a change in ownership, was the *Santa Fe Daily New Mexican.* It is located at the Museum of New Mexico, although there are issues on microfilm at the State Library in Santa Fe. Of exceptional value because no editions of the *New Mexico Nugget,* the official Populist organ, could be found was the *San Juan Times,* edited by Populist Fred E. Holt. Issues of this newspaper for the election years 1894 through 1898 chronicle the activities of the territory's most successful People's movement, the San Juan County Populist party. These are in the editorial offices of the *Daily Times* (Farmington). Several editions of the *San Juan Times* for 1895 are also on microfilm in the University of New Mexico library. The Populist editorials in this journal are most revealing of the movement's vigor, at least for this corner of the territory. Another newspaper, independent of the territorial Populist movement but partial toward the national one, was the Spanish-language newspaper *La Voz del Pueblo,* published in Las Vegas by Felix Martinez. It is in bound volumes at the State Records Center and Archives, along with the informative *Albuquerque Daily Citizen,* a conservative pro-gold Republican journal, and the *Albuquerque Democrat,* which by its political partisanship lived up to its name. Other newspapers consulted were the *Weekly New Mexican Review* of Santa Fe and the *Las Vegas Stock Grower and Farmer,* both in the Museum of New Mexico, and the *Socorro Chieftain* and *Albuquerque Evening Herald,* clippings of which were found in the Prince collection. I also was exposed to other editorial viewpoints through other journals quoted in several of the newspapers cited. Such journals include the *New Mexico Nugget, San Juan County Index, Cochiti Call, Santa Fe Herald, Raton Range, San Marcial Bee, Lordsburg Liberal,* and *Silver City Eagle.*

Through the editorials, letters to the editor, and published party statements and platforms in the territorial press, I was able to acquire much information about the stands taken by New Mexico Populists on such issues as monopoly and free silver. These territorial journals were also searched with few results for evidences of nativism, anti-semitism, or other prejudices attributed to Populism by critical scholars.

BOOKS AND ARTICLES

Although published materials dealing directly with the Populist movement in the territory are scarce, there are secondary sources available which illuminate New Mexico's political scene during the Populist era and clarify it in relation to national politics. The books and articles I used fall logically into three categories: those written by contemporaries, recent sources about nineteenth-century New Mexico politics, and accounts, many of them analytical, about the movement outside of New Mexico. In this last category are books and articles about national developments related to Populism.

Of the contemporary accounts consulted, one of the most useful was Miguel A. Otero, *My Life on the Frontier, 1882-1897: Death Knell of a Territory and Birth of a State,* Vol. II (Albuquerque, 1939). Otero, although a partisan Republican, provides needed information about Republican feuds and White Cap activities in San Miguel County. George Curry's own story,

184

George Curry, 1861-1947: An Autobiography (Albuquerque, 1958), edited by H.B. Hening, is rich in political gossip; Curry, who later became a Republican territorial governor, was a Democratic leader in Lincoln County during the nineties. Two other sources consulted in connection with Lincoln County were George W. Coe, *Frontier Fighter: The Autobiography of George W. Coe Who Fought and Rode with Billy the Kid* (Boston, 1934), which failed to provide the information sought about the Farmers' Alliance, and the more recently published Wilbur Coe, *Ranch on the Ruidoso: The Story of a Pioneer Family in New Mexico, 1871-1966* (New York, 1969). Informative on the agricultural and stock-grazing potentialities of Lincoln County during its period of protest is the Bureau of Immigration publication edited by Max Frost entitled *New Mexico: Its Resources, Climate, Geography, Geology, History, Statistics, Present Conditions and Future Prospects* (Santa Fe, 1894). Broader in scope is the rare *An Illustrated History of New Mexico* (Chicago, 1895), which contains biographical information about Mills and another Populist leader, Elwin T. Webber. Two other general histories used were by men active in the life of New Mexico during the Populist period. Ralph Emerson Twitchell's *The Leading Facts of New Mexican History*, Vol. II (Cedar Rapids, Iowa, 1912), an indispensable reference for students of territorial history, was helpful, as was Benjamin M. Read's *Illustrated History of New Mexico* (Santa Fe, 1912). Consulted for background information, but yielding little, was the standard Hubert Hugh Bancroft, *The Works of Hubert Hugh Bancroft*, Vol. XVII: *History of Arizona and New Mexico, 1530-1888* (San Francisco, 1889).

A number of accounts about the New Mexico political situation in the late eighties and the nineties were consulted. The two most useful are Howard Roberts Lamar, *The Far Southwest, 1846-1912: A Territorial History* (New Haven, 1966) and my *New Mexico's Quest for Statehood, 1846-1912* (Albuquerque, 1968). The latter account has a chapter devoted to the silver question and its impact on Populism. Lamar's book, although brief on Populism, does provide excellent background for many of the political developments in New Mexico during this period. It reveals much about such quasi-political bodies as the Santa Fe Ring and such historical episodes as the Maxwell Land Grant controversy, which was so important to the growth of the Colfax County Farmers' Alliance. Jim Berry Pearson's comprehensive *The Maxwell Land Grant* (Norman, 1961) was also helpful in understanding the ramifications of this controversy. Two books useful for background information about San Miguel County are Milton Callon, *Las Vegas, New Mexico . . . The Town that Wouldn't Gamble* (Las Vegas, 1962) and F. Stanley (Stanley Francis Crocchioli), *The Las Vegas Story (New Mexico)* (Denver, 1951). More helpful is a study on San Miguel's White Cap phenomenon, Andrew Bancroft Schlesinger's "Las Gorras Blancas, 1889-1891," *The Journal of Mexican American History,* I (Spring, 1971) 87-130. Useful on land policy is Victor Westphall, *The Public Domain in New Mexico, 1854-1891* (Albuquerque, 1965). Particularly valuable because of the importance of newspapers in reconstructing territorial political history is Porter A. Stratton, *The Territorial Press of New Mexico, 1834-1912* (Albuquerque, 1969). General histories of New Mexico found to be helpful are Frank D. Reeve's *History of New Mexico, Vol. II* (New York, 1961), which is good in discussing such germane economic developments as the emergence of the cattle industry, and Warren A. Beck's *New Mexico: A History of Four Centuries* (Norman, 1962).

The histories consulted which deal with Populism outside of New Mexico are primarily interpretive. Some are concerned with the movement as a national one, others with the growth of Populism in one or more of its regions of strength: the South, the Midwest, or the mountain-states West. John D. Hicks, *The Populist Revolt: A History of the Farmers' Alliance and the Peoples' Party* (Minneapolis, 1931) is still the most valuable source of information about the national movement. Richard Hofstadter's handling of Populism in *The Age of Reform: From Bryan to F.D.R.* (New York, 1955) is important as a revisionist treatment, summing up as it does many of the criticisms of Populism rendered by such scholars as Oscar Handlin, Victor Ferkiss, and Max Lerner. Hofstadter's work was significant in stimulating in me a great interest in what constituted the essence of the New Mexico movement, although his interpretations have been under considerable attack. Useful as a corrective to Hofstadter are Norman Pollock, *The Populist Response to Industrialist America: Midwestern Populist Thought* (Cambridge, 1962) and Walter T.K. Nugent, *The Tolerant Populists: Kansas Populism and Nativism* (Chicago, 1963), both of which provide excellent insights into the Midwestern movement. Clarifying the role of Populism, particularly in the South, is C. Vann Woodward's essay, "The Populist Heritage and the Intellectual," *The American Scholar,* LIX (Winter, 1959-60), 55-72. Another account that influenced me, because it tried to show eastern, even European, roots of western Populism, was Chester McArthur Destler's "Western Radicalism, 1865-1901: Concepts and Origins," *Mississippi Valley Historical Review,* XXXI (December, 1944), 335-68. Helpful in putting into perspective the 1896 election were Robert F. Durden, *The Climax of Populism* (Lexington, 1965); Stanley L. Jones, *The Presidential Election of 1896* (Madison, 1964); and H. Wayne Morgan, *From Hayes to McKinley: National Party Politics, 1877-1896* (Syracuse, 1969). Donald L. Kinzer's *An Episode in Anti-Catholicism: The American Protective Association* (Seattle, 1964) was also useful because the American Protective Association, even in Spanish-speaking Roman Catholic New Mexico, was an issue in at least two of the territory's elections during the nineties.

Turning to more regional or state studies of the Populist movement, there are two illuminating studies of Kansas Populism which I consulted: Michael J. Brodhead, *Persevering Populist: The Life of Frank O. Doster* (Reno, 1969) and O. Gene Clanton, *Kansas Populism: Ideas and Men* (Lawrence, 1969). But in the mountain-states West, unfortunately, the number of published studies is not comparable to those devoted to the Kansas movement. A welcome exception is Thomas A. Clinch's *Urban Populism and Free Silver in Montana: A Narrative of Ideology in Political Action* (Missoula, 1970). Certainly other monographic studies of Populism in the states and territories of the mountain West are needed in order to understand the nature and the role of the People's party in this region. There are, however, a number of good articles on aspects of Western Populism, such as G. Michael McCarthy, "Colorado's Populist Leadership," *The Colorado Magazine,* XLVII (Winter, 1971), 30-42 and David B. Griffiths, "Populism in Wyoming," *Annals of Wyoming,* XL (April, 1968), 56-67. Also presenting the Wyoming background is Lewis L. Gould's monograph, *Wyoming: A Political History, 1868-1896* (New Haven, 1968). Gould's book not only illuminates the relationship of Wyoming's People's party to the two major parties, providing insights which I was able to use in my own study, but it also contains a good analysis of how Wyoming functioned under the territorial system. Three other studies that helped to put New Mexico's territorial status in better perspective for me are the monograph, Earl S. Pomeroy, *The Territories and the United States, 1861-1890: Studies in Colonial Administration* (Philadelphia, 1947), and two articles, Frederick Jackson Turner, "The Problems of the West," *The Atlantic Monthly: A Magazine of Literature, Science, Art, and Politics,* LXXVII (September, 1896), 290-300 and Kenneth N. Owens, "Patterns and Structure in Western Territorial Politics," *The Western Historical Quarterly,* I (October, 1970), 373-92.

These books and articles are by no means inclusive of all the sources I consulted. They do include, however, those most germane or most frequently used. Secondary accounts not mentioned in this essay are included in the notes whenever cited.

UNPUBLISHED DISSERTATIONS AND MASTER'S THESES

The number of unpublished graduate studies pertaining to New Mexico Populism is disappointingly small. There are, however, four studies, two of which were most helpful to me. Walter John Donlon, "LeBaron Bradford Prince, Chief Justice and Governor of New Mexico Territory, 1879-1893" (Ph.D. dissertation, University of New Mexico, 1967) was of assistance in clarifying the relationship of the night-riding White Caps with the Knights of Labor and People's party of San Miguel County. Valuable for providing the economic background of New Mexico Populism was Herbert Theodore Hoover, ''Populism and the Territories'' (Master's thesis, New Mexico State University, 1961). For related developments in Colorado, John Foster Powers, '' 'Blaine and Free Coinage': Factionalism and Silver in the Republican Pre-Convention Campaign of 1892 in Colorado'' (Master's thesis, Colorado State College, 1968) proved useful. David Burke Griffiths, ''Populism in the Far West, 1890-1900'' (Ph.D. dissertation, University of Washington, 1967) makes an important contribution to the overall background of the Populist movement in the West.

OTHER SOURCES

I am indebted to the descendents of two important figures associated with New Mexico Populism or the protest agitation that preceded it. Mrs. Louise Coe Runnels of Capitan, New Mexico, a granddaughter of Jasper N. Coe, the Lincoln County Farmers' Alliance leader and one-time president of the territorial Alliance, and Mrs. Wilbur Coe of Glencoe, New Mexico (related to the Coe family by marriage) were both helpful in confirming the identity of the Alliance leader (see note 13, Ch. 2). Mrs. R.V. Boyle, daughter-in-law of the Santa Fe Populist Arthur Boyle, and her friend Marion Dockwiller, both of Santa Fe, rendered a similar service. They confirmed that there was no other Arthur Boyle in Santa Fe during the nineties to be confused with the Santa Fe Populist Boyle.

Related primarily to protest agitation in New Mexico were the Herrera brothers, leaders of the White Cap movement in San Miguel County. Their living relatives, Mrs. Ruth Brito and her son and daughter-in-law Mr. and Mrs. Al Brito, were most helpful in supplying information about them in an interview.

NOTES

1

NEW MEXICO: SEEDBED FOR POPULISM?

1. Howard R. Lamar, *The Far Southwest, 1846-1912: A Territorial History* (New Haven, 1966).

2. Robert W. Larson, *New Mexico's Quest for Statehood, 1846-1912* (Albuquerque, 1968). See Chapter 11.

3. An exception is a rather recent monograph on Montana Populism: Thomas A. Clinch, *Urban Populism and Free Silver in Montana: A Narrative of Ideology in Political Action* (Missoula, 1970).

4. Walter T.K. Nugent, *The Tolerant Populists: Kansas Populism and Nativism* (Chicago, 1963). More recently two valuable accounts of Kansas Populism have been published, O. Gene Clanton, *Kansas Populism: Ideas and Men* (Lawrence, 1969) and Michael J. Brodhead, *Persevering Populist: The Life of Frank Doster* (Reno, 1969). Both add substantially to our understanding of Populism in the Jayhawker State, but in neither account is the author especially concerned with interpreting the movements in relation to the overall development of American liberalism.

5. John D. Hicks, *The Populist Revolt: A History of the Farmers' Alliance and the People's Party* (Minneapolis, 1931).

6. Norman Pollack, *The Populist Response to Industrial America: Midwestern Populist Thought* (Cambridge, 1962).

7. Particularly germane because it responds directly to the criticism of Populism by revisionists is C. Vann Woodward's "The Populist Heritage and the Intellectual," *The American Scholar,* LIX (Winter, 1959-60), 55-72. This perceptive essay is also included in Woodward's *The Burden of Southern History* (Baton Rouge, 1960), pp. 141-66.

8. Richard Hofstadter, *The Age of Reform: From Bryan to F.D.R.* (New York, 1955), p. 50.

9. For the text of the act see "Organic Act Establishing the Territory of New Mexico: Approved September 30, 1850," *New Mexico Statutes Annotated,* compiled and annotated by Stephen B. Davis, Jr., and Merritt C. Mechem (published by authority; Denver, 1915).

10. Lewis L. Gould, *Wyoming: A Political History, 1868-1896* (New Haven, 1968), p. 20.

11. Frederick Jackson Turner, "The Problem of the West," *The Atlantic Monthly: A Magazine of Literature, Science, Art, and Politics*, LXXVIII (September, 1896), 295.

12. Prince to J.J. Trujillo, L. Bradford Prince Papers, State Records Center and Archives, Santa Fe. Hereafter cited as Prince Papers.

2
THE LINCOLN COUNTY FARMERS' ALLIANCE

1. Assessment Roll of Real Estate and Personal Property in the County of Lincoln, 1888, State Records Center and Archives, Santa Fe. Hereafter cited as A.R., Lincoln County.

2. Victor Westphall, *The Public Domain in New Mexico, 1854-1891* (Albuquerque, 1965), pp. 68-69.

3. A.R., Lincoln County, 1888.

4. The *Nogal Nugget.* The *Nugget* is in the newspaper collection of Theodore B. Mills, a leading territorial Populist, which was donated to New Mexico Highlands University by his son Byron T. Mills. The Mills Collection will only be cited hereafter when a new journal is introduced. See William Swilling Wallace's "A Check List of Western Newspapers in the Mills Collection," *New Mexico Historical Review*, XXX (April, 1955), 1-17, to get an idea of the extent of this remarkable accumulation of Western newspapers.

5. Westphall, *The Public Domain in New Mexico*, p. 82.

6. Located in the History Library, Museum of New Mexico, Santa Fe. Hereafter cited as History Library, M.N.M., when a new journal is introduced.

7. This organization adopted several names before it finally became officially known as the National Farmers' Alliance and Industrial Union.

8. The *Nogal Nugget*, September 27, 1888.

9. The town of Nogal had only fifteen people in 1884, according to the *Colorado, New Mexico, Utah, Nevada, Arizona and Wyoming Gazetteer and Business Directory, 1884*, Vol. I (R.L. Polk and A.C. Danser, Publishers), no page numbers. Copy of directory located in History Library, M.N.M.

10. The *Nogal Nugget*, September 27, 1888.

11. August 23, 1888.

12. Max Frost (ed.), *New Mexico: Its Resources, Climate, Geography, History, Statistics, Present Conditions and Future Prospects,* official publication of the Bureau of Immigration (Santa Fe, 1894), p. 212, History Library, M.N.M.

13. Identifying the vigorous Lincoln County Alliance leader as Jasper N. Coe, of the prominent Coe family, was not an easy task, but fortunately the writer received the complete cooperation of Mrs. Louis Coe Runnels, Jasper's granddaughter, and Mrs. Wilbur Coe, both of whom still live in Lincoln County. In the territorial press Coe's name always appeared with his initials J.N. rather than his given name, Jasper. His granddaughter was able to supply his full name, Jasper Newton Coe; thus the names designated by the initials J.N. were finally identified. As additional proof, Jasper's name appears as J.N. on the assessment rolls of Lincoln County alongside his kinfolk, Frank and George. Mrs. Wilbur Coe to Larson, October 10, 1969; Mrs. Louise Coe Runnels to Larson, January 23, 1970; A.R., Lincoln County.

14. Philip J. Rasch, "Feuding at Farmington," *New Mexico Historical Review,* XL (July, 1965), 215-16. The two most complete accounts of the Lincoln County War are William A. Keleher, *Violence in Lincoln County, 1869-1881* (Albuquerque, 1957) and Robert N. Mullin (ed.), *Maurice Garland Fulton's History of the Lincoln County War* (Tucson, 1968).

15. Wilbur Coe, *Ranch on the Ruidoso: The Story of a Pioneer Family in New Mexico, 1871-1966* (New York, 1969), p. 145.

16. For details about the San Juan range war see Rasch, "Feuding in Farmington," pp. 216-29. In the Lincoln assessment rolls, where the last names of property owners are listed alphabetically, the two brothers and their famous cousin are named one right after the other. In the 1886 and 1889 rolls the order of their names was determined by the location of their property holdings. Thus, Jasper, who settled between Frank and George, was listed between the names of his two kinfolk. A.R., Lincoln County. For another account of the adventures of the Coe family see George W. Coe, *Frontier Fighter* (New York, 1934).

17. A.R., Lincoln County, 1888.

18. The *Nogal Nugget,* September 27, 1888, and other issues.

19. Lamar, *The Far Southwest,* p. 196.

20. The problem of inadequate land surveys was particularly acute from 1876 to 1896, when federal money appropriated for surveying purposes was insufficient to meet the needs of settlers or to support the reforms demanded, according to Thomas G. Alexander in a perceptive paper entitled "The Federal Land Survey System and the Mountain West, 1870-1896," which was delivered before the Conference on the History of the Territories on November 3, 1969, in Washington, D.C. and published in John Porter Bloom (ed.) *The American Territorial System* (Athens, Ohio: 1973) pp. 145-60.

21. Westphall, *The Public Domain in New Mexico,* pp. 32-36, 100-111.

22. The *Nogal Nugget,* August 16, 1888.

23. July 19, 1888, History Library, M.N.M.

24. As quoted in *Weekly New Mexican Review* (Santa Fe), July 19, 1888.

25. August 16, 1888.

26. Westphall, *The Public Domain in New Mexico,* pp. 78-79.

27. August 16, 1888.

28. Lamar, *The Far Southwest,* pp. 136-51; Larson, *New Mexico's Quest for Statehood,* pp. 141-44. The term "Smooth Steve," used by Lamar in his book, is an especially appropriate description of this skillful lobbyist and politician. Elkins was one of the promoters of the territory's first incorporated cattle company, the Consolidated Land, Cattle Raising and Wool Growing Company of San Miguel County, which was organized in 1872. See Frank D. Reeve, *History of New Mexico,* II (New York, 1961), 211.

29. The *Nogal Nugget,* August 16, 1888.

30. The White Oaks journal was quoted and upbraided in the August 16, 1888, issue of the *Nugget.*

31. October 4, 1888.

32. The *Nogal Nugget,* August 16, 1888.

33. Ibid., August 16, 1888.

34. Quoted in Hicks, *The Populist Revolt,* p. 437 (Appendix E).

35. August 23, 1888. The price differential cited for the cost of wire fencing and cotton cloth was taken from a newspaper called the *Herald,* the location of which was not given. Two statements by Cleveland, one claiming that "trusts are the natural offspring of a market artifically restricted" and the other pointing to the problem of surpluses caused by the "unjust taxation" of the protective tariff, were published in the October 4, 1888, issues of the *Nugget.*

36. Hofstadter, *Age of Reform,* pp. 20-21, 72-81 and *passim.* The anti-semitism of struggling agrarians is particularly stressed.

37. October 4, 1888.

38. September 27, 1888.

39. September 6, 1888.

40. August 16, 1888. Also *Santa Fe Herald* as quoted in the September 6, 1888, issue of the *Nugget.*

41. August 16, 1888.

42. Larson, *New Mexico's Quest for Statehood,* pp. 164, 341.

43. *Santa Fe Herald* as quoted in September 6, 1888, issue of the *Nugget.*

44. *Colorado, New Mexico . . . Gazetteer and Business Directory, 1884.*

45. *Lincoln Independent* as quoted in the *Nogal Nugget,* October 4, 1888.

46. *Gallup Gleaner* as quoted in ibid.

47. A minor alteration was made in this quote, which also appeared in October 4 issue of the *Nugget,* in order to correct a typographical error.

48. The *Nogal Nugget,* November 8, 1888. Results showed Joseph with substantial margins in the county tabulations with Democrats doing very well in legislative races throughout the territory.

49. Ibid.

50. Robert G. Athearn, *High Country Empire* (New York, 1960), p. 144.

3
THE STRUGGLE IN COLFAX COUNTY

1. Chapter locations and Alliance officers are listed in an official directory published in the *Raton Weekly Independent* on January 5, 1889, and other issues. Mills Collection.

2. The *Nogal Nugget,* August 16, 1888. No issues of the *Wagon Mound Settler* could be located.

3. *Raton Weekly Independent,* March 16, 1889.

4. Reeve, *History of New Mexico,* II, 211. A most useful account of the cattle industry in New Mexico is included in Reeve's chapter entitled "The Range Industry."

5. Lamar, *The Far Southwest,* pp. 49-51, 141-43. Two detailed accounts of the complex history surrounding these grants are William A. Keleher, *Maxwell Land Grant: A New Mexico Item* (Santa Fe, 1942) and Jim Berry Pearson, *The Maxwell Land Grant* (Norman, 1961).

6. Reeve, *History of New Mexico,* II, 218.

7. Lamar, *The Far Southwest,* pp. 143-44, 152-53; *Raton Weekly Independent,* February 23, 1889.

8. Pearson, *The Maxwell Land Grant,* pp. 72-73. The company, weakened by anti-grant opposition which it did not completely anticipate, suffered serious losses in the Panic of 1873. By 1875 it saw its securities drop to four or five cents on the dollar.

9. Lamar, *The Far Southwest,* pp. 145-46.

10. Ross to John O'Grady, March 26, 1887, as quoted in Larson, *New Mexico's Quest for Statehood, p. 142.*

11. Larson, *New Mexico's Quest for Statehood,* pp. 143-44.

12. Coe, *Ranch on the Ruidoso,* pp. 1-2.

13. Lamar, *The Far Southwest,* pp. 152-54; Larson, *New Mexico's Quest for Statehood,* p. 138.

14. Frank Warner Angel, special investigator of the Department of the Interior and Department of Justice, filed a report accusing Axtell of such a plot. He used a letter from Axtell to Benjamin Stevens, territorial district attorney, as prime evidence. See Larson, *New Mexico's Quest for Statehood,* pp. 138, 337; Calvin Horn, *New Mexico's Troubled Years: The Story of the Early Territorial Governors* (Albuquerque, 1963), pp. 189-94.

15. August 30, 1888, Museum of New Mexico.

16. February 16, 1889.

17. *Raton Weekly Independent,* February 23, 1889.

18. E.D. Spencer to editor, the *Nogal Nugget,* August 16, 1888.

19. *Trinidad Citizen,* as quoted in the *Independent* and editorial in the same issue, February 16, 1889.

20. As quoted in the *Nogal Nugget,* September 27, 1888.

21. February 16 and 23, 1889.

22. *Raton Weekly Independent,* February 16, 1889.

23. Telegram from Hon. Edwin B. Franks to *Raton Weekly Independent,* February 23, 1889.

24. In the veto message, cited in the February 23 issue of the *Independent,* Ross was particularly critical, because the court could not inquire into the motives behind affidavits filed by witnesses in support of a change of venue. The absence of a provision which would allow the prosecution to file a counter affidavit also was criticized.

25. Ralph Emerson Twitchell, *The Leading Facts of New Mexican History* (Cedar Rapids, Iowa, 1912), II, 500.

26. Fountain was elected speaker by a vote of 15 to 8. New Mexico, Legislature, *Proceedings of the House of Representatives of the Territory of New Mexico,* 28th Sess. (Santa Fe, 1889), p. 7. Chaves was again chosen president of the Council, without serious opposition, after L.C. Fort, Republican leader from San Miguel County, was made temporary chairman. New Mexico, Legislature, *Proceedings of the Legislative Council of the Territory of New Mexico,* 28th Sess. (Santa Fe, 1889), pp. 7, 8.

27. Walter John Donlon, "LeBaron Bradford Prince, Chief Justice and Governor of New Mexico Territory, 1879-1893" (unpublished Ph.D. dissertation, Department of History, University of New Mexico, 1967), pp. 167-68.

28. New Mexico, Legislature, *Acts of the Legislative Assembly of New Mexico,* 28th Sess. (Santa Fe, 1889), p. 184. Chapter 77, the change-of-venue law, is printed on pp. 183-84. The law is still in effect, although court interpretations have somewhat modified its original intent.

29. As quoted in the *Nogal Nugget,* August 16, 1888.

30. August 16, 1888.

31. Mills to Prince, September 8, 1891, as quoted in Donlon, "LeBaron Bradford Prince," p. 280.

32. November 17, 1888.

33. The *Nogal Nugget,* September 27, 1888.

34. November 17, 1888.

35. The bill was introduced in the Territorial Council by Colonel George Pritchard, a Republican leader from San Miguel County. See New Mexico, *Acts of the Legislative Assembly . . . ,* pp. 235-40, for details about Pritchard's bill.

36. Larson, *New Mexico's Quest for Statehood,* pp. 155-60, 166, 167-68. The charge that big landowners had shifted the tax burden to stock grazers and farmers was made by Governor Ross in an editorial in the *Deming Headlight.* It was written after the governor was replaced and had returned to his old vocation as a newspaperman.

37. October 4, 1890.

38. The *Santa Fe Sun,* November 15, 1890.

39. October 25, 1890.

4

THE SAN MIGUEL PEOPLE'S PARTY

1. December 11, 1889, Prince Papers.

2. *Weekly New Mexican Review* (Santa Fe), August 30, 1888, Mills Collection.

3. Miguel A. Otero, *My Life on the Frontier, 1882-1897: Death Knell of a Territory and Birth of a State* (Albuquerque, 1939), II, 248.

4. April 15, 1890, Prince Papers.

5. August 12, 1890, as cited in Donlon, "LeBaron Bradford Prince," pp. 225-28.

6. Donlon, "LeBaron Bradford Prince," pp. 225, 228, 230-31, 233. Mills translated the White Cap threat in a letter to Prince on July 19, 1890. Letters dealing with fence cutting and Prince's reaction to the White Cap depredations are found in a special folder in Prince's Papers, the White Cap Folder.

7. For additional information about the governor's background before coming to New Mexico, see Donlon, "LeBaron Bradford Prince," pp. 7, 10-11, 17, 19, 21, 25 and Arie W. Poldervaart, *Black-Robed Justice* (Publications in History of the Historical Society of New Mexico, Vol. XIII, Santa Fe, 1948), p. 111.

8. Poldervaart, *Black-Robed Justice,* p. 110.

9. Five document cases dealing with Prince's mining ventures are found among the Prince Papers.

10. The *Santa Fe Sun,* October 25, 1890, Mills Collection.

11. M.A. Otero, *My Life on the Frontier,* II, 4, 263-65.

12. Governor Prince has been called The Father of New Mexico Statehood because of his diligent efforts in behalf of New Mexico's admission. See Larson, *New Mexico's Quest for Statehood,* p. 144 and *passim.* Prince even wrote a book on the territory's long statehood fight: *New Mexico's Struggle for Statehood: Sixty Years of Effort to Obtain Self Government* (Santa Fe, 1910).

13. Donlon, "LeBaron Bradford Prince," p. 225; Larson, *New Mexico's Quest for Statehood,* pp. 162-63.

14. Donlon, "LeBaron Bradford Prince," pp. 229-30.

15. Donlon, in his very thorough study of Prince as governor and chief justice of the territory, found no evidence that Noble contributed the money requested by Prince or that any convictions resulted from the legal action launched against the defendants in the four cases of fence cutting on lands homesteaded or pre-empted. Fiske admitted his failure to prosecute in a letter to Prince on December 18, 1891.

16. In collaboration with the Nationalists, who were members of the Nationalist clubs inspired by Edward Bellamy's utopian novel, *Looking Backward,* the Knights were most effective in giving vigorous support to the transportation plank of the Omaha platform. See Chester McArthur Destler, "Western Radicalism, 1865-1901: Concepts and Origins," *Mississsippi Valley Historical Review,* XXXI (December, 1944), 354-55.

17. Otero, *My Life on the Frontier,* II, 248-49.

18. *Las Vegas Daily Optic,* July 23, 1890, as cited in Donlon, "LeBaron Bradford Prince," p. 236.

19. The harsh evaluation of Nicanor was provided by Charles A. Siringo, the famous Pinkerton agent who conducted an undercover investigation of the White Caps. Donlon, "LeBaron Bradford Prince," p. 254. Otero, who has one of the best descriptions of the colorful Pablo Herrera in print, cites Pablo's prison record on pp.

250-51 of his autobiography. The living relatives of the Herrera brothers dispute these unfavorable characterizations. They assert that the criticisms of Nicanor were due more to his willingness to stand up to Anglos than to his admittedly quick temper. As for Pablo, his conviction for murder was to them most unfair. Pablo was involved in a fight he did not provoke and was merely defending himself. Interview with Mrs. Ruth Brito and her son and daughter-in-law, Mr. and Mrs. Al Brito of Denver, February 27, 1972.

20. John K. Martin, Frank C. Ogden, and J.B. Allen to Powderly, August 8, 1890, as cited in Donlon, ''LeBaron Bradford Prince,'' p. 233.

21. For a discussion and analysis of these early tensions see Larson, *New Mexico's Quest for Statehood,* pp. 70-71, 320-21.

22. Otero, *My Life on the Frontier,* II, 254.

23. The *Santa Fe Sun,* November 1, 1890.

24. *Las Vegas Daily Optic,* October 18, 1892. The only known description of the founding of the new party is provided by Blake in this edition of the *Optic.* Issues of the paper are on microfilm in the Special Collections Division, University of New Mexico Library, Albuquerque, which will be cited hereafter as U.N.M. when a new journal is introduced.

25. The *Daily New Mexican* (Santa Fe), September 20 and 27, 1876, History Library, M.N.M. Invoking the name of the people in behalf of any cause or organization was quite common in San Miguel County. The *Las Vegas Daily Optic* was called the ''People's Paper'' in its September 20, 1892, issue and in other editions.

26. August 16, 1888.

27. *Las Vegas Daily Optic,* October 18, 1892.

28. Benjamin M. Read, *Illustrated History of New Mexico* (Santa Fe, 1912), pp. 760-61 (Martinez's own copy, now in the possession of Dr. Myra Ellen Jenkins, state historian, State Records Center and Archives, Santa Fe); *Southern Pacific Coast Directory, 1888-9* (San Francisco, no date), p. 468.

29. *Santa Fe Daily New Mexican,* September 8, 1890, History Library, M.N.M.

30. *Las Vegas Daily Optic,* October 18, 1892.

31. *Las Vegas Daily Optic,* October 18, 1892, and November 1, 1894.

32. Donlon, ''LeBaron Bradford Prince,'' p. 236.

33. *An Illustrated History of New Mexico* (Chicago, 1895), pp. 377-78.

34. *An Illustrated History of New Mexico,* p. 378.

35. Milton W. Callon, *Las Vegas, New Mexico . . . The Town that Wouldn't Gamble* (Las Vegas, 1962), pp. 102-3. The New Mexico and Pacific Railroad Company, builder of the Santa Fe, filed a suit against Mills and other citizens who had reneged on their notes. The company later dropped the suit, deciding to solicit for "outright gifts" for the cost of railroad construction. Mills, always the promoter, gave one.

36. Otero, *My Life on the Frontier,* II, 252. When Otero was appointed clerk of the Fourth Judicial District, the Romero and Lopez factions each advanced candidates for the position of county clerk, still held by Otero. The two groups acted with such aggressiveness that Byron Mills, a competent man and apparently not a political renegade like his father, was appointed by Otero to be his deputy county clerk. Mills could collect and keep all the emoluments of the office, which would remain, however, in Otero's possession. The two factions protested Otero's right to hold both offices, and asked Justice O'Brien to remove him as district clerk, a demand which O'Brien "indignantly" refused.

37. *An Illustrated History of New Mexico,* p. 378.

38. *Southern Pacific Coast Directory, 1888-9,* p. 469.

39. There is a large and varied collection of real estate newspapers in the Mills Collection at the New Mexico Highlands University, including such journals as *American Real Estate Guide* (New York), *Real Estate Journal, The New South* and the *Virginia Real Estate Index* of Richmond.

40. A ledger entitled "T.B. Mills and Co.," located in the Mills Collection, contains descriptions and prices for the La Puressima and San Felipe grants in northern Mexico and the Jose Sutton and Vallecito grants in New Mexico.

41. *Sante Fe Daily New Mexican,* July 2, 1890.

42. The *San Juan Times* (Farmington), September 28, 1894, microfilm copy, editorial office of the *Daily Times* of Farmington.

43. *Business Directory of the Principal Towns of Central and Southern California, Arizona, New Mexico, Southern Colorado, Kansas, etc., 1882-3* (Oakland, no date), p. 319. Mills published the newspaper in Las Vegas with a man named Hadley.

44. Hubert Howe Bancroft, *The Works of Hubert Howe Bancroft,* Vol. XVII: *History of Arizona and New Mexico, 1530-1888* (San Francisco, 1889), 749. The small 35-page volume, published in Las Vegas, must have been welcomed in a territory where the mining craze was especially strong during the eighties.

45. T.B. Mills, Exposition commissioner, *New Mexico: San Miguel County, Illustrated.* Prepared for the World's Exposition at New Orleans in 1884-85 (Las Vegas, 1885), History Library, M.N.M.

46. Mills to A.A. Jones, May 10, 1893, folder entitled "Personal Correspondence August[,] 1884-March 9[,] 1912," A.A. Jones Papers, State Records Center and Archives, Santa Fe. The Western Columbian Club included as officers vice-presidents from Arizona, Colorado, Idaho, Kansas, Missouri, Montana, Utah, and Wyoming.

47. *An Illustrated History of New Mexico,* p. 378; Mills, *New Mexico: San Miguel County, Illustrated,* p. 1.

48. *Las Vegas Daily Optic,* October 18, 1892. Also, as part of the general organization of the new party, the chairmen of the precinct committees were placed on the party's county committee.

49. O'Brien to Prince, August 22, 1890, as quoted in Donlon, "LeBaron Bradford Prince," p. 237. The italics are mine.

50. As quoted in Donlon, "LeBaron Bradford Prince," p. 236.

51. Joseph was endorsed by the Knights of San Miguel County during the 1890 election campaign. The *Santa Fe Sun,* November 1, 1890. In a letter to his son-in-law, Ambrosio Valdez, two years later, Joseph admitted his warm association with the Knights, acknowledging with gratitude their past support. January 30, 1893, trans. from Spanish, Joseph Folder, Marion Dargan Papers, Special Collections Division, U.N.M., Albuquerque.

5
1890 — YEAR OF CHALLENGE

1. Herbert Theodore Hoover, "Populism and the Territories" (unpublished Master's thesis, Graduate School, New Mexico State University, 1961), p. 9. Hoover effectively analyzes the economic roots of Populism in the territories of New Mexico, Arizona, and Oklahoma.

2. Hicks, *The Populist Revolt,* pp. 69-72.

3. Hoover, "Populism and the Territories," p. 9.

4. Prince to John W. Noble, Prince Papers.

5. Hoover, "Populism and the Territories," p. 33; Jack E. Holmes, *Politics in New Mexico* (Albuquerque, 1967), p. 9. Holmes analyzes population patterns from 1880 to 1960 with some attention to occupations, agricultural or otherwise, and much attention to ethnic backgrounds. See pp. 9-16.

6. Hoover, "Populism and the Territories," pp. 38-39.

7. The average interest rate in economically depressed Kansas in 1890 was only 8.15 percent.

8. L. Bradford Prince, *A Concise History of New Mexico* (Cedar Rapids, Iowa, 1914), p. 204.

9. U.S. *Congressional Record,* 51st Cong., 1st Sess., 1890, Part 3, p. 2993; Hoover, "Populism and the Territories," pp. 55-56.

10. Hoover, "Populism and the Territories," pp. 41, 47-48, 50.

11. Larson, *New Mexico's Quest for Statehood,* p. 164.

12. Donlon, "LeBaron Bradford Prince," p. 240.

13. The policy of the federal government under the Bland-Allison Act had been to purchase the minimum number of silver dollars each month; thus the treasury took only 24 million dollars' worth of silver off the market yearly. The Sherman Silver Purchase Act increased the amount of silver purchased by as much as 17 million ounces. See Hicks, *The Populist Revolt*, pp. 206-7.

14. Donlon, "LeBaron Bradford Prince," p. 240.

15. Larson, *New Mexico's Quest for Statehood*, p. 167.

16. *Santa Fe New Mexican*, October 6, 1890, Dargan Papers.

17. Lamar, *The Far Southwest*, pp. 196-97.

18. The *Santa Fe Sun*, November 1, 1890.

19. The accusation by the *New Mexican* of Democratic responsibility for White Cap terrorism was cited in the November 1 issue of the newspaper's bitter crosstown rival, the *Sun*.

20. November 1, 1890.

21. November 1, 1890. During the month of October the *New Mexican* reported on four occasions that the Democratic Executive Committee had struck a bargain with the White Caps, whereby the masked society was promised $1,400 for its support and an additional $1,400 if Joseph obtained a majority of one thousand in San Miguel County. See Donlon, "LeBaron Bradford Prince," p. 238.

22. Undated newspaper clipping sent to writer by Louise Coe Runnels, granddaughter of Jasper N. Coe, on January 23, 1970. The story about the *Nugget* was prompted by the excavation of the newspaper's old site, which was almost destroyed by a new highway project. All that remained was a stone foundation, 60 by 70 feet; the building itself was probably constructed of wood, as were many of the hastily erected frontier structures. Some of the actual metal type was recovered.

23. Kenneth N. Owens, "Patterns and Structure in Western Territorial Politics," *The Western Historical Quarterly*, I (October, 1970), 377, 386-92. Three classifications of territorial party systems were suggested by Owens, the one-party, two-party, and "no-party" systems. In the no-party system, major parties cooperated in a coalition which made real political partisanship negligible.

24. The *Santa Fe Sun*, October 18, 1890.

25. The *San Juan Times* (Farmington), May 17, 1895. Issue on microfilm located in the Special Collections Division, U.N.M., Albuquerque.

26. As quoted in the *Santa Fe Sun*, October 18, 1890. The editor of the *Sun*, J.H. Crist, sympathized with the position of the *Index*, but disagreed with the newspaper's proposed strategy. He recommended that, in the future, each county elect conferees who would meet in a district conference to elect Council candidates. Because Rio

Arriba County had more than four times as many voters, it was entitled to a Council seat in 1890, but San Juan should have a senator once every three terms. The candidate nominated by the Rio Arriba Democrats, Alexander T. Sullenberger, was superior to Pedro Y. Jaramillo, the Republican candidate, because, in Crist's opinion, Jaramillo was a land-grabber.

27. Donlon, "LeBaron Bradford Prince," p. 224.

28. November 8, 1890.

29. The *Santa Fe Sun*, November 15, 1890.

30. The *Santa Fe Sun*, November 8, 1890.

31. George Curry, *George Curry, 1861-1947: An Autobiography*, ed. H.B. Hening (Albuquerque, 1958), pp. 69-70.

32. Donlon, "LeBaron Bradford Prince," p. 224. According to the *Tribune Almanac for 1894*, p. 356, there was another Populist besides Mills on the Council.

33. The *Santa Fe Sun*, November 15, 1890.

34. Donlon, "LeBaron Bradford Prince," p. 241.

35. Fred A. Shannon, *American Farmers' Movements* (Princeton, 1957), p. 69.

36. New Mexico, Legislature, *Proceedings of the Legislative Council of the Territory of New Mexico*, 29th Sess. (Santa Fe, 1891), pp. 8, 117.

37. Education was vital to the growth and success of the agrarian protest in the West and the South. The purpose of lecturers in the Northern and Southern Alliances was to disseminate information through meetings and study groups. In this way farmers would know the causes of their economic and social problems and support the organizational programs that would supposedly cope with these problems. A better school system was advocated, especially by the leaders of the Northern Alliance who, in their December 6, 1889, platform, stated that the "stability of our government depends upon the moral, manual and intellectual training of the young, and we believe in so amending our public school system that the education of our children may inculcate the essential dignity necessary to be a practical help to them in after life." Hicks, *The Populist Revolt*, p. 429. With no effective public school system operating in New Mexico, Mills was acting in the spirit of this widespread agrarian belief when he supported educational reform in the Twenty-ninth assembly.

38. *Proceedings of the Legislative Council . . .*, pp. 8, 9, 11, 30.

39. Ross also accused Catron and his allies of fighting public education in order to keep the people ignorant. Alluding to their opposition to the education bill introduced by Russell A. Kistler of Las Vegas, the former governor, in a January 5, 1890 letter to Congressman C.H. Mansur of Missouri, referred to Catron and the Republican leaders as that "Class of men, who seek to keep the people in ignorance that they may be more easily ruled." Pamphlet entitled "The New Mexico Statehood Proposition," Edmund G. Ross Papers, State Records Center and Archives, Santa Fe.

40. *Proceedings of the Legislative Council . . .* , p. 29. Mills was also on the Judiciary, Internal Improvements, Roads and Highways, Militia, Mines and Public Lands, Privileges and Elections, Irrigation, and Rules committees. He did not, however, serve on the important Railroad and Municipal and Private Corporations committees. His exclusion from these two committees was crucial in view of the fact that he was championing rail regulation and trying to protect the Las Vegas Community Grant.

41. Donlon, "LeBaron Bradford Prince," pp. 246, 249-50.

42. February 16, 1891, Prince Papers.

43. Twitchell, *The Leading Facts of New Mexican History* II, 509-10; Donlon, "LeBaron Bradford Prince," pp. 250-52.

44. McParland to Prince, July 27, 1891, Prince Papers. The picture of a human eye with the slogan "We Never Sleep" beneath it, which distinctively marked the stationery of this most famous organization of "private eyes," was found on this highly confidential letter to the governor.

45. Donlon, "LeBaron Bradford Prince," pp. 252-56; Twitchell, *The Leading Facts of New Mexican History,* II, 510. For a discussion of the widely publicized Borrego-Chavez feud, in which Chavez was assassinated and Borrego was hanged despite a vigorous legal defense on his behalf by Catron, see pp. 510-13 in Twitchell's history of New Mexico.

46. Otero, *My Life on the Frontier,* II, 250-51.

6

THE 1892 ELECTION

1. Hicks, *The Populist Revolt,* pp. 207-16, 223-30. Hicks' accounts of the Cincinnati and St. Louis conventions are still among the best and most detailed available.

2. *Las Vegas Daily Optic,* October 18, 1892.

3. *Tribune Almanac for 1894,* p. 356.

4. *Las Vegas Daily Optic,* October 18, 1892.

5. Donlon, "LeBaron Bradford Prince," pp. 238-39.

6. F. Stanley states that the leader of the society, Vicente Silva, was the "prototype of the Prohibition gangster of the Roaring Twenties." *The Las Vegas Story (New Mexico),* (Denver, 1951), p. 196.

7. Otero called the party the *Partido del Pueblo Unido. My Life on the Frontier,* II, 171-72.

8. According to Otero, Herrera was also a labor agitator who, after finishing his term in the House, reorganized the White Caps to make new trouble. A warrant for his arrest was given to Lopez's brother, Felipe, who met Pablo near the courthouse and, without uttering a word, pulled a pistol and killed him. Nothing was ever done to Felipe for this act and, as Juan Jose Herrera was too old, the *Gorras* lost their aggressive leadership and faded. See *My Life on the Frontier*, II, 251.

9. Twitchell, *The Leading Facts of New Mexican History*, II, 520.

10. Larson, *New Mexico's Quest for Statehood*, p. 143. The claim was made by the *Santa Fe New Mexican* in its January 13, 1883, issue.

11. Lamar, *The Far Southwest*, p. 197.

12. John Foster Powers, " 'Blaine and Free Coinage': Factionalism and Silver in the Republican Pre-Convention Campaign of 1892 in Colorado" (unpublished Master's thesis, Department of History, Colorado State College, 1968), p. 92.

13. Letter cited in Powers, " 'Blaine and Free Coinage,' " p. 179.

14. Prince to Nobel, April 23, 1892, Prince Papers.

15. M.W. Mills to Prince, April 11, 1892, as cited in Donlon, "LeBaron Bradford Prince," p. 282.
16. Prince to J.J. Trujillo, January 2, 1892, Prince Papers.

17. The slogan was displayed on badges worn by members of the Colorado delegation at the Republican national convention in Minneapolis. Powers, " 'Blaine and Free Coinage,' " p. 190.

18. Otero, *My Life on the Frontier*, p. 258.

19. Contents of Vigil's affidavit, dated April 15, 1892, quoted in Donlon, "LeBaron Bradford Prince," p. 292. Otero had another version of this controversial incident. He stated that Vigil had been lured into an empty freight car by a so-called friend for a few drinks, only to be abandoned and locked in during the crucial period. The story of the weird abduction was also carried in the *Santa Fe Daily New Mexican,* April 20, 1892, Prince Papers.

20. Prince to Noble, April 23, 1892, Prince Papers.

21. *Santa Fe Daily New Mexican,* April 20, 1892, Prince Papers; Donlon, "LeBaron Bradford Prince," p. 287.

22. April 23, 1892, Prince Papers.

23. Curry, *George Curry, 1861-1947: An Autobiography*, pp. 71-72.

24. Powers, " 'Blaine and Free Coinage,' " p. 205.

25. *Dictionary of American Biography* (20 vols., New York, 1930-58), VII, 609. The popular Gresham, who gained a reputation among reformers because of his fight against the protective tariff, could have had the support of major party leaders in Illinois and Indiana if he had accepted the Populist nomination.

26. M.W. Mills to Prince, August 2, 1891, as cited in Donlon, "LeBaron Bradford Prince," p. 279.

27. Prince to Noble, April 23, 1892, Prince Papers.

28. August 2, 1891, as cited in Donlon, "LeBaron Bradford Prince," p. 280.

29. Curry, *George Curry, 1861-1947: An Autobiography*, p. 72.

30. As late as 1915 the Hispanos of New Mexico constituted 57 percent of the territory's population. Holmes, *Politics in New Mexico*, p. 10. Today the Spanish-speaking population is approximately 28 percent, significant but no longer to the same degree. Robert W. Larson, "The Profile of a New Mexico Progressive," *New Mexico Historical Review*, XLV (July, 1970), 233, 242. M.W. Mills in his August 2, 1891, letter to Prince concerning Catron's candidacy, wrote that the Republicans had no native candidate who "could carry the Mexican people even equal to Joseph." Consequently, it was necessary that they choose an acceptable "American," such as Catron or Prince.

31. *Las Vegas Daily Optic,* October 18, 1892.

32. October 11, 1892.

33. October 14, 1892. Copies of the *Democrat* are located in the State Records Center and Archives, Santa Fe.

34. October 15, 1892.

35. *Las Vegas Daily Optic,* October 13, 1892. According to the *Optic,* Blake was so outraged that he left for Albuquerque "in disgust."

36. These charges were contained in a letter Blake wrote to the editor of the *Optic,* which was reprinted on October 18, 1892.

37. Candidates nominated by the People's party for the House were J.J. McMullen, Jose Ramon Maestes, and Tomas Gonzales. *Las Vegas Daily Optic,* October 13, 1892.

38. *Las Vegas Daily Optic,* October 17, 1892. Another development that disturbed Romero was the nomination of E.H. Salazar, Lorenzo Lopez's son-in-law. The selection was another example of the increasing dominance of the Lopez wing of the feuding family. See October 13, 1892, issue of the *Optic.*

39. October 15, 1892.

40. *Albuquerque Democrat,* November 12, 1892.

41. October 21, 1892.

42. November 3, 1892.

43. *Albuquerque Democrat,* October 4, 1892. The *Democrat* even had a Republican rival for Catron's alleged Senate bid, Frank Springer. But, in the opinion of the partisan daily, neither man had a chance. The first state legislature would elect two Democrats to the national body. October 27, November 1, 1892.

44. Catron believed that some of his landholdings could even triple in value, if New Mexico were admitted. Larson, *New Mexico's Quest for Statehood,* p. 145.

45. *Albuquerque Democrat,* November 3, 1892.

46. The resolutions of the Grant County Democrats were quoted in the October 13 issue of the *Democrat.*

47. Donlon, "LeBaron Bradford Prince," p. 319. Serious friction existed between Prince and Morrison. Prince asserted in an April 23 letter to Secretary of the Interior Noble that all of Harrison's appointees had been loyal to the president "except Morrison, who has always been a Blain [sic] man." Prince Papers.

48. *Albuquerque Democrat,* October 20, 1892.

49. *Albuquerque Democrat,* October 18, 1892.
50. November 10, 1892.
51. *Las Vegas Daily Optic,* September 29, 1892.
52. August 31, 1892, as quoted in Donlon, "LeBaron Bradford Prince," pp. 318-19.

53. Undated article from *Santa Fe New Mexican* showing county-by-county tally for 1892 election located in the Prince Papers.

54. *Tribune Almanac for 1894,* p. 356. The delegate vote by counties for the 1888, 1892, and 1894 races is provided in this volume.

55. *Albuquerque Democrat,* November 6, 9, and 11, 1892.

56. *Tribune Almanac for 1894,* p. 356.

57. Undated article from the *Santa Fe New Mexican,* Prince Papers.

58. Otero, *My Life on the Frontier,* II, 262-63.

59. November 9, 1892.

60. Martinez's prediction, signed by him, was in an open letter to Harvey B. Fergusson in the November 10, 1892, issue of the *Albuquerque Democrat.*

61. *Tribune Almanac for 1894,* p. 356.

62. Two Independent Republicans, one from the House and one from the Council, presumably from the faction-ridden county of Bernalillo, were also listed in the party breakdown. *Tribune Almanac for 1894,* p. 356.

63. *Daily New Mexican* (Santa Fe), December 23, 1892, as cited in Donlon, "LeBaron Bradford Prince," p. 322.

64. Chapter 76, sec. 1 in New Mexico, Legislature, *Acts of the Legislative Assembly of the Territory of New Mexico,* 30th Sess. (Santa Fe, 1893), p. 141.

65. "Prepayments of poll-tax shall not hereafter be a prerequisite or qualification for the right to vote." Chapter 2 on p. 18.

66. Chapter 19, *Acts of the Legislative Assembly . . . ,* p. 33

67. Joint Memorial III filed in the Territorial Secretary's office on February 17, 1893, in *Acts of the Legislative Assembly . . . ,* p. 160.

68. See Chapter 5 for a discussion of Mills' railroad regulation bill and his other legislative activities.

69. *Acts of the Legislative Assembly . . . ,* p. 37.

70. Curry, *George Curry, 1861-1947: An Autobiography,* pp. 75-76. Others in the delegation to see Cleveland were Judge Thornton, J.H. Crist, Fall, Fergusson, Neil B. Field, Granville A. Richardson, W.B. Childers, N.B. Laughlin, Rafael Romero, and Charles B. Eddy. Although Eddy was a Republican, he was in the cattle business with Cleveland's law partner.

7
THE POPULIST TERRITORIAL BID

1. August 31, 1894. Most of the issues of the *San Juan Times* cited hereafter are from the microfilm collection of the *Daily Times* (Farmington).

2. *Las Vegas Daily Optic,* November 1, 1894.

· 3. September 18, 1894.

4. August 29, 1894.

5. The *San Juan Times* (Farmington), September 28, 1894.

6. The writer was unable to discover why Mills was given that title. He was a Civil War veteran, but he never achieved the rank of colonel while serving in the Union army.

7. *Evening Citizen* (Albuquerque), August 29, 1894.
8. *Southern Pacific Coast Directory, 1888-9* (San Francisco, no date), p. 447.

9. *Southern Pacific Coast Directory, 1888-9,* p. 444; the *Albuquerque Daily Citizen,* November 4, 1898. An advertisement for Keleher's business published in the *Citizen* a few years after the Populist bid of 1894 indicates the diversity of his commercial activities. He dealt in harnesses, saddles, whips, and horse medicine in addition to hides and woolen goods.

10. October 15, 1894. The *Cochiti Call* characterized the Populist party as being "Col. Stamm's and Col. Brady's populist party," an interesting designation since Mills was living near Cochiti. The newspaper also warned other territorial journals not to continue ridiculing the new party as they might be greatly shocked when the "ides of November roll around." The *Call* as quoted in the *Daily Citizen* (Albuquerque), August 29, 1894. No information about Brady could be found. This informational dearth was a problem encountered with many Populist leaders, suggesting that a number of them were common people with little political background.

11. The Gallup *Gleaner* as quoted in the *San Juan Times* (Farmington), September 7, 1894.

12. The *San Juan Times* (Farmington), August 10, 1894. The committee set September 15 as the day of the primaries and September 22 as the day for the county convention. August 24, 1894.

13. The *San Juan Times* (Farmington), August 10, 1894.

14. A ballot for the People's party of Sierra County, enclosed in a March 28, 1956, letter from Edward d'Oench Tittmann to the New Mexico Historical Society of Santa Fe, was found in the Prince Papers. Tittmann penciled in the information about Murphy and West in his letter to the historical society.

15. September 13, 1894.

16. September 28, 1894.

17. The Populists in their St. Louis platform resolved that the "question of female suffrage be referred to the legislatures of the different States for favorable consideration." See Hicks, *The Populist Revolt,* p. 439. Mills' advocacy of women's rights did not go quite so far as endorsing suffrage, but, considering the bias of Hispano males against such reforms, his record was an admirable one.

18. September 1, 1894.

19. Reprinted in the *San Juan Times* (Farmington), September 7, 1894.

20. The *Daily Citizen* (Albuquerque), September 13, 1894.

21. The *San Juan Times* (Farmington), September 7, 1894.

22. The *Evening Citizen* (Albuquerque), September 7, 1894.

23. Mills' call was reprinted in the *San Juan Times* (Farmington), September 17, 1894.

24. The *Daily Citizen* (Albuquerque), September 14, 1894; the *San Juan Times* (Farmington), September 28, 1894. Among the responsibilities of the executive committee was the charge to fill the vacancies of the unrepresented counties.

25. Hofstadter asserted in his book, *The Age of Reform,* p. 101, that Populist leadership was not drawn from the ranks of farmers, but rather from "professional men, rural editors, third-party veterans, and professional reformers." A recent study of Colorado Populism has shown that Professor Hofstadter was correct about the predominantly urban background of Populist leaders. In Colorado the most prevalent occupations of important Populists were real estate, retail marketing, law, and education. There were also a number of newspaper editors. See G. Michael McCarthy, "Colorado's Populist Leadership," *The Colorado Magazine,* XLVII (Winter, 1971), 35-37. Hicks also recognized the tendency of farmers to elect people from urban occupations, such as lawyers and other professional persons, to represent them in the third-party movement. See *The Populist Revolt,* p. 151.

26. According to Edward d'Oench Tittmann, Murphy was the first sheriff of Sierra County. See Sierra County Populist ballot for 1894 enclosed in Tittmann's letter to the New Mexico Historical Society of Santa Fe, dated March 28, 1956, in the Prince Papers.

27. Populist campaign broadside printed in Spanish, Election of 1894 folder, Prince Papers. The writer italicized the word "all" in his translation.

28. The *Daily Citizen* (Albuquerque), September 14, 1894; the *San Juan Times* (Farmington), September 28, 1894; Populist campaign broadside, trans. from Spanish, Prince Papers.

29. September 28, 1894.

30. September 28, 1894. Brief accounts of the nomination fight also were carried in the September 14 and 26 issues of the *Daily Citizen* (Albuquerque).

31. The *Daily Citizen* (Albuquerque), September 26, 1894.

32. September 15, 1894.

33. September 14, 1894.

34. September 18, 1894.

35. October 6, 1894.

36. Salazar, an angry reformer proud of his native heritage, took his mother's maiden name.

37. September 22, 1894, trans. from Spanish.

38. September 15, 1894.

39. September 28, 1894.

40. Populist campaign broadside, trans. from Spanish, Prince Papers.

41. September 15, 1894.

42. As quoted in the *Daily Citizen* (Albuquerque), September 15, 1894.

43. Sierra Populist ballot enclosed in letter from Tittmann to the New Mexico Historical Society, March 28, 1956, Prince Papers.

44. September 14, 1894.

45. September 28, 1894.

46. The *San Juan Times* (Farmington), September 14, 1894. Von Buddenbrock was made a member of the executive committee at a meeting held in Aztec in August. The *San Juan Times* (Farmington), August 24, 1894.

47. August 24, September 14 and 21, 1894. One representative was also allowed for each fraction of ten.

48. The *Evening Citizen* (Albuquerque).

49. The *Daily Citizen* (Albuquerque), September 14, 1894.

50. As quoted in the *Daily Citizen* (Albuquerque), September 22, 1894.

51. The *San Juan Times* was confident as late as August 31. " 'As San Miguel county goes, so goes the territory' is a territorial axiom,'' the *Times* declared. ''As that county is going solidly for the People's party, we may look for a Populist victory this fall.''

52. The *Evening Citizen* (Albuquerque), September 19, 1894.

53. October 30, 1894.

54. The *Daily Citizen* (Albuquerque), September 17, 1894.

55. Larson, *New Mexico's Quest for Statehood,* pp. 169-70.

56. The *Daily Citizen* (Albuquerque), September 17, 1894.

57. Curry, *George Curry, 1861-1947: An Autobiography,* p. 80.

58. The *Daily Citizen* (Albuquerque), September 18, 1894.

59. Quoted in the *Daily Citizen* (Albuquerque), September 21, 1894.

60. Resolutions quoted in the *Chieftain* (Socorro), October 26, 1894; the *Daily Citizen* (Albuquerque), September 26, 1894; *Albuquerque Evening Herald,* undated; and two undated newspaper articles. Prince Papers.

61. The *Chieftain* (Socorro), October 26, 1894, Prince Papers. Because of Joseph's noisy efforts to gain admission, his lack of success was severely rebuked. Criticism of his alleged opposition to public education was accompanied by a strong endorsement of public schools and "universal education" in the Socorro platform.

62. The *Chieftain* (Socorro), October 26, 1894, and other papers, Prince Papers. Criticism against Cleveland's Indian policy and the closing of Ft. Marcy were also among the harsh indictments against the Democrats printed in the *Daily Citizen* on September 18.

63. As cited in the *Chieftain* (Socorro), October 26, 1894.

64. The *Daily Citizen* (Albuquerque), September 21, 1894.

65. The assessment was George Curry's, then a Democrat and a candidate for the Territorial Council in 1894. Curry, *George Curry, 1861-1947: An Autobiography,* p. 80.

66. Democrats were blamed for the 1,500,000 laborers thrown out of work during the depression and the "one calamity after another" which had occurred since Cleveland took office. See Socorro resolutions in the *Chieftain* (Socorro), October 26, 1894, and other newspapers, Prince Papers.

8
THE 1894 CAMPAIGN

1. Campaign broadside, trans. from Spanish, Prince Papers; the *San Juan Times* (Farmington), October 26, 1894. under the headline: "An Able and Inspiring Address by M.P. Stamm: Reasons for the Organization of Our Third Party and Why It Deserves Success." Quotations will be from both Spanish and English versions.

2. September 28, 1894.

3. Campaign broadside, trans. from Spanish, Prince Papers; the *San Juan Times* (Farmington), October 26, 1894.

4. August 17, 1894.

5. August 31, 1894.

6. "Declaration of Principles," undated, Executive Committee, Populist Party, Precinct 11, Grant County, Prince Papers. Members of the committee were S.S. Birchfield, E.A. Schultz, Frank Bowman, and R.C. Miller.

7. November 10, 1894.

8. Cited in the *Chieftain* (Socorro), October 26, 1894. See Chapter 7, p. 98 .

9. August 31, 1894.

10. Quoted in November 16, 1894, issue.

11. August 31 and other issues, 1894. In almost every issue of the *San Juan Times* these advertisements were included, along with a report of the New Mexico Bureau of Immigration promoting the county's agricultural potential. Also, during the election, the Populist platform of 1892 was reprinted in every issue.

12. "Declaration of Principles."

13. September 14, 1894.

14. "Declaration of Principles."

15. August 31, 1894.

16. *Wealth Maker* as quoted in August 31 issue.

17. November 2, 1894.

18. The *San Juan Times* (Farmington), August 17, 1894.

19. Ibid., August 31, 1894.

20. Joseph W. Taylor to Catron, October 24, 1894, Thomas B. Catron Papers, Special Collections Division, U.N.M., Albuquerque. Hereafter cited as Catron Papers.

21. August 31, 1894.

22. August 31, 1894. The story about the opposition of Eastern senators to Arizona statehood was carried in the *San Francisco Chronicle.*

23. October 20, 21, 22, 1894.

24. "Declaration of Principles."

25. August 24, 1894. The address was delivered by a Dr. A. Coleman.

26. October 30, 1894. The *Optic* was supporting the *San Francisco Chronicle* in its opposition to an amendment to the California constitution forbidding alien land-ownership when it waged its attack. The controversy over alien landownership continued for another two years or so. For a brief discussion of the dispute in 1896 see Larson, *New Mexico's Quest for Statehood,* p. 191.

27. August 31, 1894.

28. Undated, Grant County, Prince Papers.

29. May 27, 1893.

30. Quoted in Otero, *My Life on the Frontier,* II, 255.

31. August 17, 1894.

32. August 31, 1894.

33. Gould, *Wyoming: A Political History,* pp. 206-7.

34. Donald Kinzer, *An Episode in Anti-Catholicism: The American Protective Association* (Seattle, 1964), pp. 102-3, 156.

35. Questionnaire entitled "A Prompt Response to this Communication is Requested" with reply to be sent to A.A. Leyton of East Las Vegas, October 8, 1894, Catron Papers. The issues in the questionnaire were formulated in Washington on August 28, 1894, by delegates of various patriotic organizations. There was space at the bottom for the candidate's signature and the date of his reply.

36. Pamphlet found in folder entitled Election of 1894, Prince Papers. Although Joseph was regarded widely as the embodiment of almost everything a good New Mexico Hispano should be, he rarely attended church, was divorced and remarried, and was active in a Masonic order. Larson, *New Mexico's Quest for Statehood,* p. 164.

37. The *San Juan Times* (Farmington), November 2, 1894.

38. October 18, 1894.

39. September 26, 1894.

40. September 28, 1894.

41. *Chaffee County Record* as quoted in August 31, 1894, issue.

42. September 17, 1894.

43. September 25, 1894.

44. William Watson, an attorney from White Oaks in Lincoln County, wrote Catron that he had asked the Republican territorial committee for such literature. September 24, 1894, Catron Papers.

45. September 17, 1894. The *Optic* also declared that, because Democrats believed in a tariff for revenue only, they would even tax items *not* made in this country, forcing the customer to pay the foreign price plus the tax or tariff duty. September 22, 1894.

46. The *Daily Citizen* (Albuquerque), September 26, 1894.

47. A.B. Laird of Silver City to Catron, November 4, 1894, Catron Papers.

48. November 4, 1894.

49. The *San Juan Times* would not let Catron forget his association with Francisco Gonzales y Borrego, who was indicted in June of 1894 for the murder of former Santa Fe sheriff, Francisco Chavez. The term Thomas Borrego Catron was used in at least one issue. October 12, 1894. See Chapter 5, p. 62 and note 45.

50. Major points made by Mills in his interview were carried in the November 2 issue of the *Las Vegas Daily Optic.*

51. October 26, 1894.

52. Laird to Catron, November 4, 1894, Catron Papers.

53. Watson to Catron, September 24, 1894, Catron Papers.

54. William B. Baly of Tularosa to Catron, October 30, 1894, Catron Papers.

55. "Declaration of Principles." Grant County should be considered a swing county rather than a Democratic one. Joseph lost it in 1892 by five votes out of 1,883 cast.

56. Hugo Seaburg of Springer to Catron, October 5, 1894, Catron Papers. Apparently a law partner of M.W. Mills, whom he said was in Kansas City, Seaburg appeared to share his colleague's low opinion of native New Mexicans. The tenor of his note to Catron and the way he used the term "Mexicans" would lead one to suspect he had such a bias.

57. September 22, 1894, trans. from Spanish.

58. September 28, 1894.

59. The *Chieftain* (Socorro), October 26, 1894, Prince Papers. The *Chieftain* made the questionable assertion that newspapers always reflect the sentiments of their readers. The implication was that with the *Times* and *Index* opposing Joseph his cause was doomed. The journal also predicted that Joseph would lose his home county, Taos.

60. H.A. Groves of Aztec to Catron, October 13, 1894, Catron Papers. Catron's correspondent urged the Republican candidate to visit the county before the election.

61. September 24, 1894, Catron Papers.

62. A.C. Vorhees of Raton to Catron, September 26, 1894; J.C. Hill of Clayton to Catron, October 2, 1894; W.W. Boyle of Clayton to Catron, October 5, 1894, Catron Papers.

63. Fort served as temporary chairman of the Council while that body was organizing itself. *Raton Weekly Independent,* January 5, 1889.

64. October 3, 1894, Catron Papers.

65. Otero, *My Life on the Frontier,* II, 257. The elderly victim was on his way to Indian Territory when Faulkner asked to join him and help him care for his team of horses. Faulkner later killed the old man in his sleep with an ax and buried him in a shallow grave. Prosecuting a surly individual for such a deed is bound to redound to the benefit of a district attorney.

66. When Catron was maneuvering to control the New Mexican delegation to the Republican national convention in 1892, he promised the citizens of Clayton and Folsom a new county. M.W. Mills to Prince, April 11, 1892, as quoted in Donlon, "LeBaron Bradford Prince," p. 282.

67. Fort writes Catron in his October 3 letter of the great discontent that many Union Democrats felt toward Joseph. One gets the impression in studying Union County politics that the leaders of the county People's party were really disgruntled Democrats rather than committed Populists.

68. October 3, 1894, Catron Papers.

69. Mills' interview with the *New Mexican* as cited in the *Las Vegas Daily Optic*, November 2, 1894, Catron Papers.

70. *Santa Fe New Mexican*, undated, Election of 1894 folder, Prince Papers.

71. Larson, *New Mexico's Quest for Statehood*, p. 183. George Curry, then a Democrat, cited the importance of these two factors.

72. T.A. Finical to Catron, November 8, 1894, Catron Papers. Finical, who reported the banners, was an influential leader in the county. "With you in Cong. and S.B. Elkins in the Senate, we confidently expect that our [statehood] promises will be carried out to the letter."

73. *Santa Fe New Mexican*, undated, Prince Papers.

74. *Las Vegas Daily Optic*, November 10, 1894.

75. The *Evening Citizen* (Albuquerque), November 12, 1894. The name of the fortunate Democrat was Henry V. Harris.

76. Only one candidate on the Union ticket was defeated. *Las Vegas Daily Optic* as cited in the *Evening Citizen*, November 12, 1894.

77. November 9, 1894.

78. November 16, 1894.

79. November 9, 1894.

80. November 17, 1894, trans. from Spanish. Although Martinez, the publisher of the newspaper, was an opportunist, his journal's denunciation of Mills and the Populists did not mean he had totally forsaken Populism. The September 8 issue of *La Voz del Pueblo* had nothing but praise for Davis H. Waite, the Populist governor of Colorado. It referred to him as the "most extraordinary man in the American union."

81. The *Evening Citizen* (Albuquerque), November 12, 1894.

9
CONFUSION OVER FUSION

1. The *Evening Citizen* (Albuquerque), December 31, 1894.

2. Ibid.; Larson, *New Mexico's Quest for Statehood*, p. 199. Although territorial politics had always tended toward the tumultuous, the alleged Democratic theft of the Thirty-first Legislative Assembly was not forgotten. In the campaign of 1896, Republican gatherings denounced the Democratic action. The Republican *Daily Citizen* of Albuquerque favorably commented on one resolution of condemnation. "The San Miguel County republicans did exactly right in denouncing by resolution the outrageous and illegal act of Secretary Miller in swearing in as members of the last legislature men who had no shadow of title to their positions." September 23, 1896.

3. New Mexico, Legislature, *Acts of the Legislative Assembly of New Mexico*, 31st Sess. (Santa Fe, 1895), p. 109. Memorial approved on February 13, 1895.

4. May 17, 1895. An ordinance enacted which prohibited the peddling of fruit and farm products in Durango by growers further infuriated the *Times*. It called the measure a "restraint of legitimate trade." Consequently, small producers in New Mexico had to cope with what they regarded as another form of monopoly. May 31, 1895.

5. For a reform newspaper the *Times* continued to sound like a local chamber of commerce. Calling San Juan County the "Finest Fruit Country in the World," the Populist newspaper carried advertisements to promote the orchard land around Farmington. It also reprinted on a regular basis exerpts from a report by the New Mexico Bureau of Immigration boasting of the county's great agricultural potential.

6. May 30, 1895.

7. "Missouri lost as much in falling prices in consequence of silver demonetization as the whole silver output of Colorado," Bland also asserted in his speech. Attacks on demonetization by other prominent persons were carried in this story.

8. A copy of the "Resolution for the Appointment of a National Silver Committee," which was adopted by the Memphis convention, was found in the Prince Papers.

9. For more detailed informat on regarding the background of Joseph and Fergusson see Larson, *New Mexico's Quest for Statehood*, pp. 183-84, 189-190.

10. *Southern Pacific Coast Directory, 1888-9*, p. 448. Moving from Wheeling, West Virginia, Fergusson practiced law in White Oaks before he came to Albuquerque in 1883.

11. March 3, 1894, Prince Papers.

12. Prominent bimetallists were to give talks on Silver Day, scheduled for September 11. Undated news clipping, Prince Papers.

13. Copies of this July 19, 1895, letter were apparently sent to prominent bimetallists. Prince Papers.

14. Undated issue, p. 214, Prince Papers. An October 19, 1895, letter from Morton Frewen, prominent Wyoming cattleman and silverite, was also printed in this issue.

15. The petition, dated January 23, 1896, was in the form of a resolution, Prince Papers.

16. Quoted in the *Albuquerque Daily Citizen,* September 12, 1896.

17. The critic was the noted economist, college educator, and statistician, General Amasa Walker, who favored bimetallism, but through international agreement. He opposed unilateral silver coinage by the United States. Typewritten paper entitled ''Arguments,'' Prince Papers.

18. Typed statement about the Trans-Montane League, Prince Papers.

19. Clipping of a review of Prince's book in the *Brooklyn Citizen,* September 27, 1896, Prince Papers. The review was favorable, *The Money Problem* being praised for its ''clearness of apprehension.'' The book cost twenty-five cents a copy.

20. Prince's letters to these men, all of them written on August 15, received replies. Warren to Prince, August 19, 1896; Mondell to Prince, August 25, 1896; A.J. Russell, Wolcott's secretary, to Prince, August 18, 1896; McKinley to Prince, August 26, 1896. Prince Papers.

21. Larson, *New Mexico's Quest for Statehood,* pp. 185-86.

22. Kirk H. Porter, *National Party Platforms* (New York, 1924), p. 203.

23. H. Wayne Morgan, *From Hayes to McKinley: National Party Politics, 1877-1896* (Syracuse, 1969), pp. 500-501.

24. Hicks, *The Populist Revolt,* pp. 350-53.

25. On September 6, 1894, Greaves had written to Holt from California, commending him for the ''straightforward'' and ''moderate tone'' of his newspaper. As for the Populist party, ''a party rapidly recruiting among the masses,'' Greaves felt it would receive the fair consideration of every man ''whose mind is not narrowed by partisan claims and who seeks the liberal advancement of the people.'' The *San Juan Times* (Farmington), September 21, 1894.

26. Porter, *National Party Platforms,* pp. 181-87.

27. Hicks, *The Populist Revolt,* pp. 360-66; Porter, *National Party Platforms,* pp. 196-200. Chapter two of Robert F. Durden's *The Climax of Populism: The Election of 1896* (Lexington, 1965) also provides an excellent account of the 1896 Populist national convention.

28. *Albuquerque Daily Citizen*, September 3, 1896. Daniel Griffin, chairman of the New York delegation at the Indianapolis convention, wired Cleveland at Buzzard's Bay informing him of the strong, "unmistakable" desire of the convention delegates to nominate him.

29. *Albuquerque Daily Citizen*, September 9, 1896. Pro-gold Democrats met in Albuquerque, on August 22, to organize a territorial party, select members for an executive committee, and choose delegates to their August 29 territorial convention. Childers and Schofield were elected at the convention as delegates to the Indianapolis meeting. The *Chieftain* (Socorro), August 23, 1896, Prince Papers.

30. September 2, 1896.

31. September 1 and 9, 1896.

32. *Albuquerque Daily Citizen*, September 3, 1896. Palmer had been a party bolter before. As a Republican who was disgusted with the corruption of the Grant administration, he joined the Liberal Republicans in 1872. Eventually he became a Democrat, attending the Democratic national convention in 1884 as a delegate. *Dictionary of American Biography*, Vol. XIV (New York, 1934), 186-87.

33. September 8, 1896.

34. Notices appeared in local papers where the Populist organization was strong with news of those meetings where delegates to the Las Vegas meeting would be selected. In Bernalillo County, for instance, W.W. McClellan, the county chairman, called for Populists to meet in the office of W.A. Skinner at 8 o'clock on Tuesday evening, September 15, to elect eight delegates to the Populist territorial convention. *Albuquerque Daily Citizen*, September 14, 1896.

35. Mills' active politicking was described with bitterness by M.P. Stamm in an interview which appeared in the *Albuquerque Daily Citizen*, September 24, 1896.

36. *Albuquerque Daily Citizen*, September 16, 1896.

37. September 21, 1896.

38. On September 24, the Sierra Populists met at Hillsboro and passed resolutions demanding fusion with the Democrats on both the national and local levels. *Santa Fe Daily New Mexican*, October 2, 1896.

39. *Albuquerque Daily Citizen*, September 16, 1896. There was also speculation that three legislative tickets would be presented to the voters of San Juan County, while Populists and Democrats would support the Democratic nominee for delegate unless Populists should nominate their own candidate in Las Vegas on September 23.

40. September 23, 1896.

41. September 11, 1896.

42. September 4, 1896.

43. The *Daily Citizen* was convinced that Fergusson would win the nod from both Populists and Democrats at their territorial conventions. September 9, 1896.

44. A biographical sketch of Boyle appeared in his obituary published in the *Santa Fe New Mexican,* March 17, 1910. A good account of his father-in-law, William Blackmore, and Arthur Boyle's personal and business relationship with him, can be found in Herbert O. Brayer's *William Blackmore* (Denver, 1949). See introduction and pp. 5, 30, and 122. Blackmore handled the large Sangre de Cristo Grant in southern Colorado and northern New Mexico. To confirm that Arthur V. Boyle, the Populist, was also Boyle, the land speculator, the 1896 Assessment Roll for Santa Fe County was checked. There was only one Boyle listed, Blanche Boyle, Arthur Boyle's wife. State Records Center and Archives, Santa Fe. A letter to Boyle's daughter-in-law, Mrs. R.V. Boyle, validated the information in the assessment roll. To her knowledge there was only one Boyle family in Santa Fe at this time. Larson to Mrs. R.V. Boyle, October 2, 1969 and Marion Dockwiller, writing for Mrs. Boyle, to Larson, October 20, 1969.

45. Boyle was most active. At one time he was receiver for the Canon de Chama Grant. He once served as an agent for the British-owned Rio Arriba Land and Cattle Company. Rio Arriba District Court Records, Civil, Case No. 209, State Records Center and Archives. Boyle was an agent for the Colorado Mortgage and Investment Company of London (Ld.) and New Mexico agent for the Arkansas Valley Land and Cattle Company. Boyle to Fiske and Warren, November 9, 1885, Eugene A. Fiske Papers, State Records Center and Archives, Santa Fe. Boyle advertised himself as an agent for English capitalists. *Colorado, New Mexico, Utah, Nevada, Arizona, and Wyoming Gazetteer and Business Directory, 1884,* I, 348, Museum of New Mexico, Santa Fe. Boyle was also an agent for Australian investors, and declared himself to be an investigator of Spanish and Mexican land grants. *Santa Fe Daily New Mexican,* May 2, 1883. As for his Republican background, Boyle was a Republican candidate for the Santa Fe school board in 1890, but was removed from contention because he had not taken out his second citizenship papers. *Santa Fe New Mexican,* January 7, 1890. Both news items were supplied by Mrs. J.K. Shishkin, retired research editor for the Museum of New Mexico. Shishkin to Larson, September 2, 1969; February 27, 1970.

46. Boyle was a director of the International Trunk Railway in 1883. *Santa Fe New Mexican Review,* June 14, 1883. In 1881, he and Thomas B. Catron and Charles H. Gildersleeve incorporated the Santa Fe Progressive and Improvement Company, a real estate development firm. Catron and Gildersleeve were key members of the Santa Fe Ring. *Daily New Mexican,* February 19, 1881. Boyle became secretary and treasurer of this land development company. *Santa Fe Daily New Mexican,* March 6, May 15, 1881. The four news items in this note were sent to writer by Mrs. J.K. Shishkin. October 1, 7, 28, 1969 and April 30, 1970.

47. *Santa Fe Daily New Mexican,* January 27, 1883; Shishkin to Larson, February 11, 1970.

48. August 17, 1896, Prince Papers. Catron knew about Burns' role in the move to win the nomination for Prince. A political supporter from Chama wrote him that Burns ''strongly favored'' Prince's nomination and wanted the entire Rio Arriba delegation instructed to support the former governor. W.E. Broad to Catron, September 16, 1896, Catron Papers.

49. September 18, 1896, Prince Papers.

50. R.L. Baca to Prince, September 25, 1896, Prince Papers.

51. Joseph E. Watrous to Prince, September 22, 1896, Prince Papers.

52. G.W. Hartman to Prince, September 14, 1896, Prince Papers.

53. E.W. Eaton to Prince, September 16, 1896, Prince Papers.

54. The *San Juan Times* (Farmington), September 18, 1896.

55. Handwritten resolution in folder entitled ''Silver Issue and the Populist Party, 1889-1900,'' Prince Papers.

56. H.H. Betts to Prince, September 22, 1896. Prince Papers.

57. R. Hudson to Catron, September 20, 1896, Catron Papers.

58. Amado Chaves to Prince, September 10, 1896, Prince Papers.

59. September 13, 1896, Prince Papers.

60. Frank W. Clancy to Prince, October 7, 1896. Prince Papers.

61. September 22, 1896.

62. According to interview with Stamm published in the *Albuquerque Daily Citizen*, September 24, 1896.

63. *Albuquerque Daily Citizen*, September 1, 1896.

64. According to the *Santa Fe Daily New Mexican*, September 23, 1896, Wagner by convention time was a leader in the fight to win the nomination for Fergusson, along with Stamm and a J.B. Allen. There was talk that the pro-Prince delegates and the pro-Fergusson delegates might compromise on a middle-of-the-roader acceptable to both sides.

65. Interview with Stamm in the *Albuquerque Daily Citizen*, September 24, 1896; *Santa Fe Daily New Mexican*, September 23, 1896.

66. *Santa Fe Daily New Mexican*, September 25, 1896.

67. Hadley was reported as wanting the Republican nomination for delegate. Joseph E. Watrous to Prince, September 22, 1896, Prince Papers. Perhaps, like Prince, he was willing to consider both the Republican and Populist nominations, but lacking political strength he agreed to support Prince instead.

68. *Santa Fe Daily New Mexican*, September 25, 1896.

69. These proposals were among the twenty-six planks that made up the platform drafted by the Las Vegas gathering. *Santa Fe Daily New Mexican,* September 25, 1896. The 1896 national platform of the People's party was reprinted in Porter, *National Party Platforms,* pp. 196-200.

70. In the national platform the call for public projects appeared as follows: "In times of great industrial depression, idle labor should be employed on public works as far as practicable."

71. A statement to this effect, almost identical in language, was incorporated in the national platform drafted in Saint Louis. But the plank in the Saint Louis platform referred specifically to the settlement of public lands under the National Homestead Law. It also included Indian reservations "when opened for settlement." When references were made to land grants in the national platform, it was to lands granted to transcontinental railroads ("the Pacific railroad companies") rather than to Spanish or Mexican land grants. See Porter, *National Party Platforms,* pp. 198-99.

72. The Populists at their St. Louis meeting, two months earlier, demanded that alien landownership be prohibited, thus clinging to their position in the 1892 platform, when they demanded that the government reclaim land owned by aliens. Porter, *National Party Platforms,* pp. 169, 198.

73. Platform as published in the *Santa Fe Daily New Mexican,* September 25, 1896. This declaration, the nineteenth plank in the Las Vegas platform, was an abbreviated version of a forceful statement which appeared in the national platform.

74. Stamm interview in *Albuquerque Daily Citizen,* September 24, 1896; *Santa Fe Daily New Mexican,* September 25, 1896. Rumors that Stamm would bolt, if Prince were chosen, circulated before the names of candidates were put into nomination. *Santa Fe Daily New Mexican,* September 23, 1896.

75. *Albuquerque Daily Citizen,* September 24, 1896. The *Daily Citizen* remarked amusingly the following day that "Col. Stamm is more than ever convinced that eternal vigilence is necessary to keep [the] populist party in existence."

76. September 28, 1896.

77. *Santa Fe Daily New Mexican,* September 25, 1896.

78. September 25, 1896.

79. September 24, 1896.

80. Blake's letter to Prince was written on T. B. Mills' business stationary, indicating that Mills had forgiven Blake's desertion of the Populist cause in 1894. Prince Papers.

81. As quoted in the *Santa Fe Daily New Mexican, September, 25, 1896.*

82. Quoted in Larson, *New Mexico 's Quest for Statehood,* p. 186.

83. *Albuquerque Daily Citizen,* September 28, 1896; *Santa Fe Daily New Mexican,* September 28, 1896.

84. *Santa Fe Daily New Mexican,* September 28, 1896.

85. September 26, 1896.

86. *Albuquerque Daily Citizen,* September 28, 1896.

87. Curry, *George Curry, 1861-1947: An Autobiography,* pp. 93-94.

88. *Lordsburg Liberal* as quoted in the *Albuquerque Daily Citizen,* September 21, 1896.

89. *Albuquerque Daily Citizen,* September 25, 1896.

90. *Santa Fe Daily New Mexican,* September 30, 1896.

91. Llewellyn to Prince, September 27, 1896, Prince Papers.

92. September 28, 1896.

93. September 30, 1896. The Albuquerque newspaper's response was to the pro-silver *Rocky Mountain News.*

94. Enclosed in a letter from Cross (first name not given) to Prince, October 5, 1896, Prince Papers.

95. Biographical Sketch of Webber in *An Illustrated History of New Mexico* (Chicago, 1895), p. 635.

96. Cross to Prince, October 5, 1896.

97. *Santa Fe Daily New Mexican,* October 7, 1896.

98. The manifesto of the territorial committee of the People's party, which was dated October 7, was signed by Webber as chairman and Mills as secretary.

99. Largely as a result of Catron's opposition, Prince was defeated by Joseph in his bid for delegate in 1884. A split in the Republican party gave Prince 9,930 votes to 5,192 for William L. Rynerson, leading a faction of Republican bolters. The Republican schism allowed Joseph, who polled 12,271 votes, to win his first term as delegate. Larson, *New Mexico's Quest for Statehood,* p. 143; Twitchell, *The Leading Facts of New Mexican History,* I, 499-500.

100. October 6, 1896. The editorial writer claimed to have known Prince well for fifteen years.

101. October 16, 1896.

102. October 14, 1896.

103. October 23, 1896. Childers, who had been appointed United States attorney during the last months of the Cleveland administration, was regarded by Democrats and Populists as the man behind the Dame nomination. The *New Mexican,* in its October 14 issue, called the territorial convention of the Gold Democrats "a Childers convention." As national committeeman for the new party, Childers organized the "sound money democrats" in his own county, Bernalillo. He then helped to establish organizations in other counties. *Albuquerque Daily Citizen,* September 17, 1896.

10

"THE SILVER CRAZE"

1. Frost to Catron, October 17, 1896, Catron Papers. The man quoted by Frost was Colonel R. Hudson, a member of the Republican central committee of Grant County, who also used the term "Free Silver Craze" in a letter sent to Catron after the election. November 7, 1896.

2. J. D. Kello to Catron, October 18, 1896, Catron Papers.

3. Mills to Catron, November 6, 1896, Catron Papers.

4. August 29, 1896, address quoted in the *Albuquerque Daily Citizen,* September 1, 1896.

5. Platform of Sierra County People's party as quoted in the *Santa Fe Daily New Mexican,* October 2, 1896.

6. Two Silver Democratic tickets enclosed in the following documents: a letter from R.A. Nickle, chairman of the Silver Democratic Central Committee of Sierra County, and Thomas Murphy, secretary, to territorial secretary Lorion Miller, October 23, 1896, and an October 26, 1896, certification of the joint convention signed by Thomas Murphy, chairman of the People's party; R. A. Nickle, chairman of the Democratic party; and Otto E. Gertz, secretary. Records of the Office of Secretary of State, State Records Center and Archives, Santa Fe. Copies of the above documents were sent to writer by Dr. Myra Ellen Jenkins, state historian for New Mexico, September 12, 1969.

7. Copy of Populist ticket enclosed in letter from Edward L. Bartlett to Catron, October 28, 1896, Catron Papers; *Santa Fe Daily New Mexican,* November 9, 1896.

8. October 28, 1896.

9. October 25, 1896, Catron Papers.

10. October 23, 1896.

11. *Albuquerque Daily Citizen,* September 22, 1896. According to the September 17 issue of the *Citizen,* the *Las Vegas Daily Optic* tried to pressure the Republican gathering to endorse Bryan, the silverite, instead of McKinley. A number of Populists, Democrats, and Bryan men attended the convention to disrupt it with "noise and racket," but were defeated despite their "yells."

12. *Santa Fe Daily New Mexican,* October 19 and 23, 1896; Curry, *George Curry, 1861-1947: An Autobiography,* p. 95.

13. Miguel A. Otero to Catron, October 31, 1896, Catron Papers. Otero, in response to a $700 check sent by Catron to cover Catron's campaign expenses in San Miguel, conceded that he had been compelled to draw upon an "additional authorization" of $300 because of the closeness of the race.

14. October 17, 1896, Catron Papers.

15. A. W. Thompson to Catron, October 31, 1896, Catron Papers.

16. The *San Juan Times* (Farmington), September 25, 1896. Spanish-speaking candidates nominated for county office by the San Juan Populists were J. E. Manzaneres and J. Real for commissioners, Ramon Labato for probate judge, a candidate named Garcia for assessor, and F. M. Salazar for surveyor.

17. November 6, 1896. Jaquez and Garcia were listed as Democrats in the November 16 issue of the *Santa Fe Daily New Mexican.*

18. October 23, 1896.

19. J. D. Kello, member of the San Juan Republican Central Committee, to Catron, October 28, 1896, Catron Papers.

20. The *San Juan Times* (Farmington), October 23, 1896. Stivers supported Republican S. R. Blake for the House, Democrat John W. Brown for sheriff, and Populist William McRae for county clerk.

21. November 6, 1896.

22. October 13, 1896.

23. October 16, 1896.

24. As quoted in the *Santa Fe Daily New Mexican,* September 25, 1896.

25. September 4, 1896.

26. September 5, 1896.

27. September 28, 1896.

28. September 12, 1896.

29. As quoted in the *Albuquerque Daily Citizen,* September 29, 1896.

30. September 29, 1896.

31. Porter A. Stratton, *The Territorial Press of New Mexico, 1834-1912* (Albuquerque, 1969), pp. 25, 210.

32. *Las Vegas Daily Optic,* March 20, 1896, as quoted in Larson, *New Mexico's Quest for Statehood,* p. 190.

33. October 17, 1896.

34. August 21, 1896.

35. Pamphlet enclosed in October 12, 1896, letter to Catron, Catron Papers.

36. Discussed in a letter from Dr. A. L. Mahaffey to Catron dated October 30, 1896, Catron Papers.

37. Mrs. J. D. Perkins, president of a women's pro-silver organization in the territory, wrote Prince on October 1, 1896, requesting that he send her fifty copies of his book at his "earliest convenience." Prince Papers.

38. The *San Juan Times* (Farmington), October 16, 1896.

39. The former governor apparently did some selective campaigning for a few of his friends. See D. P. Carr to Prince, November 9, 1896, Prince Papers.

40. Mary Baird Bryan thanked Prince for sending the booklet to her husband and for the "kind words" in his accompanying letter. Mrs. Bryan to Prince, October 11, 1896, Prince Papers.

41. Hanna thanked Prince for his "very complimentary letter" and his analysis of the New Mexico vote in correspondence sent to Prince six weeks after the election. December 14, 1896, Prince Papers.

42. The letter from Saint and his associates was reprinted in the October 26 issue of the *New Mexican.*

43. J. E. Sheridan, proprietor of the *Enterprise,* to Catron, October 12, 1896, Catron Papers.

44. J. H. Overhulls and citizens of Bland to Catron, October 19, 1896, Catron papers. "If you can't meet with us[,] write us," Overhulls wrote for his friends in the mining district.

45. October 29, 1896.

46. As quoted in the *Albuquerque Daily Citizen,* September 29, 1896.

47. As quoted in the *Santa Fe Daily New Mexican,* October 12, 1896.

48. Also quoted in the *New Mexican.* See October 14, 1896, issue.

49. September 16, 1896, and other issues.

50. November 2, 1896.

51. *Santa Fe Daily New Mexican,* October 16, 1896.

52. Catron's motto, according to the hostile *New Mexican,* was "Viva los Borregos." October 14, 1896.

53. October 14, 28, and 30, 1896.

54. October 28, 1896.

55. *Intelligencer Post* clipping dated July 11, 1897. Typed report on the organization and activities of the Trans-Montane League also discussed in Chapter 9 on p. 123.

56. The *Santa Fe Daily New Mexican* on September 4, 1896, carried a story on a Democratic meeting in Missoula, Montana, which agreed to fusion on terms proposed earlier by the state Populist conference committee. A clipping in the Prince Papers (probably from a New Mexico journal) had a story with an October 6 dateline telling of a struggle in Colorado between the silver Republicans and the regular Republicans or "McKinleyites" over possession of the party emblem, the American Eagle. Populists and Democrats were arranging a fusion ticket in Wyoming on the basis of two Democratic electors to one Populist elector, according to a September 22, 1896, story in the *Citizen.* The Albuquerque journal had earlier, on September 3, taken some solace in the fact that Terence V. Powderly, the former Knights of Labor leader, had declared for McKinley. Another item of interest in the *Citizen* was a September 11 story showing that the Nevada Republican party had placed a plank in its platform calling for the "free coinage of the American product of silver," a step later taken by New Mexico Republicans.

57. October 30, 1896. Marion Butler, chairman of the Populist national committee, arranged in the name of the committee to distribute Donnelly's address to the press.

58. R. Hudson to Catron, November 7, 1896, Catron Papers.

59. Carl N. Degler, *The Age of the Economic Revolution, 1876 to 1900* (Glenview, no date), pp. 142-43. For a comprehensive study of the 1896 national campaign with particular emphasis on pre-convention proceedings, see Stanley L. Jones, *The Presidential Election of 1896* (Madison, 1964).

60. *The World Almanac and Encyclopedia, 1899* (New York, 1899), p. 427.

61. Callahan defeated the Republican candidate for territorial delegate, Dennis T. Flynn, by a vote of 27,435 to 26,267. U.S. Congress, Senate, *Official Congressional Directory, . . . ,* 55th Cong., 1st Sess., 1897, Dec. 1, p. 140.

62. Smith polled 6,065 votes to Doran's 4,090. U.S. Congress, *Official Congressional Directory,* Senate Doc. 1, p. 140. O'Neil's candidacy in 1894 had cost the Democrats the office of territorial delegate, Republican Nathan O. Murphy winning with only 42 percent of the vote. Jay J. Wagoner, *Arizona Territory, 1863-1912: A Political History* (Tucson, 1970), p. 309.

63. Certificate of Election, Election Records, Records of the Office of Secretary of State. A county-by-county breakdown of the 1896 delegate vote is included in this certification of election results made by territorial secretary Lorion Miller on December 3, 1896.

64. Undated article from the *Santa Fe Daily New Mexican,* Prince Papers. Results by county of 1894 delegate race included in this article, along with percentage total for each candidate.

65. Certificate of Election, Records of the Office of Secretary of State.

66. George B. Barber to Catron, November 5, 1896, Catron Papers.

67. Certificate of Election, Records of the Office of Secretary of State. Catron was reported as irate in the November 11 issue of the *New Mexican,* feeling that Fergusson's two-vote majority was achieved through fraudulent means. One hundred and seventy-five votes in two San Miguel precincts allegedly were illegal.

68. Certificate of Election, Records of the Office of Secretary of State.

69. F. W. Parker to Catron, November 6, 1896, Catron Papers.

70. Anderson to Catron, November 14, 1896, Catron Papers. Grant County tally in Certificate of Election, Records of the Office of Secretary of State.

71. Certificate of Election, Records of the Office of Secretary of State. *Citizen* editor Thomas Hughes commended Catron after the election for the fine showing he made in Bernalillo, where Albuquerque resident Fergusson was popular. Hughes and W. T. McCreight, publishers of the *Albuquerque Daily Citizen,* to Catron, November 12, 1896, Catron Papers.

72. *Santa Fe Daily New Mexican,* November 13, 1896; Certificate of Election, Records of the Office of Secretary of State. Gold Democrats were hopelessly out of step with New Mexico voters. Dame received only twelve votes in his home county of Santa Fe and, according to the November 6 issue of the *New Mexican,* only one vote in his hometown, Cerrillos. He was not on the ballot in Dona Ana, Rio Arriba, and San Juan counties. *Santa Fe Daily New Mexican,* November 16, 1896.

73. Curry, *George Curry, 1861-1947: An Autobiography, p.* 95.

74. Certificate of Election, Records of the Office of Secretary of State.

75. House Journal (unpublished), p. 2, Legislative Papers, State Records Center and Archives, Santa Fe.

76. Page 2, Legislative Papers. The Council Journal is unpublished.

77. Curry, *George Curry, 1861-1947: An Autobiography,* p. 95.

78. With Fergusson's almost 4 to 1 margin in silver-producing Sierra County, for instance, one can assume that the Populist-Democratic silver fusion ticket in Sierra had little difficulty in winning most of the county offices.

79. *Santa Fe Daily New Mexican,* November 9, 1896. Catron associate, Republican Charles A. Spiess, won the seat on the Territorial Council for which Boyle was a candidate.

80. The San Juan Populists carried every office in the county except the offices of sheriff and school superintendent. Their candidate for sheriff, A. H. Dunning, lost in his re-election bid to a Democrat by only twenty votes. Their candidate for school superintendent, L.B. Burnham, was defeated by a Republican. *Santa Fe Daily New Mexican,* November 10 and 16, 1896.

81. The *San Juan Times* (Farmington), November 6, 1896. Joseph and Locke were elected to represent San Juan and Rio Arriba counties in the Council. *Times,* November 13, 1896.

82. D. P. Carr to Prince, November 9, 1986, Prince Papers.

83. Mills to Prince, November 8, 1896, Prince Papers.

84. Mills died in New York ten years later, in September, 1906. *Santa Fe Daily New Mexican,* September 15, 1906.

85. November 13, 1896. The *Times* speculated that if the Denver Rio Grande Railroad were to build a branch line to Farmington the line would probably be extended to Albuquerque. Thus, San Juan would be connected with the "outside world."

11
THE TWILIGHT OF POPULISM

1. As quoted in Larson, *New Mexico's Quest for Statehood,* p. 191.

2. Lamar, *The Far Southwest,* p. 197.

3. Larson, *New Mexico's Quest for Statehood,* p. 192. For a discussion of Fergusson's role as a delegate in Congress, including his involvement in the passage of the Fergusson Act and his statehood efforts, see pp. 192-94.

4. The *Albuquerque Daily Citizen,* October 18, 1898.

5. Clinch, *Urban Populism and Free Silver in Montana,* p. 154 and subsequent pages.

6. New Mexico, Legislature, *Acts of the Legislative Assembly of the Territory of New Mexico,* 32d Sess. (Santa Fe, 1897), pp. 17, 23, 111-12, 140.

7. Another provision relating to dead livestock required railroads responsible for the death or injury of a stock animal to pay the owner the market value of the animal within 90 days or risk a suit. New Mexico, *Acts of the Legislative Assembly . . . ,* pp. 46, 60.

8. The *Albuquerque Daily Citizen,* September 30, October 1, 1898. Luna was a Rough Rider captain who benefited from the popularity enjoyed by almost all Rough Riders as a result of their participation in the Spanish-American War. Luna's promising political career ended abruptly with his death in the Philippines campaign. Curry, *George Curry, 1861-1947: An Autobiography,* pp. 124, 127.

9. October 11, 1898.

10. October 13, 1898.

11. The *Albuquerque Daily Citizen,* October 18, 1898. The *Citizen* chided Democratic papers for giving Fergusson the credit for wool protection. The Democrats in Congress, it insisted, solidly opposed the tariff on wool. It took the initiative of a Republican congressman, Nelson Dingley, Jr., to get the protection measure before the House. October 20, 1898.

12. September 24, 1898.

13. The *Albuquerque Daily Citizen,* October 13, 1898.

14. October 19, 1898.

15. Larson, *New Mexico's Quest for Statehood,* p. 194. Fergusson's accompanying announcement that the New Mexico Rough Riders were on their way to Cuba provoked loud applause in the House.

16. The *Albuquerque Daily Citizen,* November 12, 1898.

17. For an analysis of the Curry-Roosevelt relationship see Robert W. Larson, "Ballinger vs. Rough Rider George Curry: The Other Feud," *New Mexico Historical Review,* XLII (October, 1968), 271-90.

18. The *Albuquerque Daily Citizen,* October 31, 1898.

19. November 2, 1898.

20. October 19, 1898.

21. According to the *Citizen,* Democrats gave themselves "bodily" to the "sorehead" Republicans, called Independents, in return for their pledge to support Fergusson's re-election. October 15, 1898. Also see the October 22, 26, and 27 issues of the *Citizen.*

22. The *Albuquerque Daily Citizen,* November 4, 1896.

23. October 21, 28, 1898.

24. October 28, 1898.

25. October 21, 1898.

26. October 28, 1898.

27. *The World Almanac and Encyclopedia,* 1899, p. 455.

28. November 11, 1898.

29. Two of the nine Populists designated themselves as Silverites. In the previous session, the Fifty-fifth, there were twenty-one Populists, four fusionists, and three members of the Silver party. See *The World Almanac and Encyclopedia, 1899*, pp. 416, 420.

30. In the November 14 issue of the *Albuquerque Daily Citizen* the delegate election was characterized as being too close to call. In the final tally Perea received 535 votes to Fergusson's 512.

31. *The World Almanac and Encyclopedia, 1899, p. 455*.

32. The *Albuquerque Daily Citizen*, November 10, 1898.

33. In 1896 Fergusson carried the county, 677 to 168 votes. But in 1898 his support diminished, the vote being 495 for Fergusson to 317 for Perea.

34. Perea won the county by a vote of 2,550 to 2,114. See *The World Almanac and Encyclopedia, 1899*, p. 455, for a comparison of Fergusson's 1896 and 1898 Bernalillo tallies.

35. The *Albuquerque Daily Citizen*, November 10, 1898.

36. *The World Almanac and Encyclopedia, 1899*, p. 455.

37. November 12, 1898.

38. The *Albuquerque Daily Citizen*, November 15, 1898.

39. Read, *Illustrated History of New Mexico*, p. 760.

40. Simpson's statement following his defeat was symbolic of the discouragement of Populist leaders during this twilight year of 1898. ''I shall seek office no more. I shall at the expiration of my term in Congress retire to my cattle ranch at Medicine Lodge, and participate only to help out the populist party whenever my services are in demand.'' The *Albuquerque Daily Citizen*, November 12, 1898.

41. November 12, 1898.

42. The *Albuquerque Daily Citizen*, November 15, 1898.

12
NEW MEXICO POPULISM IN RETROSPECT

1. *Santa Fe Daily New Mexican*, September 23, 1896. Ordinarily thought of as a Republican journal, the *New Mexican* in 1896 was Democratic. See chapters 9 and 10 *passim*.

2. Prince Papers.

3. Shannon, *American Farmers' Movements*, p. 72.

4. October 13, 1896, Prince Papers.

5. Gould, *Wyoming: A Political History,* pp. 250-55.

6. *Southern Pacific Coast Directory, 1888-9,* p. 468. Martinez listed as his two business lines in the directory ''real estate and land grants.''

7. Pollack in comparing the Populist movement with Marxism, although insisting that ''Populism was certainly not Marxism,'' does see important similarities. ''For each, industrial capitalism meant alienated man — man divorced from himself, his product, and humanity.'' Pollack, *The Populist Response to Industrial America,* p. 68 and *passim.*

8. Hofstadter, *The Age of Reform,* p. 101.

9. A situation unlike the one in Colorado, where, in 1892, there were two private lawyers, one town attorney, and two county judges among the leaders of the state Populist party. McCarthy, ''Colorado's Populist Leadership,'' *The Colorado Magazine,* XLVIII, 39. For more discussion of this article see chapter 7, note 25.

10. Nugent, *The Tolerant Populists,* p. 238. To underscore these two terms Nugent used them, or variations of them, throughout the summation of his book in the last chapter.

11. September 15, 1894. For details of this charge, which had such important political overtones, see Chapter 7, p. 94 .

Constitution of 1889, 32-33, 52, 53, 56
Co-operative Company of Nogal, 17-18
Corruption, attacked, 102
Court of Private Land Claims, 4, 53, 82
Cox, Jacob D., 23
Cox and Peacock cattle company, 7
Crime of '73, 97, 105, 120, 144, 150, 215 n 7
Crist, Jacob D., 32, 58, 200 n 26, 206 n 70
Cuba, 134, 228 n 15
Curry, George, 58, 97, 155, 162, 214 n 71

Daily Populist (Denver), 121
Dakota territories, 32, 34
Dame, W. E., 141, 149, 153, 154, 222 n 103, 226 n 72
De Baca, Manuel C., 36
Deflation, 34, 49-50, 105, 120, 173, 176
Deming, 78, 160
Democratic party: philosophy of, 3-4; elections, 14, 17, 31, 53-59, 72-73, 78-82, 95, 97-99, 109, 111-18, 135, 144-55, 160-65; conventions, 15, 53, 72, 74-75, 97, 137, 160; platforms, 15, 53, 72, 97, 125, 137, 160; supports protest, 31-34, 47, 53, 57-58, 95, 163, 177-78; endorses free coinage, 53, 68, 94, 97, evaluation of, 168-71. See Gold Democrats
Denver, Colo., 109
Denver Republican, 147
Denver and Rio Grande Railroad, 103, 156, 227 n 85
Department of the Interior, U.S., 3, 39
Depression of 1893, 85, 98, 101, 104, 105-6, 109, 120, 160, 210 n 66
Dona Ana County, 8, 16, 42, 76, 114, 154, 226 n 72
Dow, E. A., 91
Duncan, James S., 145, 154
Dunning, A. H., 227 n 80
Durango, Colo., 120, 156, 215 n 4
Dwyer, J.W., 21, 31, 161

Economy, Populists advocate, 96, 134
Eddings, F. M., 90
Eddy, Charles B., 7, 12, 33, 206 n 70
Eddy County, 9, 15, 80, 153, 164

Education, 30, 32, 52, 59-61, 62, 77, 82, 89, 97, 107-8, 160, 171, 201 n 37
El Capitan Land and Cattle Company, 7
Elections. See Democratic party, Populism, Republican party
Electoral college, 91, 92
El Paso, Texas, 69, 165
El Sol de Mayo, 68
Elizabethtown, 21, 23
Elkins, Stephen B., 12, 23, 25, 69, 71-72, 111, 192 n 28, 214 n 72
Evans, J. M., 91

Fall, Albert Bacon, 74, 97, 137, 206 n 70
Farmers' Alliance: territorial, 8-22, 26-31, 50, 56, 95, 161, 177; national, 50, 59, 65
Farmers' Mutual Benefit Association, 65
Farmington, 88, 156, 227 n 85
Fergusson, Harvey B.: political activities, 74-75, 97, 112, 121, 127, 128, 133, 137, 206 n 70, 215 n 10, 219 n 64; candidate for delegate, 137, 138-39, 140-41, 144-45, 148-50, 152, 153-55, 168, 171, 172, 226 n 67; incumbent delegate, 158, 160-62, 164-65; evaluation of, 173, 174
Ferguson Act, 158
Field, James G., 73, 75, 82
Field, Neil B., 206 n 70
Finical, T. A., 214 n 72
First National Bank of Santa Fe, 23
Fiscal extravagance, 110-11
Fiske, Eugene A., 39, 70-71, 196 n 15
Flora Vista, 57, 88
Flushing, N.Y., 38
Flynn, Dennis T., 225 n 61
Folsom, 70, 214 n 66
Foraker, C. M., 130
Foraker, Joseph Benson, 130
Forsha, John T., 155
Fort, Lewis C., 115, 194 n 26, 213 n 63, 214 n 67
Fort Marcy, 97-98, 210 n 62
Fort Union, 39
Foster, Charles, 101
Free silver. See Silver issue
Frewen, Morton, 216 n 14
Frontier, influence of, 50, 175